CHAUCER'S ENGLAND.

VOL. I.

AMS PRESS
NEW YORK

GEOFFREY CHAUCER.

CHAUCER'S ENGLAND.

BY

MATTHEW BROWNE.

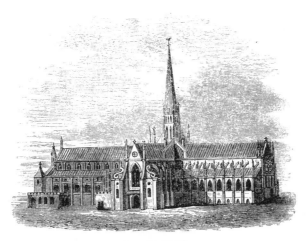

OLD SAINT PAUL'S.

IN TWO VOLUMES.

VOL. I.

LONDON:

HURST AND BLACKETT, PUBLISHERS,

13 GREAT MARLBOROUGH STREET.

1869.

The right of Translation is reserved.

Reprinted from a copy in the
collections of the Harvard University Library

Reprinted from the edition of 1869, London
First AMS EDITION published 1970
Manufactured in the United States of America

International Standard Book Number:
Complete Set: 0–404–01139–X
Volume 1:   0–404–01140–3

Library of Congress Number: 74–113566

AMS PRESS INC.
NEW YORK, N.Y. 10003

CONTENTS

OF

THE FIRST VOLUME.

CHAP.   PAGE

   I. THE POET OF THE CANTERBURY TALES   .   .   1

  II. THE STORY AND THE PILGRIMS   .   .   .   85

 III. CHIVALRY   110

  IV. THE GAY SCIENCE 144

   V. FEMALE TYPES IN CHAUCER   174

  VI. MERRY ENGLAND   201

 VII. THE HEART OF ENGLAND   236

VIII. MOTLEY   263

  IX. MEDIÆVAL NUDITARIANISM   279

THE TABARD INN.

CHAPTER I.

THE POET OF THE CANTERBURY TALES.

WHO is not familiar with the image of Chaucer, as it
stands in the copies of one or other of the existing
portraits? That of Occleve is the most common,
and is supposed to be the only genuine portrait in
existence; but all the portraits which claim to
have any degree of authenticity resemble each other
so much that it is easy to identify them with the

description given of himself by the poet in the *Canterbury Tales*. For instance, a portrait which was engraved in Todd's *Illustrations of the Lives and Writings of Gower and Chaucer*, and is now, according to Sir Harris Nicolas, in the possession of Lord Francis Egerton; this painting (in a copy of the *Canterbury Tales*) represents Chaucer on horseback, booted and spurred,—a little man, ' round of shape,' dressed in a long dark robe, with a hood to it. A portrait, which Sir Harris Nicolas thinks is not older than the reign of Queen Elizabeth (Additional MS. 5141 Brit. Mus.), shows how early the daisy had become associated with Chaucer's name, for that flower is painted in the corner as an emblem. Occleve's affectionate words about his ' deere maistir and fadir Chaucer ' are well known :—

> ' Althogh his lyfe be queynt, the resemblaunce
> Of him hath in me so fresshe lyflynesse,
> That to putte othir men in remembraunce
> Of his persone, I heere his lyknesse
> Do make, to this ende in sothfastnesse,
> That thei that have of hym lest thought and mynde,
> By this peynture may ageyn him fynde.'

In the portrait prefixed to this volume, engraved from Occleve's painting (Harleian MSS. 4866), Chaucer is represented in half-length against a background of green tapestry. His hair and beard are both grey, the latter being forked under the chin in the way so commonly observed in the portraits of the time, the dress and hood are dark, and a 'knyf harnessed' hangs from his neck; his eyes are downcast, according to his own description of himself. The hands are very small, the right being extended with the forefinger pointing outwards, and the others closed upon the palm, under the thumb; an attitude of monition apparently, in keeping with the suggestion of the string of beads suspended on his left hand. Doubts have been raised— very unnecessarily—about the authenticity of the disclaimer which in the poet's name, but with some undramatic confusion between him and the parson, is given at the end of the Parson's Tale.* But small con-

---

* 'God have mercy on me and forgeve me my giltes, and nameliche my translaciouns and of endityng in worldly vanitees, whiche I revoke in my retracciouns, as is the book of Troyles, the book also of Fame, the book of twenty-five Ladies, the book of the Duchesses, the book of seint Valentines day and of the Parlement of briddes, the Tales of Caunterbury, alle thilke that sounen into synne, the book of the Leo, and many other bokes, if thay were in my mynde or remembraunce, and many a song and many a leccherous lay, of the whiche Crist for his grete mercy forgive me the synnes. But of the translacioun of Boce de consolacioun, and other bokes of consolacioun and of legend of lyves of seints, and Omelies, and moralitees, and devocioun, that thanke I oure Lord Jhesu Crist, and his moder, and alle the seintes in heven, bisekyng hem that thay fro hennysforth unto my lyves ende sende me grace to biwayle my gultes, and to studien to the savacioun of my soule, and graunte me grace and space of verray repentaunce, penitence, confessioun, and satisfaccioun, to don in this present lif, thurgh the benigne grace of him, that is king of kynges and prest of alle prestis, that bought us with his precious blood of his hert, so that I moote be oon of hem at the day of doom that schal be saved; *qui cum Patre et Spiritu Sancto vivis et regnas Deus per omnia secula. Amen.*'

fusions of the kind (and this is not the only one) go for
nothing in an unfinished work like the *Canterbury
Tales ;* and it was in strict keeping with the spiritual
etiquette or regimen of chivalric manners and literature, that a poet should, before he died, recant or
express his grief for having written romances of love,
fighting, feasting, jousting, and 'all manere delyt of
the world, the fleisch, and the divel.' This was so
strictly the proper thing to do, that it is impossible to
conceive Chaucer omitting it—unless he had died suddenly. In the Romance literature we find the *carrière*
of the Troubadour unmistakably defined. In the fine
spring morning, when the birds sing in the grove, particularly in the month of May,—because that was dedicated to the Virgin Mary,—he begins his career of a
minstrel, with a gay paltock on his back and a guitar
slung to his shoulder. The business of his life's day is
'minstralcie.' He is to sing of love, ladies, knights,
flowers, birds, sunshine, and the like, not forgetting
the stock figures of course, Tristram and Iseult aux
blanches mains, Lancelot du Lac, and Queen Guinevere.
All his life he is to compose verses of 'corrage' and
' delyt,' tinkling his guitar in bower, and hall, and tilt-
yard. But as the evening draws on, he is to reflect
that the Church does not look with a kindly eye upon
'delyt' of any sort ; and he is to take care and write
something to say how very sorry he is for having
written songs of love and knighthood. The state of
mind and feeling which could receive so incoherent a

theory of life is not intelligible to us; but it was beyond question a matter of course in Chaucer's time. And however he may have intended to ridicule troubadour poetry in his ' Rhyme of Sir Topas,' he was too receptive a person not to take to that portion of the faith of his time which made repentance and bead-telling and a hortatory disposition the proper things in an old man. We, who look upon faith, devotion, and repentance of wrong-doing as things for the whole of a man's life, and not for his old age only, cannot help smiling at the mediæval view of the subject. But we must take care not to smile unkindly. The whole theory of life and duty in those days was one of classification of persons, functions, seasons, foods, and occupations. That one part of life was intended to be more religiously lived out than another would not seem so very absurd to a man whose church told him to eat no flesh on Wednesdays and Fridays, and gave him absolution for confessed sin upon penance done as often as he liked to come for it. In the Middle Ages caste was moral as well as social and civic. The knight was to put lance in rest; the clerk was to be learned, ' morall of sentaunce;' the parson was to preach, and to be a great deal more religious than his people; while those that 'ben seculare' may, by the side of all this, do pretty much as they please. This is the organisation of life; virtues and offices are divided and apportioned; and the Church overlooks the motley throng with blessing or ban in her power. I do not see any reason to doubt that the disclaimer or recantation of which we have been speaking, is Chaucer's own.

The poet is preserved to us then by Occleve, in the guise of a penitent; and I confess, though, perhaps, some of my criticisms do not seem to correspond with the confession, I have felt some delicacy, in dealing with the man Chaucer, as to the hypothesis of character upon which I should proceed. Nothing can be more capricious than the manner in which the biographers choose or reject at pleasure quasi-biographic indications in the poetry and prose of Chaucer; but it is quite plain that the moods of his writings vary as his years change; and as I do not believe in any entity called ' the interests of literature,' or ' the interests of morality,' which ought to prevail over the duty of absolute simple justice and loyalty, even to a dead man, I am not at all sure what image of Chaucer I ought to be most anxious to leave upon the reader's mind; for his own wishes in such a matter should, unquestionably, have much weight. No man can know another man as that other man knows himself: and I am unalterably of opinion that a human being's estimate of his own character and worth is usually far more truthful than the best estimate that can be made by all the ingenuity of his friends put together. After all, however, Chaucer deliberately gave his writings to the world pretty much as they stand in print at this day, and we must take him as they represent him; from his early youth —

' When I was yong at xviii yere of age
  Lusty and light, desirous of plesaunce —'

to the time of his maturity—

' I am a married man, and yet
  Thou art a merry man, quoth Wat—'

and so on, to the time of his old age, when he was
' hoor and round of schape,' and ended his days by
inditing, if we are to trust the record, ' when he was
on his death-bed in great anguish,' the verses beginning—

' Flee fro the pres and duelle with sothfastnesse.'

His visible figure, at all events, stands plainly before us—a large head, a little body, but with broad
shoulders, and small extremities.   His physical energy
must have been enormous—in terms of physiology, he
must have had large viscera—to support the incessant
and varied labour of his life.   His writings alone are
voluminous, and though of course varying in merit,
they are of unflagging force.   Considering the state of
the English language and literature of the time, it is
plain that he could not have produced his poems without possessing an immense amount of the independent
originating power of genius.   And if the *Testament of
Love* is not in at least some parts a translation or
paraphrase, Chaucer was not only a poet but a meta-
physician.   Otherwise no acquaintance with the philo-

sophy of his time would have carried him safely over the sensitive ground which he sometimes touches with logical sure-footedness in that remarkable book. Besides this, we have to take into account that Chaucer was not only a man of letters, but, after the manner of younger times than ours, a soldier and a man of affairs. However difficult then we may find it to discriminate between the strictly autobiographical and the merely fanciful references to himself which abound in his writings, we are forced to receive as gospel what he says in the prologue to the *Legend of Good Women :*—

> ' On bokes for to rede I me delyte,
> And in myn herte have hem in reverence
> So hertely that ther is game noon,
> That fro my bokes maketh me to goon.'

The business of biography is, of course, to tell the truth ; and yet I sympathize with Tyrwhitt, who does not like people who are ' fascinated with the charms of a barren page and a meagre collection of dates.' I am intensely of Chaucer's opinion that men ought—

> .   . ' To yeve credence
> To olde stories and doon hem reverence,
> And that men mosten more thyng beleve
> Than they may seen at eighe or elles preve.'

In other words, I think that all tradition of persons which is not incoherent with verified facts of record, should be received into our belief, unless it affirms impossible things. I think, therefore, that the older biographers of Chaucer, like Leland and Urry, deserve careful attention.

On the question of Chaucer's parentage the testimony is absurdly conflicting. That he was of noble birth ; that his father was a rich vintner ; that his father was a merchant ; that his father was a knight — all these statements have been made with confidence. But the statement of Urry, that Chaucer was the son of a John Chaucer who followed in the train of Edward III. to Flanders and Cologne ; and that he was taken notice of in his childhood by the king and queen, partly in consideration of his father's services, and partly on account of his own attractive qualities, seems to me the most probable.

I might well pause here to notice how small comparatively is the amount of trustworthy biography which has reached us from the early years of English history. No doubt it is true in one sense that, as Mr. Tennyson puts it, the individual withers, and the world is more and more ; but in our literature the ' individual' is indemnified by the prevalence of biography, autobiography, and minute character sketching, which goes on in books of fact and books of fiction. In earlier days the case was quite otherwise ; the ' individual' was more, but it was by making his mark on the time — his friends do not think of writing his life, or if they do, it is in such a way that nobody can make anything of it. It is impossible, think of it how we may, not to feel surprised that the idea of a life in detail, with the necessary *pièces justificatives* for posterity did not occur to any of the immediate survivors of men like Chaucer, Shakspeare, and Milton. Their minds ran in those days upon portraits, monuments, and commendatory verses; and few people, if any, appear to have suspected that future generations could care to know the history of a prominent man's youth, the details of his marriage, or what sort of appetite he had at breakfast.

Of the poet himself we have a portrait in outline by his own hand, which, besides agreeing minutely with Occleve's picture, has in a high degree the quality of physiognomical significance. It occurs at the close of the Prioress's Tale : —

> ' Whan sayd was this miracle, every man
> As sober was, that wonder was to se,
> Til that oure host to jape he bigan,
> And than at erst he loked upon me,
> And sayde thus: " What man art thou ?" quod he.
> " Thou lokest as thou woldest fynde an hare,
> For ever upon the ground I se the stare.
>   " Approche ner, and loke merily.
> Now ware you, sires, and let this man have space.
> He in the wast is schape as well as I ;
> This were a popet in an arm to embrace
> For any womman, smal and fair of face.
> He semeth elvisch by his countenaunce,
> For unto no wight doth he daliaunce.
>   " Say now som what, sins other folk han said ;
> Telle us a tale and that of mirthe anoon."

" Host," quod I, " ne beth nought evel apayd,
For other tale certes can I noon,
But of a rym I lerned yore agoon."
" Ye, that is good," quod he, " now schul we heere
Som deynté thing, me thinketh by thy cheere." '

Here, it will be noticed, we have the *downcast* look,
as people call it, which is so often said by ordinary
critics in physiognomy to distinguish minute observers
— ' they look as if they saw nothing, and all the while
they see everything, and remember it '—that is a kind
of countenance with which we are, I think, most of us
familiar. Downcast is not perhaps the word to apply
to the peculiar look in question, but we can see what
the host Harry Baily *meant* by saying that Chaucer
was always looking on the ground, as if he expected to
see a hare run by. The fact is, people of quick observation and retentive memory have commonly eyes that
are prominent, and which take in a good deal even
when the lid is dropped. In such people the lid is
often dropped for obvious reasons—in the first place,
they are meditative, and in the second, they are self-
conscious and often full of humour. In laughter the
eyes are half shut; in the first stages of humorous
sensibility the lids are slightly dropped over the eye-
balls. Hence a man like Chaucer would naturally be
described by a rough observer like Harry Baily as
' staring on the ground.'

It is worth notice that this (so-called) downcast
look belonged to Richardson the novelist, a man who

resembled Chaucer in nothing but power of minute observation, patience, and latent humour; of the last,
however, possessing comparatively very little.   Still
Richardson's own portrait of himself, forwarded in pen
and ink to one of his lady correspondents, is worth
quoting, for the sake of the parallel which does exist,
or at least, in order to illustrate the remark that men
of minute observation often have this ' downcast' trick
of the eye with them.   Richardson describes himself
as ' short, rather plump, about five feet five inches high,
smooth-faced . . . . . walking so as to seem to steal away
the ground ;' and bringing his observation to bear upon
an object of interest from the feet, and so proceeding
upwards. Chaucer's description of himself, taking what
is expressed along with what is implied in the host's
challenge is admirable :—

> ' Approche ner, and loke merily ! '

says he; and then, with a double contradictory reference to the smallness of the pilgrim's height, and the
roundness of his waist, bids the other pilgrims to make
room for him : —

> ' Now ware, you sires, and let this man have space ! '

He is a ' popet' for a woman to dandle.   He is ' small
and fair of face,' and yet

> ' He in the wast is schape as well as I.'

Such a speech as Falstaff might have made to little Richardson.   And then

> ' He seemeth elvisch by his countenance,
> For unto no wight doth he daliaunce ;'

in which we have, probably, besides the small figure and latency of manner, a reference to the largeness of the head as compared with that of the chest.   I should say that if the figure of Douglas Jerrold were altered to suit the portrait of Occleve, we should have a very good idea of the appearance of Chaucer.

Challenged by the host, the elvish man brightens up, and there is something very natural in the patronizing manner of the former, and also in his evident enjoyment of the promise there was in the new story-teller's face : —

> ' " Say now som what, sins other folk han said ;
> Telle us a tale and that of mirthe anoon."
> " Host," quod I, " ne beth nought evel apayd,
> For other tale certes can I noon,
> But of a rym I lerned yore agoon."
> " Ye, that is good," quod he, " now schul we heere
> Som deynte thing, me thinketh by thy cheere."

And then, as we know, the elvish man begins the ' Tale of Sir Thopas ;' though only to be roughly interrupted by Harry Baily, and cut short before he has reached the middle.

To his fatness Chaucer refers more than once in his

other poems. In a well-known roundel of his, the line—

      ' Since I fro Love escaped am so fat,'

occurs three times, and in the verses to Scogan, he says—the reference being of course to Cupid—

> He wol nat weth his arwes been ywroken
> On thee ne me, ne noon of your figure;
> We shul of him have neyther hurte nor cure.
>
> ' Now certes, frend, I drede of thyn unhappe,
> Lest for thy gilte the wreche of love procede
> On alle hem that ben hoor and round of shappe.'

It is unnecessary to add that fat was against all the canons of the court of love. One of the commandments in Chaucer's own " Court " is ' to fast.' It is equally contrary to the spirit of knighthood, and indeed, the soldierly spirit. In modern times the only people who must not get fat are jockeys; but in an earlier and sterner time the Gauls punished the soldier whose waist-belt protruded in the rank; we need not pursue the subject into trivialities of illustrations.

It is admitted on all hands that Chaucer must have been born of well-to-do parents, and that his education was that of a gentleman; but the strenuous manner in which he maintains, in more than one place in his writings, the truth that a man's rank is determined by what he is and does, and not by his birth, might be supposed to imply an oblique reference to his own origin, if we did not know how uncertain such conclusions are. Chaucer's was a revolutionary age; it is difficult not to believe that the radicalism of those times was greatly in excess of any proof of it which remains; for there is a whiff or wind of social insurgence blowing through all its literature. The impression made upon my own mind is that Chaucer was the son of a court favourite, and a favourite himself; and if my fancy insists on adding other particulars with respect to his origin, I need not produce them here.

In the "Court of Love," the poet, speaking dramatically, says—

> ' Philogenet I called am fer and nere,
>   Of Cambridge, clerke —,'

but of course we cannot infer positively that Chaucer was ever at Cambridge University. It is asserted by Leland that Chaucer was a clerk of Oxford (and that he finished his education in Paris), and the frequent references to Oxford and its neighbourhood in the poet's writings, give some colour to this statement. It is believed that

> ' The morall Gower and philosophical Strode,'

to whom Chaucer dedicates *Troilus and Creseide* were both educated at Oxford, and Godwin and others conjecture that the three men became acquainted at Oxford University. These uncertainties are so tedious that I hardly know whether to repeat or not Speght's anecdote that Chaucer, being at that time a law student of the Inner Temple, was once fined two shillings for thrashing a Franciscan Friar in Fleet Street. Nothing is more likely than that Chaucer, when young and full of pluck, perhaps wine, should beat a friar; and Leland confirms Speght in the statement that Chaucer had been a student in 'the college of the lawyers,' to say nothing of the fact that Mr. Buckley told Speght he had seen the record of the fine of two shillings in the Inner Temple. But on the other hand, Thynne, who ought to have known, asserts that ' lawyers were not of the Temple till the latter part of the reygne of Edward III.,' at which time the poet was in his maturity.

Up to August 1866 then it was safe for any biographer of the poet to state that there was no record of Chaucer's existence until 1359.

But in August 1866, Mr. Bond, through the *Fortnightly Review,* informed us that he had "lately" had the fortune to meet the name of Geoffrey Chaucer in some fragments of a contemporary 'Household Account;' the fragments being 'two parchment leaves which had, some three or four centuries ago been pasted down to the covers of an ancient manuscript purchased a few years since by the British Museum, and now known as the Additional MS. 1862.' Mr. Bond goes on to say, that when the volume was rebound these fragments might have been cast away as worthless but for a rule strictly observed in the British Museum of preserving *every* scrap of old writing, whether it appear valuable or not—a circumstance which I mention merely for its intrinsic interest. The leaves, in being adapted to the purpose of lining the whole binding of the MS., had been mutilated and defaced, but Mr. Bond found them perfectly legible, and of the facts which they supply in reference to Chaucer the interest is extreme. Of course I shall not do Mr. Bond's ingenious paper the injustice of referring to it any further than my purpose requires. But the account was kept for the Countess Elizabeth, then the wife of Prince Lionel, who was the third son of King Edward III. The lady had herself been brought up by Queen Philippa, upon the choice of the king himself, and, at nine years old, she was betrothed to the young Prince Lionel. In 1352 she married him. Her mother was Maud, sister of Henry, first Duke of Lancaster. She seems to have lived at Hatfield, which was then royal property; but, like most royal or distinguished personages in those days (unless they were in prison), she seems to have been always moving about from one part of the country to another. During the three or four years over which the account extends, Mr. Bond finds her at Southampton, at Reading, at Stratford-le-Bow, at Campsey, at London again, at Woodstock, at Doncaster, at Windsor, at Hertford, at Anglesea, in Liverpool, in London again, at Reading again, in London again, ' feeing the keepers

of the lions in the Tower,' and lastly, again at Hatfield.
In the winter of 1357, John of Gaunt was apparently
at Hatfield, ' for new-year's gifts are presented by the
Countess to John of Gaunt's cook and clerk of the
kitchen.' Now in April 1357, the lady is in London,
preparing for the festival of Easter, and also for assist-
ing at the feast of St. George, to be held at Windsor
with great pomp, to celebrate the recent foundation of
the Order of the Garter. At this time there is an entry
in the account of ' a paltock, or short cloak, a pair of
red and black breeches, and a pair of shoes,' for Geoffrey
Chaucer. At the same time there are entries of articles
of dress for Philippa Pan, which Mr. Bond thinks is
probably a contraction for *panetaria*, or mistress of
the pantry.

We have Chaucer's own testimony, given in the
Scrope and Grosvenor Case, to the fact that in the year
1359 he fought under Edward III. in the French expedition, and was taken prisoner. What we gather in
addition from Mr. Bond's discovery is, that it was in
the retinue of Prince Lionel that the poet went to
France. Of course, if he was born in 1328, he was
thirty-one at this time ; if Mr. Bond is right in fixing
the date of his birth at about 1340, he was only nineteen. If Chaucer was born in 1340, he was married
very early, for it is almost certain that he was
ransomed upon the peace of Chartres in 1360 ; and it
is nearly as certain that he was married to his wife
Philippa in that year. There is scarcely the shadow of

a doubt that the 'Parliament of Birds' relates to the marriage of John of Gaunt with the Lady Blanche of Lancaster, who, in the poem, puts off the marriage for a year. Now the marriage took place in 1359, and this would make Chaucer the author of the poem in question when he was eighteen. But in the poem called 'The Dream,' which still more certainly relates to the same marriage, we have Chaucer representing, in the true Romance vein, John of Gaunt and Lady Blanche, with the other lords and ladies, interceding with his own mistress on his behalf, and she finally relents, also in the true Romance fashion, and agrees to marry him. Tyrwhitt and Urry say that he was married in 1360; and Sir Harris Nicolas, who says in one place that it was about June, 1367, when Chaucer married 'Philippa, one of the ladies in attendance upon the Queen,' quotes in another place a pension to 'Philippa Chaucer una Domicellarum Cameræ Philippæ Reginæ Angliæ,' of ten marks per annum for life, on the 12th of September, 1366. The exact date of his marriage is not, however, so curious or so disputed a question as the exact lady whom he married. Sir Harris Nicolas disposes absolutely of the notion that one Philippa Picard was Chaucer's wife, by quoting a record of a pension to Philippa Pycard, expressly by that name, in January, 1370, when the poet must have been married at the least four years. The fact is, the frequency with which the name Philippa was given to girls in honour of Queen Philippa of Hainault, is rather confusing. But the idea of some previous biographers, that the alliance with Philippa Picard originated Chaucer's close relations with John of Gaunt is disposed of by Mr. Bond's discovery. John of Gaunt was at Hatfield during the three years over which the account extends, and the poet's connexion with him was probably of some standing at the time of his marriage. The lady to whom all the evidence points as Chaucer's wife is Philippa Roet, sister of Catherine Swynford, whom John of Gaunt made his wife in due form, after he had sustained conjugal relations with her for several years without the form.

Some points upon which tradition was tolerably strong, though the evidence expected by the scientific historian was wanting, while they were plausible and natural in themselves, have been made yet more plausible by the discovery of Mr. Bond. Godwin was in his usual fashion eloquently positive, merely upon the strength of internal probabilities, that Chaucer met Petrarch at Padua, and there probably received from him the story of ' Patient Griselda.' One of the points Godwin made was, that it was otherwise an unaccountable circumstance that Chaucer should insert in the Clerk's Tale the name of Petrarch, as the person from whom he had it, when it was from Boccaccio's Italian that Petrarch had translated the tale into Latin. Godwin says, ' It is plain Chaucer did this, because he was eager to commemorate his interview with this venerable patriarch of Italian letters, and to record the pleasure he had reaped from his society. Chaucer could not do this more effectually than by mentioning his having learned from the lips of Petrarch a tale which had been previously drawn up and delivered to the public by another. We may defy all the ingenuity of criticism to invent a different solution for the simple and decisive circumstance of Chaucer having gone out of his way, in a manner which he has employed on no other occasion, to make the Clerk of Oxenford confess that he learned the story from Petrarch ; and even assigned the exact place of Petrarch's residence in the concluding part of his life.' There is perhaps only one other obvious solution, and that is a base one. It *might* be suggested that Chaucer was willing to hide out of sight, so far as ignoring them would do it, numerous supposed obligations to Boccaccio. But it is scarcely incontestable that he incurred any such obligations; and if he did, the middle ages had no literary code or etiquette which made the acknowledgment of such debts at all necessary. Upon this question Sir Harris Nicolas seems to me—I say it with much respect—to hit rather wide of the mark. In the first place, the fact which he mentions, namely, that two English envoys in 1404 could not speak French when in France for the purposes of their embassy, by no means goes to prove that Chaucer could not, with his versatility and power, speak and read Italian quite easily. There is no need to be one of ' those indiscriminate worshippers of genius who endow their idols with all human attainments;' but, though Sir Harris Nicolas does not appear to appreciate the fact, the difference in the attaining or acquiring faculties possessed by a man like Chaucer, and those of any other man then in England, would be as the difference in height between Chimborazo and Primrose Hill. Is it too much to say that Chaucer's brain was more superior to that of, for instance, a man like Edward II., than such a man's brain was superior to an anthropoid ape's? A first-class mind is like a many-sided mirror, which catches reflections more than it wishes or needs; or like Ezekiel's living creatures, with eyes before and behind. But besides this, Sir Harris Nicolas surely mistakes the point, when he remarks, ' Unless, then, it be assumed against probability that Italian, of which there is no proof that Chaucer knew anything, was as familiar to him as Latin, which language there is evidence that he knew well, a sufficient reason is formed for his having taken the tale from Petrarch's translation, rather than from the *Decameron.*' But the point is not where Chaucer took the tale from, but what he *says* about taking it. Godwin's question remains pertinent, ' Why did Chaucer go out of his way to *say* that the tale was learned of a particular person, at a particular place?' Far more forcible is the remark of Sir Harris Nicolas, that the theory of the poet's having learned the tale from Petrarch at Padua, is very different from the apparent suggestion of a passage near the end of the Clerk's Tale : —

‘ Every wight in his degree
Shulde be constant in adversitee,
As was Griselde, therefore Petrark writeth
This storie, which with high stile he enditeth.’

This however, though differing, is not inconsistent;
and Speght and Godwin, who maintain that Chaucer
met Petrarch in Italy, are decidedly confirmed by
Mr. Bond’s discovery, which makes it probable that
Chaucer, being part of the suite of Prince Lionel, was
present at the Prince’s marriage with Violanta, daughter
of Galeazzo, Lord of Milan, which was celebrated at
Milan in the year 1369, and there met Petrarch. On
the whole, my own reading of the case would be that
the imaginative, sensitive Godwin caught in Chaucer’s
words a tone or accent which others have missed in the
intentness of their criticism. The probability is that
Chaucer did meet Petrarch, and was anxious to record
the meeting. And that, whether Petrarch told him of
the story in person, or not (which is indifferent to
either theory), he read it in Petrarch’s version, and
then, as a compliment to a great man with whom he
had exchanged courtesies, added that Petrarch had
himself ‘ with high style indited the story :’ *q. d.* ‘ I saw
Petrarch, who spoke to me of this story, which he has
himself written out.’

Chaucer was on the Continent in the king’s service
in 1370, and the usual letters of protection granted
him by the king are quoted by Sir Harris Nicolas. In
1372 he went to Genoa, being joined in a commission

with John de Mari and James Pronan (?), 'to treat with
the Duke, citizens, and merchants of Genoa, for the
purpose of choosing some port in England where the
Genoese might form a commercial establishment.' He
received an advance of money from the Royal Exchequer
for his expenses—the entry in the Issue Roll beginning,
'Galfrido Chaucer armigero Regis misso in secretis ne-
gociis domini Regis versus partes transmarinas, &c.' He
went to Florence while in Italy, and was in England again
within a year, because on the 22d of November, 1373,
we find him receiving his pension ' per manus proprias'
on that day.   Sir Harris Nicolas, the most cautious of
his biographers thought, and with good reason, that
there was nothing unlikely in the presumption that
Chaucer went to Padua for his own pleasure, the records of the payment of his expenses naturally mentioning only the places to which the royal errand carried him.   We now see from Mr. Bond's discovery
that there is reason to believe that Chaucer did make
Petrarch's acquaintance at Milan in 1369,* although
the same reason which makes the payments for his
attire rather low in scale, might lead to the omission
of his name from the contemporary lists of the suite of
Prince Lionel.   And there is so much fervour in the
manner in which Petrarch's name is mentioned in
the Clerk's Tale, that it is very probable he afterwards

---

* And that, although there appears to be no mention of
Chaucer in the Rolls of the Tower as having been in the retinue
of Prince Lionel.

went to Padua to meet the illustrious Italian, of whom he speaks in this warm, almost personal manner :—

> ' I wil yow telle a tale, which that I
> Lerned at Padowe of a worthy clerk,
> As proved by his wordes and his werk.
> He is now deed, and nayled in his chest,
> Now God give his soule wel good rest !
> Fraunces Petrark, the laureat poete,
> Highte this clerk, whos rethorique swete
> Enlumynd al Ytail of poetrie,
> As Linian did of philosophie,
> Or lawue, or other art particulere ;
> But deth, that wol not suffre us duellen heere,
> But as it were a twyncling of an ye,
> Hem bothe hath slayn, and alle we schul dye.
> But forth to telle of this worthy man,
> That taughte me this tale, as I bigan,
> I say that he first with heigh stile enditith
> (Er he the body of his tale writith)
> A proheme.'

It will be observed that at the beginning, just as at the close, direct reference is made to Petrarch's having written the tale as well as taught it to the clerk ; so that there could not have been anything inconsistent, as Sir Harris Nicolas hints there was, in the statements that the tale was known to Chaucer as written, besides having been taught him personally by Petrarch. Sir Harris Nicolas appears to have overlooked this parallel passage at the opening : *

* See his *Life of Chaucer*, pp. 27, 28.

' Fraunces Petrark, the laureat poete,
Highte this clerk　.　.　.　.
That taughte me this tale, as I bigan,
I say that he first with heigh stile enditith
(Er he the body of his tale writith)
A proheme.'

One of the most curious points in debate about the
life of Chaucer turns upon the reading to be given to
his *Testament of Love.*　　Gower, in his *Confessio
Amantis,* makes Venus say this :—

' And grete wel Chaucer, when ye mete,
As my disciple and my poete ;
For in the floures of his youthe,
In sundry wyse, as he wel couthe,
Of dytees and of songes glade,
The whiche he for my sake made,
The lande fulfylled is over alle ;
Whereof to him in specyalle,
Above all other, I am most holde.
Forthy now in his dayes olde
Thou shalle him telle this message,
That he uppon his latter age,
To sette an end of al his werke,
As he whiche is myn owne clerke,
Do make his Testament of Love,
As thou hast done thy shrift above,
So that my court yt may recorde.'

This *Testament of Love* is one of the most deeply
interesting of Chaucer's works, and takes the very
highest rank as a proof of his intelligence and varied

knowledge. But it is in substance and form a long allegory interspersed with dialogue between Love and the Poet, and long speeches, often very beautiful ones, addressed by Love to him, he being represented as a prisoner, slandered, deserted, and in fear that his mistress should believe the slanders, and desert him in his disgrace. The lady of the allegory is Marguerite, as all Chaucer's ladies are ; and though her face is half hidden between the 'wimples' and 'folds' of the allegory, she remains for the reader a positive human figure, who was chosen by the romancist as his mistress, and the lady of his vows, to whom his *love* was due, according to the fashion of the middle ages, as distinguished from fidelity to the conjugal bond. But then those portions of the work in which the lady shows manifestly as a real woman seem to me incapable of being torn from those portions in which the poet is represented as an actual prisoner in debt and in disgrace. From the passages which are given in another place, every reader can judge for himself whether or not facts are embedded in the allegory, however, difficult it may be to make sense of them in connexion with the known dates of established facts in Chaucer's life.

In 1386, Chaucer being then one of the knights of the shire for the county of Kent, sat in the parliament which assembled at Westminster on the 1st of October in that year. It seems admitted on all hands that Chaucer's object in attending this Parliament, if not in entering the House of Commons, was to support the party who adhered to John of Gaunt, Duke of Lancaster, his friend; and it is supposed that his dismissal in December of the same year from his offices of Comptroller of Customs and Comptroller of Petty Customs in the port of London was due to the displeasure of the king or the king's party at the part taken by the poet on the Duke of Lancaster's side of the questions of the day. At all events, his dismissal quickly followed the sitting of a Commission appointed in November to inquire into the management of the departments of the Subsidies and Customs; and Adam Yerdeley and Henry Gisors were appointed in his place.

A glance at the extracts from the *Testament of Love* will make quite intelligible what follows. When John of Northampton was elected Lord Mayor of the City of London in 1382, it has been supposed, or rather stated with confidence, that Chaucer exerted himself actively to promote the election of this man, who was on the Duke of Lancaster's side, and, like the Duke, a Wyckliffite. Riots followed the election, fomented probably by the clergy of the city; the court party interfered to put them down; there was some blood shed, and John of Northampton was arrested and sent to Corfe Castle. Now by those who maintain that the *Testament of Love* contains a genuine narrative of facts, it is assumed, on its authority, that process was issued for the purpose of taking Chaucer also into custody; that, being alarmed in time, he fled to the island of Zealand, where he helped, with his purse and otherwise, some of his companions who had taken refuge in Zealand for the same reason ; that his trustees in England 'cut off his supplies and embezzled his income;' and that the inconvenience thus occasioned to him forced him to return from exile to England, upon which he was arrested immediately and sent to the Tower, where he remained for three years ; but that, in May 1389, King Richard II. pardoned and released him, upon condition that he should give such testimony against those who had been associated with him on his side of the struggle in the City as would lead to their impeachment. It is taken for proved upon the same evidence, namely, that of the *Testament of Love* that the poet accepted the terms, and did actually betray his friends into the hands of the government.

Upon all this Mr. Robert Bell makes the following remarks :—

'Mr. Campbell, speaking of this incident, pleads on behalf of Chaucer that however easy the lessons o uncapitulating fortitude may be outside the walls of a prison, they are hard when 'read by the light of a dungeon.' Before this plea in extenuation had been urged, however, it should have been ascertained what were the revelations made by Chaucer, and who it was he betrayed. Certainly not the Duke of Lancaster, and as certainly not John of Northampton, who received a full pardon from the crown in the following year.

Yet it was assumed that Chaucer had turned approver against his associates, not only in the absence of a particle of evidence as to the confidence he violated, or the consequences of its violation, but in the face of the facts that at this very time his friends were restored to power, instead of being punished on his testimony, and that he was himself again taken into their favour and protection, instead of being discarded by them, as he must have been had he acted so basely.'

As I do not think the question about the *Testament of Love* can be considered as disposed of, it is perhaps worth while to remark that this reasoning does not appear very conclusive. It is surely within the limits of possibility that, though John of Northampton was pardoned next year, Chaucer might have given evidence, which he was more or less justified in giving, against other persons whose names are lost to us, and who were disturbers of the public peace, deserving of no particular consideration, and, to use a colloquialism, scarcely worth one's powder and shot. Quite conclusive upon the subject of the dates of Chaucer's presumed flight, return, imprisonment, and release, are however the criticisms of Sir Harris Nicolas, who finds, from the Issue Rolls of the Exchequer, that from 1380 to May 1388, Chaucer must have been in London, because he took his pension half-yearly at the Exchequer with his own hands for all the years between those dates. 'It is certain,' says Sir Harris Nicolas, ' that he held both his offices in the Customs from May

1382 until about December 1386; that in November 1384, he was permitted to be absent from his duties on his private affairs for one month; that in February 1385 he obtained the further indulgence of being allowed to exercise his office of Comptroller of the Subsidies by deputy; and that at the very moment when he is supposed to have been a prisoner in the Tower, he was sitting in Parliament as a knight of the shire for one of the largest counties in England.' This, I repeat, is obviously conclusive, so far as the dates are concerned; but the same reasons, or rather feelings (demanding a *rationale*), which make one unable to miss the real woman in the Marguerite of this *Testament* compel one to find a tangible meaning, however obscure, in Chaucer's references to his disgrace, his banishment or imprisonment, and his extreme anxiety lest his mistress should believe any of the slanders against which he takes such pains to defend himself. After making large allowances for the irrelevant genius of the allegory of the middle ages, I find it utterly impossible to make anything but a gross absurdity out of the *Testament of Love* unless there lie embedded in it such facts as these:—that Chaucer got into trouble for the part he took in certain civic disputes in London;* that he gave some testimony or other against

---

* In estimating the closeness of Chaucer's connexion with the City of London, which is referred to so strongly in this *Testament* we must not forget the entry in the *Liber Albus*, which makes him the lessee of the Aldgate Bar.

certain connexions in relation to those disputes, for doing which he was charged with infidelity to his friends; that he defended himself on the ground that his duty to the public order and justice, which required his testimony, was superior to the obligations of friendship ; and that he maintained that on any footing those friends had no right to complain, because they had forfeited some of the rights of friendship by ingratitude, dishonesty, and breaches of trust. That all this may refer to certain events connected with his dismissal from the Customs in 1386, is, perhaps, possible; and it never struck me that the *imprisonment* referred to in the *Testament of Love* was anything but a metaphor common enough in literature of that order.

When the Duke of Lancaster's party was once more predominant in the reign of Richard II., we again find Chaucer at court, and shortly afterwards he is appointed clerk of the King's Works at Westminster Palace, the Tower, the Castle of Berkhamstead, and the Royal Manors of Kennington, Eltham, Sheen, Byfleet, Childern Langley, and Feckenham, at the Royal Lodge of Hathenburgh in the New Forest, at the Lodges in the Parks of Clarendon, Childern Langley, and Feckenham, and at the Mews for the King's Falcons at Charing Cross. He held this office only two years, being expressly allowed to perform the duties of them by deputy. He was dismissed in 1391, when we find another person filling his place ; but the cause of his dismissal is not recorded. It is not at all improbable that he was scarcely active in the fulfilment of his duties.

In the latter part of his life we find Chaucer frequently receiving his pensions in advance, and by the hands of others, which looks as if they had been pledged beforehand ; and there are passages in his writings which conclusively prove that he knew personally, and also keenly, what poverty was. But immediately on his accession to the throne, Henry IV. granted him a yearly pension of forty marks, in addition to his other pensions. During the last ten or fifteen years of his life he had been engaged in preparing the *Canterbury Tales ;* but by this time (1399) he was, we may presume, incapable of much activity of any kind. In 1398 letters royal are granted him, to save him from arrest for debt, and in the same year a tun of wine ; he having many years previously received a grant of a ' pitcher ' of wine from King Edward III.

During the last three years of his life he was resident in London, and in 1399 he took a lease of a house in the Garden of the Chapel of the Blessed Mary, at Westminster, which is said to have occupied the site of the existing chapel of Henry VII. On the 25th of October, 1400, he died, and was buried in Westminster Abbey.

Chaucer had two sons. Lewis, for whom he wrote a treatise on the Astrolobe, died, as is believed, very young—at all events, his history is not traceable.

Thomas held various offices under the crown during his father's life, was member of Parliament for Oxfordshire between 1402 and 1429, was Speaker of the House of Commons in 1414, was one of the Royal Commissioners appointed to negotiate the marriage of Henry V. with Katherine of France, and was engaged at the battle of Agincourt. This Thomas Chaucer had one child, Alice, who was twice married, the second time to the Duke of Norfolk (who was beheaded for treason in 1450), to whom she bore three children. But, so far as can be traced, the line of the morning-star of English poetry has long ago been extinct.

All the biographers are at sixes and sevens upon the age of Chaucer when he died. It matters little where one begins to look at so puzzling a subject, and as a specimen of the uncertainty of some of the evidence, even when supplied by the poet himself, we will take a jocular little poem, called *L'Envoy de Chaucer à Scogan.* The verses begin by saying that the statutes of heaven are broken, and that the seven planets are weeping and wailing, Venus in particular threatening to drench the earth with her tears, which produce a 'deluge of pestilence.' For this, Scogan is told he is to blame, because when his 'lady saw not his distress,' he 'gave her up at Michaelmas.' Chaucer then goes on to tell Scogan that Cupid, in his displeasure, had dropped his acquaintance, and adds,—

' He wol nat with his arwes been ywroken
  On thee ne me, ne noon of youre figure;
  We shul of him have neyther hurte nor cure,

' Now certes, frend, I drede of thyn unhappe,
  Lest for thy gilte the wreche of love procede
  On alle hem that ben hoor and rounde of shappe.'

This intimates that Chaucer was both grey and
stout.   Then he refers to ' Olde Grisel,' adding, that
his muse had gone to sleep, and that he never thought
to wake her again, though when he was young he ' put
her forth.'   Now this poem is with obvious reason supposed to refer to the ' Deluge of Pestilence,' or tremendous rain that fell in the year 1348, and was connected
in people's imagination with the Black Death.   In
Fabian's *Chronicle* we read, under the year 1348:—
' And in this xxiii. yere [*i. e.* of Edward III.] fell great
continuall rayne, from Mydsomer to Christmas, whereof ensued exceedinge floodes.   By reason whereof
the grounde was sore corrupted, so that dyvers incon-
veniences ensued upon the same, as sykenesse and other,
as in the yeres followinge shall appear . . . . . . And
aboute the ende of August the mortalite began in
dyvers places of Englande, and specially at London,
and so continued to the saide month of August next
ensuing.'

The dates even in Fabian cannot be reconciled,
unless for 23rd we read 25th; but this may pass.   Only
how are we to make out upon any hypothesis of the
time of Chaucer's birth that he was old in the

time of the Black Death? The majority of his biographers fix the date of his birth in 1328, while Mr.
Bond pushes it forward to 1340. In one case Chaucer
would have been twenty in the year of the pestilence;
in the other case only eight! Another example of the
uncertainty which attaches to such evidence as we have
is to be found in the testimony which Chaucer gave in
the case of the Grosvenor peerage, when he appeared
as a witness on behalf of Richard Lord Scrope, at Westminster, on the 15th of October, 1386. In his evidence Chaucer said that he had borne arms for twenty-
seven years, and was aged ' forty years and upwards.'
Now it has been remarked by those who are competent
to speak on such a subject, that witnesses often under-
stated their ages to the extent of ten, or even nearly
twenty years; and there has been no difficulty in as-
suming that Chaucer, at the time of the trial, was more
than fifty-six years old, instead of forty-six, as Mr.
Bond wants to make him. We know that the evidence
a man gives depends on the questions put to him, and
that preliminary questions are often answered loosely,
so that when we read ' Geoffry Chaucer, Esquire, of the
age of forty and upwards, armed for twenty-seven
years, produced on behalf of Sir Richard Scrope, sworn
and examined,' we may not unnaturally suppose that
Chaucer gave his age to the clerk or officer who admi-
nistered the oath, in general terms, such as to imply
that his testimony on a question of repute or notoriety
was worth having, which would not have been the case

with the evidence of a very young man. I do not know the exact form which was adopted in such cases, but on the faith of this document the statement of his age formed no part of the sworn evidence of the witness, and ' forty *and upwards*' may merely have meant *at the least* of such an age as to be able to look back over a good many years. As Chaucer's income depended upon the offices he held or might hold at the king's pleasure, he might not have been anxious to blazon his age if it was at all verging upon a point at which a man might be presumed to have lost some of his activity, energy, and pliancy.

The chief reason of Mr. Bond for presuming that Chaucer was only about forty-six years old in 1386, in other words, that he was born in 1340, appears to be that it is a plausible theory, founded on that very interesting discovery made by Mr. Bond himself, that Chaucer was probably a page in the household of Prince Lionel, third son of Edward III., or in the suite of his wife Elizabeth Countess of Ulster, in the years 1356, 1357, 1358, 1359 ; and for this purpose it would scarcely do to make him older than seventeen. But, if Chaucer had borne arms twenty-seven years in 1386, being then forty-six years of age, he must have begun to bear arms at thirteen, which is too early even for Chaucer's times, and scarcely leaves room for the studious years which we *must* suppose him to have passed in his adolescence, whatever force we allow to his natural genius. But besides this, in the *Confessio*

Amantis of Gower, which Gower says was written in
the year of Richard II., namely 1392, Gower expressly
says that Chaucer was ' in his dayes old,' and again, ' in
his latter age.'   Now, if Chaucer was born in 1328, he
would have been sixty-four in 1392, which accords with
Gower's description.   But if he was born in 1340, he
was of course only fifty-two when Gower wrote the *Confessio Amantis*.   It is possible that in times when
active life began so young, a man might be described
as in his latter age at fifty-two, but as at present informed I do not think it likely.

II. One of the oddest things to be met with in the
biographies of men of distinguished ability is the kind
of speculation in which the biographers indulge, as to
the manner in which great men came by their knowledge ; and when the great man is a man of genius in
the usual sense, the case becomes still more curious.
Biographers seem to forget what distinguished ability,
and much more genius, can do.   Why, what is genius?
Not the power of making efforts, though it has been
so defined, but the power of doing without visible
effort what costs other people a calculably laborious
process.   What I am now saying applies to much, if
not all, the speculation as to what Shakespeare, for
instance, knew; for though not technically a scholar, it
is probable that he knew, effectively though loosely,
much more than Ben Jonson did.   In the case of

Chaucer, speculations of this kind are still more out of place. The learned and ingenious Sir Harris Nicolas makes this remark :—' That Chaucer was not acquainted with Italian may be inferred from his not having introduced any Italian quotation into his works, redundant as they are with Latin and French words and phrases.' And to this he adds the following foot-note :— ' Though Chaucer's writings have not been examined for the purpose, the remark in the text is not made altogether from recollection, for at the end of Speght's edition of Chaucer's works, translations are given of the Latin and French words in the Poems ; but not a single Italian word is mentioned.' Now, it would be much more reasonable to say that it was utterly impossible for a man of Chaucer's ability to be ignorant of Italian. How was that possible for a man who understood Latin and French, and very often wrote in a style which, to the modern eye, suggests French a good deal more than it does English ? Surely it must be trivial to suppose that a man of the versatile genius of Chaucer, a scholar, a man of the world, a courtier, a soldier, an intimate of the royal family, a well-travelled ambassador, who had been both in France and Italy, could *help* understanding Italian, in an age when the quickening of European intellect through Italian literature was fresh, and the memory of Dante a thing of yesterday. In another page I have specified one word which seems to me like modified or mangled Italian. Familiar to us all is the couplet in which Chaucer, exactly translating a passage in the *Purgatorio* of Dante,* says :—

> ' Wel can the wyse poet of Florence
> That hatte Daunt, speke of this sentence,
> Lo, in such maner of rym is Dauntes tale :
> Ful seeld uprisith by his braunchis smale
> Prowes of man, for God of his prowesse
> Wol that we claime of him our gentilesse.'

Again (though opinions differ as to the stress to be laid upon the statement), Chaucer says that he 'learned' the Clerk's Tale from a 'worthy clerk' at Padua, 'Fraunceis Petrark, the laureate poete;' or rather he puts this statement into the mouth of the clerk of Oxenford. But I decidedly think we must take Chaucer to be speaking as if in his own person, and that it is highly probable that he conversed with and saw Petrarch in Italy—a point which has arisen already in these pages. In those days it was easier for an Englishman to talk Latin to an Italian than it is now, and Petrarch understood French ; but it is far more likely that Chaucer and he conversed in Italian, for a man like Chaucer, having a scholar's previous knowledge of the language, could have learned to talk it in a week. On the whole, I have the honour of agreeing with Mr. Wright, who thinks that Chaucer was 'well acquainted with the

---

* Purg. vii. 121.
> ' Rade volte risurge per li rami
> L' humana probitate: ed questo vuole
> Quei che la dà, perchè da se si chiami.

writings of Dante, and probably those of Petrarch,' to which I would myself, with even more confidence, add the name of Boccaccio, though Mr. Wright speaks more doubtfully of him.

III. ' What is the first broad general impression produced upon your mind by Chaucer?' To this question, put suddenly to a reader of culture and sensibility recently introduced to the poet of the *Canterbury Tales*, the answer was—' An impression of Lightsomeness.' To the question which was immediately added, ' And what is your second impression?' the answer,—not less promptly given, and with the colloquial freedom which takes little effective liberties with language,—was, ' His Englishness.'

It is not often that so much good criticism may be packed in so small a compass. Whether the Englishness (to retain the colloquialism) or the Lightsomeness ought to rank first in a just analysis of the elements of Chaucer's writings might be disputed; but inevitably the lightsomeness is first to strike the mind, because it is of the very essence of his manner. His verse is full of buoyancy; its very art is easy, the wind is not freer, it is a south-west air with a rhythm in it, and a masterly skill in the pauses. Flippancy, or even happy smartness, is easy to manage, and implies none of the highest qualities in a writer of verse; but lightsomeness or buoyancy chiefly impresses the mind when the flights taken are long enough to give the idea of

strength as well as that of elasticity.   The power of
taking a long sweep before coming to a pause, and then
of beginning again with a spring from the pausing-point,
is a well-known characteristic of the best poetry.   It is
a characteristic of which we had the last *magnificent*
example in Milton.   I do not forget the long-
resounding march and energy divine of Dryden; but
he is nearly as far below Chaucer or Milton as Leigh
Hunt is below him : a remark which I make in no
spirit of unworthy disparagement, for I love Dryden,
and all that art and happy instinct could do—one
wishes, for the sake of English literature, the success
had been as great as the desert—was done by Leigh
Hunt to restore the ' Chaucerian mood' to familiar
usage in English poetry.   But he lacked sustained
power.   How long an albatross will remain poised in
the air without apparent motion by a ship's side I
forget ; but if it had, like a sea-gull, some of the
vivacity of the swallow or the martin, it would represent the flight of the Chaucerian or the Miltonic verse
as contrasted with the swallow-flights of poets who
cannot remain long upon the wing.   It may be added,
that, while no one can fail to catch Chaucerian echoes
in Keats, they breathe so much of the peculiar balmy
music and perfume of the Elizabethan time that we
feel chiefly that they have been lingering there till they
have forgotten Chaucer.

If there are any readers of these pages who are
unaccustomed to consider the higher characteristics of

verse in the great masters, they may not perhaps be
displeased if I approach by very easy degrees the long-
breathed lightsomeness of the poetry of Chaucer.
Since his dialect is not familiar to some of us, and it is
only by a special effort that his verse can be read
musically, we will begin by lending our ears to a passage in Milton, *Paradise Lost,* Book II. :—

> ' Though all the giant brood
> Of Phlegra with the heroic race were join'd
> That fought at Thebes and Ilium, on each side
> Mix'd with auxiliar gods; and what resounds,
> In fable or romance, of Uther's son,
> Begirt with British and Armoric knights,
> And all who since, baptized or infidel,
> Jousted in Aspramont or Montalban,
> Damasco, or Morocco, or Trebisond,
> Or whom Biserta sent from Afric shore
> When Charlemain, with all his peerage, fell
> By Fontarabia   .   .   .'

This is only a portion of the sentence, which in its
complete form extends over seventeen lines of Milton's
text; but it will suffice to exhibit to the least accustomed person, especially if he will read it out loud,
what is meant by length or strength of poetic flight.
It will be observed, in reading it, that the voice is
kept in suspense, held as it were in the air over the
theme, and cannot come suddenly to a cadence ; and the
same thing will constantly occur in the reading of
Chaucer.   But, in order to obtain a full idea of the

Lightsomeness of his measure, we must add colour, vivacity, and rapid interspersed touches that seem pleasantly to threaten the mind and ear with a descent here and there; which is nevertheless withheld. For the same reason that an example of strength of wing was taken from Milton,—namely, that his dialect is at once familiar,—an example of brightness and buoyancy will now be presented from Shakespeare, King Henry IV., Part I., Act iv. Scene 1.

> ' All furnished, all in arms,
> All plumed like estridges, that with the wind
> Battle like eagles having lately bathed;
> Glittering in golden coats, like images;
> As full of spirit as the month of May,
> And gorgeous as the sun at midsummer;
> Wanton as youthful goats, wild as young bulls;
> I saw young Harry, with his beaver on,
> His cuisses on his thighs, gallantly arm'd,
> Rise from the ground like feather'd Mercury,
> And vaulted with such ease into his seat,
> As if an angel dropp'd down from the clouds
> To turn and wind a fiery Pegasus.'

These passages speak freely enough for themselves; and if the reader will imagine their characteristics in a considerable degree combined, he will have an idea of the lightsomeness of the Chaucerian music, which is the natural expression of an elastic genius.

It cannot, perhaps, be said that there is anything essentially or peculiarly English in this lightsomeness of music; it seems to me to derive direct from the

Italian, or perhaps through the French. It is too late
to complain, as Tyrwhitt has done, of any loss we may
have incurred in poetic effects by the gradual dropping
of the feminine *e* formerly sounded (considerably at
discretion I think in Chaucer's time) at the end of a
word when the next word began with a consonant; but
there is no doubt it communicated to English metre a
flavour of quantity which we now miss in our accen-
tually compounded poetry—the feet of the verse seemed
then to move on a soft springy carpet; the measure
was gentle, like a cavalier lightly supporting a lady
with the spirit of the dance in her sandals. But, if the
thorough 'Englishness' of Chaucer is not to be sought
in his measure technically considered, it is easily discovered in what adheres to his measure with a junction
which is unmistakably vital. *Le style c'est de l'homme
même*—the style, here as elsewhere, is of the man himself; and the man is every inch an Englishman. He
is not only English in the sense of being unable, apparently, to escape such things as 'frank anachronism'
in the telling of classic or foreign stories,—like a traveller who persists in treating the inhabitants of a
strange land as foreigners; he is English in the essential objectivity of his mind, and in the directness of his
touch. In other words, persons disclose themselves to
us in his poetry by what they say and do, and are not
ripped up by analysis; and the description proceeds by
strong salient touches which shirk nothing. In spite
of the influence of Wordsworth, and the absence of any

recent dramatic poetry accepted of the people, the bent of the poetic genius of England is objective; and, in spite of any unpleasant and disgraceful facts which we have been forced to learn about ourselves, we must still be permitted to say that not to shirk anything is a pre-eminent note of the English character. This note belongs in a high degree to Chaucer: hence the force of his descriptive touches; to employ a vulgarism which he himself would scarcely have disdained, he hits the right nail on the head at once. To the account of this directness of vision and touch which will shirk nothing must be laid some of that plainness of speech upon certain topics which we now call, and justly call, coarseness; to much, indeed, of what is to be found in Chaucer, we should now be justified in applying the word filthy. But 'coarseness' is decidedly an English quality; and when it does not go beyond a species of humorous bravado at odd moments in presence of facts which are punctiliously enclosed for the greater part of men's and women's time, it needs imply no depravity, or even disrespect to human life. This topic will, however, arise again; it was only necessary, in this place, to guard myself against being supposed to acquiesce in the half-sincerely apologetic handling which the subject too often receives.

The Englishness of Chaucer is, meanwhile, conspicuous in other particulars, and especially in his good fellowship. He is 'the goode felawe' of his own Wife of Bath, and something more—for the latter was, by the implications of the lady's talk, a mere boon companion. It is not true, in the sense in which the words are usually taken, that the English 's'amusent moult tristement.' They have amusements which are spiced with adventure—and long may they love them!—and even amusements in which hard blows can scarcely be escaped; there is even a sturdiness or business-like air about their play, which may pass for *tristesse*—but the national character is a root of bravery rising to a stem of strong social feeling, gnarled and twisted just above-ground with genuine fun. Said to be slow to talk, the English are good fellows through it all. To put it differently, they are before all things human and sociable. Hence, however maladroit their colonial administration may have been, they are *par excellence* colonists, missionaries, gatherers together, founders of social groups, makers of history (*i. e.* the story of men and women in groups), wherever they go. In this sense who is an Englishman more English than Chaucer? His poetry is penetrated with the social spirit. He loves the haunts of men, the places where they dwell, the episodes of mutual need that bring and keep them together; meat and drink; industry and play; the uprisings and downsittings, the incomings and outgoings of men and women. It is easy to heap up words concerning this, but simple as it seems to say that a poet is intensely human, it is really *not* easy to appreciate, much less explain the thing intended. It could not exist in company with *habitual* cruelty; but it is by no means always allied with philanthropy. Yet the openness of heart, the hostelry-keeping of the affections which we indicate when we say a man is, as Chaucer was, intensely human, is something truly divine (though that word appears antithetic), and a mighty purifying influence. Hence, it may be said of Chaucer, that even when he describes what is vicious the total effect of his writing is not impure. The same thing might be said of Fielding, again, for the same reason,—that of the abounding humanity of the man; but he is not so free from taint as Chaucer. A steady breeze of strong human feeling flows through his writing; he keeps you in the open air of life. He describes with zest, not with greed; he does not peep at wrong passion shut up in the stews. If there is any ' garden-scene,' any kissing in the ' summer-house,' at which he laughs, he laughs out like a man; he is not a grinning, eaves-dropping devil. Above all, he describes imaginatively, as if he had himself no share in the transaction, though he tastes by sympathy what is bright and joyous in it. He never says, with Mephistopheles:—

> ' I have my pleasure in it, too.'

though we shall, I fear, not be able to acquit him of unnecessary dabbling in ideas with which a chastised imagination would rather not play at all.

In the Bellows Portrait, Shakespeare was described as the prince of good fellows, and he has certainly described a good fellow in terms which might admirably well be applied to Chaucer:—

> ' Thou hast been
> As one, in suffering all, that suffers nothing—
> A man that Fortune's buffets and rewards
> Hast ta'en with equal thanks. And blest are those
> Whose blood and judgment are so well commingled
> That they are not a pipe for Fortune's finger
> To sound what stop she please.'

In this description there is more gladness and relish of life than we associate with the idea of the modern Englishman; but that is another question. This relish of life was, in Chaucer, connected, as it often is, with a versatility of energy which is not now so common as it used to be, but which was illustrated in splendid examples down to the time of Milton,—most splendidly of all in the Elizabethan times. He was a gentleman, a courtier, an ambassador, and a soldier; perhaps a man of business too, though we have no means of knowing *how* he filled the public offices which he held under the Crown during some portions of his life. His descriptions of life and pictures of character could only have come from a writer who was a man of the world (as well as a scholar and a poet); he was connected by various links with persons and events which are prominent in one of the most splendid eras of English history; and his *Canterbury Tales* contain, to repeat the *naïve* word already employed in this chapter, more

Englishness than any other poem in the language. For these reasons, he may fairly be taken as a typical person, so that no impertinence can be charged against such a title as 'Chaucer's England.'

IV. 'I never read a biography constructed from fragmentary hints,' said to me once a living writer, 'without fancying that I have the man himself looking over my shoulder, and saying, "Oh, nonsense—never mind that book—it's all stuff." ' If there is reason in this (and there is much), as applied to biography, in which the imagination throws up elaborated spans of continuation from isolated piers of fact, the application to a memoir of an era is still stronger. Much depends upon the reader's tendency to set a high value, or the reverse, upon what are called picturesque touches. Mr. Carlyle thinks it of considerable consequence, to gather from an old chronicler that, say, Abbot Samson trudged along upon a journey with his skirts thrown over his arms at the elbows; and no doubt such trifles are useful in keeping up a sense of reality. Yet it is surprising, and even astonishing, to note how rarely the most faithful diary or chronicle that we can imagine tells us the precise thing we want to know; and how regularly it happens that matter-of-fact writing starts by a million times more questions than it satisfies. Every single fact that we know or pretty certainly guess concerning the life of Chaucer is only a whet to our curiosity; and such a picture of England in his

lifetime as we can make for ourselves out of what we
know, proves a canvas upon which, under the hand of
the ' restorer' or ' cleaner,' a bit of outline or a gleam
of colour starts forward here and there; but the consent of a complete design is wanting. We all know in
our daily experience how baseless are often the assump-
tions by which we piece together into a story facts
which seem connected;—how absurd are some of our
most ingenious theories. Half the interest of half the
best plots in the world depends upon the fact that,
men may construe things clean from the purpose of
the things themselves. We are not necessarily much
the wiser for knowing with exactness a thousand facts
about the external life of a man who died seven hundred
years ago. We may know that he lived on coarse food,
dressed in coarse cloth, lived in a smoky hut, and
never saw a toothbrush; but we cannot safely conclude
that he was more sensible of physical discomfort than
any one of ourselves. A similar uncertainty must
attend our criticism of the morality of a past time, and
even of its manners or etiquette. It would be a very
poor, and often very erroneous idea of modern English
society that would be gathered from an ordinary manual
of etiquette. Books proposing rules of conduct must
be elementary, to begin with; in order to be exhaust-
ive, they must forbid a great many things which
are not supposed to be commonly done, and enjoin
others which are not generally neglected. A traveller
from another planet to this would not be justified in

concluding from the existence of the sixth commandment in the sacred books of Europeans, that we were always committing murder. I have, for my own part, a profound distrust of imaginative reconstructions of the past, in which the strictly historic element is the basis of a calculated superstructure. But, on the other hand, the spirit or poetry of a time is not necessarily difficult to realise in proportion to its remoteness. Perhaps we are in some respects nearer to the time of Chaucer than to the time of the Regency, and can understand it better. Can any imagination put sense into Beau Brummel, or make a credible living figure of him? To go a little further back, still keeping within the same characteristic limit, can anybody now living understand how the speech of Sheridan upon the impeachment of Warren Hastings could be, as it was, overwhelming in its effect upon a highly-cultivated auditory?

There is indeed a sense in which it may be said that the history of England begins about the time of Chaucer, or in his century. The solid island is here, and *was* here, before Julius Cæsar; and, though the surface of the land is changed, and the wild boar is gone from the forest, and the bittern from the marshes, and the heron from the banks of the Thames, and hundreds of generations of men and women have laid their ashes down here, and thousands of acres have been furrowed and unfurrowed, and a thousand cities have trodden out the grass and elbowed aside the trees, it may still be said that we tread the soil on which was spilt the blood of Caractacus, on which the scythed wheels of Boadicea's chariot moved to the battle-field.   But who can get up any sympathy with the Druids ?   The mistletoe does not help us, nor the mystery of Stonehenge : they are as remote as the Aztecs.   We should cut them dead if we were to meet them.   We call ourselves Anglo-Saxons when we are on our stilts, but we must pass over many years from the time of Caractacus before we can ' feel in our very bones' the England of our pride.   Mr. Carlyle, fortune-telling backwards after the manner of modern historians, pronounces it to have been a good thing that William the Norman conquered Harold.   But what school-boy ever read, or what man or woman ever remembered, the familiar words : ' As soon as William had passed the Thames at Wallingford, Stigand, Archbishop of Canterbury'—without feeling very enraged with Stigand, and thinking that Stigand ought to have cursed William with bell and book, and told him to ' get out of that?'   However the Norman did, in fact, lay his hand upon England, and left pretty strong finger-marks there.   Then come forest laws, feudalities, resistance of the Kentish men, Domesday book, the gradual remoulding of the Anglo-Saxon institutions by the supple administrative fingers of the Norman, the struggles between the kings and the kings' barons, which began the break-up of the feudal system, the resistance of offended or injured nobles and others to the forest laws, the true romances (more

representatively true, I believe, than much history) of
Robin Hood and Little John, and Adam Bell and Clym
of the Clough; and Magna Charta; and the gradual
modification of the Roman Catholic religion in practice
by the spirit of the people; and the growth of London
and Canterbury, and the fermentation of the best of
the old Anglo-Saxon elements in the noble county of
Kent; and the gradual appearance in the political
arena of ' the modern problem—the greatest happiness
of the greatest number:' the confluence of the Romance
and the English literary genius; the advent of a great
monarch; the self-adjustment and reconstruction of the
language, and its admission within courtly gates,—and
we are in the time of Chaucer. Every thing is alive.
The chimney is added to the house, the glass-window
replaces the lattice or the shutter; the gun threatens
the bow and arrow with extinction; Adam Scrivener
' lothly' lays down his penner when the click of movable
types becomes loud; dress begins to *think* of lopping
off its entangling superfluities, and suiting itself to the
wants of a people going busily to and fro; the dignity
and prestige of the priestly person is threatened, and
more remotely that of the soldier, an element clearly
traceable in the spirit of the times; lastly, religious
persecution lights the torch to burn the heretic,—and
we feel that we are in England. To-morrow the first
printing-press will be set up under the shadow of Westminster Abbey; and after the Bible, Chaucer's *Canterbury Tales* will be the first book printed. The thing

which seems least like what we now call England is the
red-handedness of religious persecution, and the odd
manner in which spiritual and secular personages jumble their functions and thwart each other on exactly
the same principles, though on exactly opposite sides
of the battle. John of Gaunt in St. Paul's, insisting
that Wycliffe shall have a chair, and Bishop Court-
ney, descended from Charlemagne, quarrelling with the
duke, who threatens to ' pluck the bishop by the hair
out of the church,' are scarcely more absurd than
Henry VIII. playing seraphic doctor and inquisitor all
in one to a poor martyr. But we perceive, in reading
the history of the time, that when we have things
got to this pass, a work of liberty is begun, which is
almost as safe as it was when Cromwell took it in hand
and made it sure for England. No part of English
history (it is trite to make the observation) has fascinated so many generous minds as the reign of Edward
III.; partly, of course, because of the admiration felt
for the character and exploits of the king himself,
love for the Black Prince, and interest in the morning-
star of English poetry; but partly also from a subtle
consciousness that in this century, or thereabouts, the
lineaments of the England to which we really belong
are first vividly traceable.

V. It would be too much to expect that Chaucer
should be above the use of the stereotyped forms of the
literature of the time. He is not. Even in what may

be called the comedy parts of the *Canterbury Tales,* he
occasionally, though rarely, adopts an unnatural trick
—the Wife of Bath, for example, is too full of explanation and speech-making for even the hypothesis or
' fable' of the poem. The well-known device of the
old-world story-tellers,—that of putting explanatory
speeches (under impossible or improbable circumstances) into the mouths of the personages in their
stories, evidently derives from the circumstance that
the supposition of the literature is that its author is
speaking to the reader. If we imagine a troubadour
or minstrel reciting the adventures of a hero or a he-
roine to a circle of listeners, we perceive it is natural
for the reciter, every now and then, to dramatize his
tale, to assume the character of the hero, and speak
in the first person singular, for the purpose of dis-
playing his emotions. Thus the ' complaynte' of the
mourning knight in the ' Boke of the Duchesse,' would
have a very different effect if given with the living
voice of the singer or reciter, from that which it now
has in print under our eyes, where all such speeches
have an intolerable stiffness of effect. A similar remark applies to another conventionalism, which is frequent in Chaucer,—that of addressing the reader with
an asseveration, an assurance that the truth, and only
the truth, is being told him,— such as, ' I wol not lye;'
' I shal you tel certayn,' and the like. For one thing,
we must remember that asseveration was a natural
ornament of style in an age when it was praise to say

of a lady and a princess that her greatest oath was 'by Saint Loy.' But besides, in the telling of a story, occasional asseveration was not unnatural to a singer or reciter, who was supposed to be carrying his listeners along with him in a perfect illusion. Modern criticism condemns in the story-teller, not only all asseveration about incident, but all meditation about the characters of the personages, as being simply destructive of the illusion; but that is because the illusion is supposed to be so slight that it will not bear a comment however oblique. A printed novel, however, which we take up or lay down as we please in our solitude, is a very different thing from a romance delivered with animation by the living voice and gesture to a number of excited listeners, who hardly know whether they believe or not. And English poetry in Chaucer had not yet outgrown this child-like hypothesis.

The enormity of the demands so often made upon the reader by the 'fable' or hypothesis of the narrator of the time, is curiously illustrated in the Frankleyne's Tale. This is one of the best told and least offensive of the whole series of the *Canterbury Tales;* it is everywhere tender and dignified, and abounds with single touches of great beauty. But, unhappily, the morality of the fable, so to speak, is too absurd to leave the narrative itself enjoyable, unless we begin by granting it of wilfulness aforethought. A married lady, passionately pursued by a lover in her

husband's absence, informs him, by way of shutting
him up from any further prosecution of his suit, that
she will listen to him in the day when he shall have
removed all the rocks from the coast of Brittany. The
lover takes this as it was intended, and prepares for
death, since the vehemence of his passion made life impossible to him. In the sequel he finds an old magi-
cian who communicates to him a spell by which he is
enabled to make it appear to the lady that all the rocks
are removed. In the meantime the lady's husband has
returned, and, hearing the facts, actually bids his wife
go and redeem her word by the sacrifice of her purity.
The catastrophe is averted, as it happens ; but note that
this is put before the reader in apparent good faith as
a case of conflict of duties, and an illustration of perfect honour. We are called upon, by what I have
called the moral hypothesis of the fable, to admire the
utter truthfulness with which the lady kept her word
to her lover. But the poet must have known all the
while that this was child's play, such as could impose
on nobody. It is mere verbal quibbling to say that
there was any promise in the case ; for the answer of
the lady, although it was, by a figure of speech, in the
form of a promise, was a denial, and was so understood
by the lover. They *both* believed the figure of speech
employed by the lady implied an impossibility. The
mutual understanding was perfectly clear. It was not
as if the lover had come to his mistress and said, ' I
can remove the rocks on the coast of Brittany — if I

do it, will you grant me your love?' In short, it is impossible to feel interested in the cutting of the *nodus*, for there was in reality none to cut. Of course these comments are not addressed to any impossibility in the story, for we are bound to grant that; but to an absurdity which remains when the story is granted.

It is, indeed, by no means certain that Chaucer—of whose seriousness of intent we are so often left uncertain—did not mean in the Frankleyne's Tale to ridicule the ethics of Troubadour and Trouvere romance, or at least that he did not write the story with a sly reference to those ethics. There is no clear burlesque or parody, as there is in Sir Thopas, but it is impossible that a shrewd man and a humourist like Chaucer should have missed the absurdity just pointed out.

VI. Of Chaucer's incessant play of sly humour the instances might be multiplied a thousand-fold. The most serious subject is never quite safe in his hands, —until he becomes old and 'morall,' if even then. When the Clerk has finished the story of Griselda, we are immediately treated—and very properly in this case—to a bit of banter, 'L'Envoye de Chaucer'—which is introduced in this way:—

' But oo word, lordes, herkneth er I go:
    It were full hard to fynde now a dayes
    As Grisildes in al a toun thre or tuo ;
    For if that thay were put so such assayes,

The gold of hem hath now so badde alayes
With bras, that though the coyn be fair at ye,
It wolde rather brest in tuo than plye.
  For which heer, for the wyves of Bathe,—
Whos lyf and alle of hir secte God meyntene
In high maistry, and elles were it scathe,—
I wil with lusty herte freisch and grene,
Say yow a song to glade yow, I wene ;
And *lat us stynt of ernestful matiere.*'

Whether the opening of the ' Legende of Goode
Women ' is meant to be quaintly serious, it would
take a keener wit than mine to determine—I confess
that to me the poet's eye seems to twinkle a little
between the lines : —

' A thousande tymes I have herde telle,
  That there ys joy in hevene and peyne in helle,
  And I accorde wel that it ys so ;
  But, natheles, yet wot I wel also,
  That ther nis noon dwellyng in this countree,
  That eyther hath in hevene or helle ybe,
  Ne may of hit noon other weyes witen,
  But as he hath herd seyd, or founde it writen ;
  For by assay ther may no man it preve.
    But God forbede but men shulde leve
  Wel more thing than men han seen with eye !
  Men shal not wenen every thing a lye
  But yf himselfe yt seeth, or elles dooth ;
  For, God wot, thing is never the lasse sooth,
  Thogh every wight ne may it not ysee.
  Bernarde, the monke, ne saugh nat al parde !'

In the Nun-priest's Tale, when Chanticleer is talk-

ing in the night toh is sultana Partlet, he slily mis-
translates his little scrap of Latin in a precisely contrary sense :—

> ' Madame Pertilot, so have I blis,
>   Of o thing God hath me sent large grace ;
>   For whan I see the beaute of your face,
>   Ye ben so scarlet hiew about your eyghen,
>   It makith al my drede for to deyghen,
>   For, al so siker as *In principio*
>   *Mulier est hominis confusio.*
>   (Madame, the sentence of this Latyn is,
>   Womman is mannes joye and mannes blis.)'

The Franklin avows that the gods had not made him
poetical, but though the next illustration may be
explained by supposing that it is said in character by
the prosaic husbandman, it is truly Chaucerian in its
sudden afterthought of plain construction :—

> ' .   .   .   The brighte sonne had lost his hewe,
>   For the orizont had reft the sonne his liht,
>   This is as much to sayn as it was nyht.'

In the ' Boke of the Duchesse' (the lady whose death
is bewailed being Blanche, first wife of John of Gaunt)
there is a passage in point which appears to puzzle the
pundits.   The poet describes the lady as one in whom
there was no guile, no coquetry, no desire of holding
admirers in the leash, no capacity of feigning (even
with her face) except in self-defence.   He then goes
on to add that she was not a woman to send a knight,

who should do her homage, upon impossible or very dis-
tant services :—

> ' Hyr lust to holde no wyghte in honde,
> Ne, be thou siker, she wolde not fonde,
> To holde no wyghte in balaunce,
> By halfe word, ne by countenaunce,
> But yif men wolde upon hir lye.
> Ne sende men into Walakye,
> To Pruise, and to Tartarye,
> To Alysaundre, ne into Turkye,
> And bydde him faste anoon that he
> Goo hoodeles into the drye se,
> And come home by the carrenare.'

The last three lines are banter, *q. d.* ' Nor send him to
fetch her a pound of green cheese from the moon' —

> ' Go hoodless into the dry sea,
>   And come back by the carrenare.'

It may perhaps be for want of vision, but I confess
that I see no obscurity here.   Of course the ' dry sea '
is an absurdity, it was meant to be so.   As for the
word *carrenare*, it is a stumbling-block, but not a
worse stumbling-block than some other adapted,
modified, or mangled words in Chaucer.   I take it to
be bad Italian for carrier or caravan.   If we suppose the
word to have been written *carratare* it is scarcely very
bad Italian.   The proper word would be *carrettiere*, a
carter; but *carretta* means cart, and *carrettare*, formed
from that for the sake of the rhyme, is not very out-

rageous license, compared with other things of the same kind to be found in Chaucer and poets of the time.

'The Wife of Bath' opens her Tale with some innuendoes that are quite to the purpose with regard to Chaucer's quietly humorous scepticism:—

> ' In olde dayes of the kyng Arthour,
> Of which that Britouns speken gret honour,
> Al was this lond fulfilled of fayrie ;
> The elf-queen, with hir joly compaignye,
> Daunced ful oft in many a grene mede.
> This was the old oppynyoun, as I rede ;
> I speke of many hundrid yer ago ;
> But now can no man see noon elves mo.
> For now the grete charité and prayeres
> Of lymytours and other holy freres,
> That sechen every lond and every streem,
> As thik as motis in the sonne-beem,
> Blessynge halles, chambres, kichenes, and boures,
> Citees and burghes, castels hihe and toures,
> Thropes and bernes, shepnes and dayeries,
> That makith that ther ben no fayeries.
> For ther as wont was to walken an elf,
> Ther walkith noon but the lymytour himself,
> In undermeles and in morwenynges,
> And saith his matyns and his holy thinges
> As he goth in his lymytacioun.
> Wommen may now go saufly up and doun,
> In every bussch, and under every tre,
> There is non other incubus but he,
> And he ne wol dorn hem no dishonour.'

It is *scarcely* easy, realist as we know Chaucer to

have been, to decide whether all this means that the
friars had driven away the fairies, or that they had
suppressed the belief in them.   No doubt the lady
intended to make the company understand that she
was of the opinion which probably the majority of
them held, namely that fairies and fairy-craft did not
exist.   But the last two lines are, as schoolchildren
say, 'all her impudence.'   The Wife of Bath was not
the person to preach up the purity of the friars ; and
nobody can doubt that her opinion and Chaucer's too,
was pretty nearly hit in the 'Song against the Friars,'
from which I have made some quotations in another
place—it would be impossible to give quite the whole
of it in a book for general reading.

Another example of Chaucer's slyness, a slyness
amounting almost to ambiguity, occurs in his comment
upon the Sompnour's or Summoner's way of estimating
an ecclesiastical malediction.   'A man's soul,' says the
Sompnour, 'is in his purse.'   'But well I wot,' says
Chaucer—

> 'But wel I woot he lyeth right in dede
>   Of cursing oweth ech guilty man to drede ;
>   For curs wol slee right as assoilyng saveth—'

in other words, that neither blessing nor ban is of any
use whatever.

In the same class of half ambiguous deliverances
we may class the description of the Miller :—

> 'Well cowde he stealen corn and tollen thries ;
>   And yet he had a thombe of gold parde.'

Upon which Tyrwhitt remarks, carrying with him the
assent of every reader, that, the allusion probably
being to the old saw, ' Every honest miller has a thumb
of gold,' the meaning of Chaucer was that this particular miller was just as honest as the rest of his trade ;
i. e. that millers were all thieves alike.

There is in the prologue, in the description of the
Monk, a touch of the species of humour I have now in
my mind, which is not so marked as some others that
have been quoted, and yet is characteristic. It relates
to the rule of monastic life ordained by St. Benedict
and others, and sanctioned by St. Augustine. Chaucer,
speaking in the Monk's person, apologizes for the easy
life he led :—

> ' What schulde he studie and make himselven wood,
>   Uppon a book in cloystre alway to powre,
>   Or swynke with his handes and laboure,
>   As Austyn bit ?   How schal the world be served ?
>   Let Austyn have his swynk to him reserved.'

Q. d. Let St. Augustine keep his rule himself, and
not plague other people with it.   Everything, in these
cases, depends upon the delicate colouring of a phrase ;
this explanation of mine (unnecessary, I dare say,) reads
flatly, but there is humour in saying,—

> ' Let Austyn have his swynk to him reserved.'

The very word ' swink' is one which we may regret
having dropped out of ' polite' use, so droll is it.   It is

only now and then a clown whom in modern days we
hear say ' sweat and swink.'

To these examples may be added one more, which
is to be found in the last line of the ' Court of Love,'
in which Chaucer, with mock gravity, thanks the god-
dess Venus that he is allowed to retain his life.   Elsewhere he refers to his ' escape' from love.

VII. The attempts, honourably designed and honourably executed, of other English poets to modernize
Chaucer as it is called, are on all hands admitted to
have been only partially successful.   Indeed, all such
attempts must be failures. When we read a translation of
a poem from another language into our own, we make a
large allowance to start with—a much larger allowance than we can make when the task of the adapter
is simply that of ' modernizing' a poem in our own
tongue, though in an antiquated form of it, where
the meanings of the majority of the words employed
by the poet are easily made out.   In truth, the
preparatory labour required for understanding and enjoying Chaucer is not to be compared with that of
acquiring a new language, the needful glossary containing at the utmost only a few hundred words.   And
we proceed upon a gross misconception if we fancy we
have got a poet's poem when we have got the thought,
story, or imagery of his writing.   In all good writing,
but most of all in poetry,—as has been often said,—
the words are not the dress, but the body of the

thought. We do not hear Chaucer the poet, unless we hear the exact music which he employed. If we drop or vary an accent, or put a thin close vowel where he inserted an open one, we miss the intention of the poet. Hence, it has been truly said that in the best specimen of the modernizing process applied to Chaucer,— that for which we are indebted to Wordsworth,— something is lost, and in that something, everything. In order to the complete enjoyment of the Chaucerian music, the reader ought undoubtedly to know a little French, a little German, and, perhaps, a little Anglo-Saxon. But a few simple rules will carry him a long way.

First. Sound softly, enough to make a syllable of it, the final *e* in a word when the rhythm requires it, as it generally does before another word beginning with a consonant. Before a vowel or an aspirate, not. Thus, the first line of the *Canterbury Tales* should be read:—

' Whan that April-le, with his schowr-es swoote.'

Second. Wherever the verse requires it for the purpose of accuracy or uniformity of beat, accentuate the word on the last syllable. Thus, the third line of the *Canterbury Tales* should be read:—

' And bathud every veyne in swich *licour*,'

the accent on the last syllable. No one who reads French will feel any difficulty in doing this in the right place.

Third. It will be obvious, upon the most cursory glance at Chaucer, or any of his contemporaries, that the termination which we now write *tion* must be read as two clear syllables : *e. g.*

> ' Yet hastow * caught a false suspec-ci-oun.'

Lastly. Although it may be contended that the verse is justified as it stands whenever the number of *accents* in lines intended to couple is the same, whatever may be the number of the syllables, always bear in mind that copyists make blunders, and particularly that Chaucer's did. Remember the poet's lines addressed ' unto his own scrivener :'—

> ' Adam Scrivener, if ever it thee befalle
> Boece or Troilus for to write new,
> Under thy long locks thou maist have the scalle,
> But after my making thou write more trew !
> So oft a day I mote thy werke renew,
> It to correct and eke to rubbe and scrape ;
> And all is thorow thy negligence and rape.'

It is true these couplets suggest that Chaucer was a careful reader and corrector of his own manuscripts ; but no care is sufficient to exclude errors in copying, as those who are accustomed to revise such work have too much reason to know.

If any reader, alarmed and repelled by the uncouth look of the strange words scattered over the pages of

---

* That is, ' Yet hast thou.'

Chaucer, is inclined to think there can be no music in him worth listening to, I invite him to read aloud, according to the preceding suggestions, but with as much flexibility of accent as he would employ if he were reading Shakspeare, the following exquisitely melodious song, from the ' Prologue to the Legend of Good Women :'—

' Hyde, Absolon, thy gilte tresses clere;
  Ester, ley thou thy mekenesse al adoune ;
Hyde, Jonathas, al thy frendly manere ;
  Penelopee, and Marcia Catoun,
  Make of your wifehode no comparysoun;
Hyde ye youre beautyes, Ysoude and Eleyne ; —
  My lady cometh, that al this may disteyne.

Thy faire body lat yt nat appere,
  Lavyne ; and thou Lucresse of Rome toune,
And Polixene, that boghten love so dere,
  And Cleopatre, with al thy passyoun,
  Hyde ye your trouthe of love, and youre renoun,
And thou, Tesbe, that hast of love suche peyne; —
  My lady commeth, that al this may disteyne.

Hero, Dido, Laudomia, alle yfere,
  And Phillis, hangyng for thy Demophoun,
And Canace, espied by thy chere,
  Ysiphile betraysed with Jasoun,
  Maketh of your trouthe neyther boost ne soun,
Nor Ypermystre, or Adriane, ye tweyne; —
  My lady cometh, that all this may disteyne.'

Leigh Hunt might well call this a strain of music fit to go before a queen !

VIII. Every now and then some reader of books writes to some periodical to express his surprise at having discovered a fresh ' original,' or ' source,' or authority for a well-known quotation or proverbial sentence. In every case that I have yet happened to notice, the labour might just as well have been spared. There are certain thoughts which all men in all ages, in all countries, have naturally ; and which naturally throw themselves into similar phraseology, whatever may be the language. *L'homme propose, mais Dieu dispose*—how many authorities or originators have we not all óf us seen turned up for this most obvious antithesis both of thought and expression! The thought is one which must occur to the human mind place it where you will, and under whatever conditions; I do not believe there is a language under the sun which would not furnish the necessary terms for the antithetical play of phrase ; and, although I do not remember seeing it there, I should make sure of finding it, or its equivalent, in Captain Burton's collection of proverbial sayings from equatorial Africa. It is with no surprise whatever that a reader accustomed to these reflections finds in the ' Goodly Ballade' of Chaucer, which occurs among the Minor Poems, the following :—

> ' Grete God disposeth
> And maketh casuel, by his providence,
> Suche thing as mannes frele witte purposeth.'

In every third page of Chaucer might be traced some

familiar sentiment in familiar phrase. I open him absolutely at random, at 'the Assembly of Foules,' and my eye is met with these lines : —

> 'The lyfe so short, the craft so long to lerne,
> Thassay so hard, so sharpe the conquering,
> The dreadful joy, alway that flit so yerne,'—

only three of them, but each one of them, especially the first and third, containing one of those 'parallels' with which literature is crowded. Of course, nobody would express any surprise at finding the *ars longa*, *vita brevis*, in this new shape ; but it would be the most natural thing in the world to find some critical writer tracing Gray's 'snatch a fearful joy' to the third line. Yet the expression 'fearful joy,' or 'dreadful joy,' is a perfectly obvious one, certain to be alighted upon by a majority of able writers ; and I have no doubt that, if it were worth while, I could find it, or the exact equivalent, in a score of authors in *every* literature.

It may just be noted in this connexion that no man is more frank in avowing, in general terms, his obligations to others than Chaucer. In his time, the very idea of originality as a supreme merit in literature had not taken possession of men's minds. The merit of a 'clerk' in those days was to know what other men had written. His own peculiar skill was shown in selection—unless he had genius, as Chaucer had, in which case the genius did its own work more or less unconsciously, and gave invention *in*—the originality was in excess of the bargain between him and his readers, but there it was.　In the Prologue to the ' Legend of Good Women,' Chaucer says : —

> ' But helpeth ye that han konnyng and myght,
> Ye lovers, that kan make of sentement ;
> In this case oght ye be diligent,
> To forthren me somewhat in my labour,
> Whether ye ben with the leef or with the flour,
> *For well I wot, that ye han herbeforne*
> Of makynge ropen, and lad awey the corne ;
> And I come after, glening here and there,
> And am full glad yf I may fynde an ere
> Of any goodly word that ye han left.
> And thogh it happen me rehercen eft
> That ye han in your fressh songes seyede,
> Forbereth me, and beth not evele apayede,
> Syn that ye see I do yt in the honour
> Of love.'

And again, in the ' Assembly of Fowls ;'—

> ' For out of the olde fieldes, as men saith,
> Cometh al this newe corne fro yere to yere ;
> And out of olde bokes, in good faith,
> Cometh al this newe science that men lere.'

This is a dictum that might easily be twisted into nonsense, since there is nothing absolutely new, or absolutely old ; but I have said in another part of this volume, that we must represent to ourselves human progress under the image of a shadow-cone, in which, at its greatest dilatation, there is nothing that was not within the outline at the beginning; whilst all proceeds by laws, recognizable, but untraceable, and for ever mysterious and sublime. In this way we may find the rudest folk-lore, the most perfect mythology, the symbolism of poetry and the most abstract philosophy at one.

To take another illustration, which relates to what some people would call the inner meaning of the word, ' gentleman.' This has acquired a secondary signification so remote from its first, that I confess myself unable to relish its application in any of the high senses in which some modern writers have attempted to give it currency. The only result in practice is, it appears to me, a nauseous double meaning. In Mr. Tennyson's ' Walking to the Mail,' there is a suggestive triplet, which naturally arises in the mind when this subject is present to it : —

> ' Kind nature is the best : those manners next
> That fit us like a nature second-hand ;
> Which are indeed the manners of the great.'

There is always something repulsive, however, in the ' second-hand' gentleness which is so common—it is so much like a *fashion,* instituted to keep human wild beasts in order, and make eating and drinking, and dressing and walking about go smoothly; and the question always thrusts itself up (however it may be answered)—' Does not the originally poor, unkind

nature show the worse, instead of the better, for this
gloss, this second-hand nature?'

In the time of Chaucer, and much later, the social
hypothesis or fiction was, that every man of gentle
blood was gentle.   Thus, in the 'Tale of Gamelyn,' we
have Adam and Gamelyn, when they have escaped from
the sheriff into the 'woode schawes,' seeking the
'maister, kyng of outlawes,' when they are tired and
hungry; and they say : —

'If that he be heende, and come of gentil blood,
  He wol geve us mete and drynk, and doon us some good.'

The 'heende' (easy, courteous) being meant, not as an
addition so much as an equivalent; *q. d.* every man
'come of gentil blood' is 'heende.'

Neither in Chaucer's time nor in another could
the difference between a 'nature kind' by origin, and a
nature kind at 'second-hand,'—wearing courtesy like a
glove over a hard hand,—escape notice or criticism.
But the fantasy of the mediæval spirit did not like to
give up the idea of the hereditary transmission of the
'gentle' spirit; so we find it resorting to a quibble,
and making the Founder of Christianity the *father* of
'gentilesse,' who transmits the 'gentilesse' to 'his
heirs,' who are they that 'doone him queme' [please
him.]   He who 'desires to be gentil' must follow
'the first father and finder of gentilesse,—the first
stock :'—

' The firste fadir and fyndr of gentilesse,
  What man desirith gentil for to be,
  Most followe his trace, and alle his wittes dresse,
    Vertue to shew, and vices for to flee ;
  For unto vertu longeth dignitee,
    And nought the revers, savely dar I deme,
  Al were he miter, corone or diademe.

This first stoke was ful of rightwisnesse.
  Trewe of his worde, sober, pitous and free,
  Clene of his gooste and lovid besynesse,
    Ageynste the vice of slowthe in honeste ;
  And but his heire love vertu as did he,
    He nis not gentil though him riche seme,
  Al were he miter, corone or diademe.

Vice may welle be heyre to olde richesse,
  But there may no man, as ye may wel see,
  Byquethe his sone his vertuous noblesse ;
    That is approperid to no degree,
  But to the firste Fader in Magestee,
    Which maketh His heires hem that doone Him queme,
  Al were he miter, corone or diademe.'

This is a composition, which, in the literary dialect of the time, is called ' a ballad ;' but the same vein of thought crops out in the Wife of Bath's Tale, in which the ugly old woman to whom the Knight is married addresses him in a similar spirit,—quoting Dante !—

    ' Ye speken of such gentilesse
  As is descendit out of old richesse,

Therfor schuld ye ben holden gentil men ;
Such arrogaunce is not worth an hen.
Look who that is most vertuous alway,
Privé and pert, *and most entendith ay*
To do the gentil dedes that he can,
Tak him for the grettest gentil man.
Christ wol we clayme of him oure gentilesse,
Nought of oure eldres for her olde richesse.
For though thay give us all her heritage,
For which we clayme to be of high parage,
Yit may thay not biquethe, for no thing
To noon of us, so vertuous lyving,
That made hem gentil men y-callid be,
And bad us folwe hem in such degré.
Wel can the wyse poet of Florence,
That hatte Daunt, speke of this sentence ;
Lo, in such maner of rym is Dauntes tale :
Ful seeld uprisith by his braunchis smale
Prowes of man, *for God of his prowesse*
Wol that we claime of him our gentilesse ;
For of our auncestres we no thing clayme
But temporal thing, that men may hurt and mayme.
Tak fuyr and ber it in the derkest hous
Bitwixe this and the mount Caukasous,
And let men shit the dores, and go thenne,
Yit wol the fuyr as fair and lighte brenne
As twenty thousand men might it biholde ;
His office naturel ay wol it holde,
Up peril on my lif, til that it dye.
Her may ye se wel, how that genterye
Is nought annexid to possessioun,
Sithins folk ne doon her operacioun
Alway, as doth the fuyr, lo in his kynde.
For God it wot, men may ful often fynde

> A lordes sone do schame and vilonye.
> And he that wol have pris of his gentrie,
> For he was boren of a gentil hous,
> And had his eldres noble and vertuous,
> And nyl himselve doo no gentil dedes,
> Ne folw his gentil auncester, that deed is,
> He is nought gentil, be he duk or erl ;
> For vileyn synful deedes maketh a cherl.
> For gentilnesse nys but renomé
> Of thin auncestres, for her heigh bounté,
> Which is a straunge thing to thy persone ;
> Thy gentilesce cometh fro God alloone.
> . . . He is gentil that doth gentil dedis.
> Than am I gentil, whan that I bygynne
> To lyve vertuously, and weyven synne.'

This is not a bad opportunity for inviting the unaccustomed reader to note how easy it is to make out
the meaning of Chaucer in spite of the antiquated
spelling. The particular passage before us is as intelligible as a paragraph in the *Times*. We receive
from our ancestors only that which some men may
' hurt and maim ;' but ' gentilesse' is divine, deriving
from God, through the incarnated Word of God. You
may bury a fire in the darkest place between here and
Mount Caucasus, and shut the door upon it, yet the
fire will burn on, as much as if it were a beacon-flame
for thousands to behold. In the same way you may
surround the divine light and fire of a gentle soul with
poverty and mean accidents ; but still, though ' gentil-
nesse' may appear to be wanting, ' gentilesce' is there :
the divine spirit inherited from God Himself. He is

gentle that does gentle deeds.   Handsome [heende] is
that handsome does.

Those who like to note coincidences, however slight
or however natural, between poets, may compare one of
the exclamations of Troilus : —

> ' O olde, unholsom, and myslyved man !
> Calkas I mene, allas ! what ayled the
> To ben a Greke, syn thow ert born Troian ?

with Juliet's : —

> ' Oh, Romeo, Romeo, wherefore art thou Romeo?
> Deny thy father and refuse thy name,
> Or, if thou wilt not, be but sworn my love,
> And I'll no longer be a Capulet.'

I am not well read enough to say whether the
remark has been made before or not, but to me it is
plain, that the ' Eve of St. Agnes ' of Keats, was suggested, though remotely only, by a portion of the machinery of *Troilus and Cressida.*   In Chaucer's poem,
Troilus is concealed by Pandarus in a closet, and then
introduced at night into the bedchamber of Cressida.

The phrase ' all and sundry,' or ' all and some,' is
familiar in Chaucer.   Take, as one example, the terms
in which the supper is spoken of in *Troilus and
Cressida* : —

> ' And after to the soper all and some,
> Whan tyme wos, ful softe thei hevn set.'

Among well-known proverbs, we recognise, at a

glance, an old friend, ' Let sleeping dogs lie,' in one line of a speech of Pandarus, in *Troilus and Cressida* : —

> ' It is not good a sleeping hound to wake.'

Here is one example of ' frank anachronism :'—

> ' Pandare, which that *in the parlemente*
> *Had herde what every lord and burges seyde,*
> And how ful graunted was, by oon assente,
> For Antenor to yelden out Cryseyde,'

and so on.

Some comment has been expended upon a line in the Reeve's Prologue : —

> ' Yet in our aisschen old is fyr i-reke,'

(even in the ashes of our old age the fire smokes); and and of course, it instantly reminds the reader of Gray's—

> ' Even in our ashes live their wonted fires.'

Gray refers to Petrarch for the original of his idea; but it is, perhaps, scarcely traceable there ; and what do we want with an ' original' at all ? In this instance, as in a thousand, the image refers itself to a commonplace of human observation, and, though it is no wonder that many poets use it, the wonder would be great indeed if no poet hit upon it.

Gratiano's reasons were like two grains of wheat in two bushels of chaff. This, agàin, is a natural image —a commonplace of human experience—sure to belong to the ordinary speech of poetry and life: accordingly, we find in Chaucer—*Troilus and Cressida :* —

> ' Eke al my wo is this, that folke now usyn
> To sey right thus, that jelosy is love ;
> And wold o [one] busshelle of jelosy excusyn,
> For that o greyn of love is in it shove.'

The proverb, ' A burnt child dreads the fire,' we find in Chaucer's version of the *Romaunt of the Rose :* —

> ' Brent child of fier hath mych drede.'

(The reader will note that ' fier' is here a dissyllable.)

The ' courage of a mouse' is an invention as old as the hills. And so is the question, ' Are you afraid he (or she) will bite ?' addressed to a timid or reluctant person. When Troilus appears loth to be led to Cressida's bedchamber :—

> ' Quod Pandarus, " Thou wrecchid mousis hert !
> Art thow agast lest she wole the byte ?
> Why, do on this furrid cloke on thi shert,
> And folow me." '

Unfortunately, we cannot from these lines draw any conclusion with respect to a question of manners that turns up subsequently ; it will not do to decide that people always went to bed in night-dresses, because Troilus wore a shirt on this occasion — the occasion being, as it was, so peculiar.

But, to pass on. We are apt to fancy that the saturation, so to speak, of literature with Biblical phrases, the modulation by Biblical accent, the moulding of sentences upon Biblical patterns, is a recent phenomenon, subsequent at least to the free circulation among the common people of a translated Bible. But a very casual reading of Chaucer and his contemporaries at once destroys the fancy, if we have once formed it. Of hundreds of instances, here is one from the Clerk's Tale, where Griselda is dismissed by her husband :—

> ' " Naked out of my fadres hous," quod sche,
> " I com, and naked moot I torne agayn." ' '

A passage which it is, of course, impossible to read without being reminded of Job, i. 21, and the version of the same thought which is given in our own ' Order for the Burial of the Dead.' And, it must be added, that in the story, as told by Boccaccio, no such words are put into the mouth of the repudiated woman, who simply says to her lord, ' I have not forgotten that you took me naked.'

Here is another example, out of the Second Nun's Tale :—

> ' And for that faith is deth withouten werkis,'

(see James, ii. 17); and yet another from the same place :—

> ' Thenk on the womman Cananee, that sayde
> That whelpes ete some of the crommes alle
> That from her lordes table ben i-falle ;'

(see Matt. xv.); and such instances might be multiplied indefinitely.

In the Prologue of the Canon's Yeman, we have, ' All that glitters is not gold,' as well as the worm in the apple :—

> ' But al thing which that schineth as the gold,
> Is nought gold, as that I have herd told;
> Ne every appel that is fair at ye,
> Ne is not good.'

Nor is it necessary, or very helpful, to go far afield for a parallel passage, as the commentators do, finding it in a writer of Latin verse who belonged to the thirteenth century ; for these again are not only familiar, they are obvious and natural, not to say inevitable forms of thought.

Among children and the vulgar to this day, the conventional question, ' How do you do ?' is often answered, in play or in sullenness, by the rhymed words, ' None the better for seeing you.' In *Troilus and Cressida* we recognise this familiar acquaintance on the lips of the lady when Pandarus comes to her bedside to inquire how she has slept :—

' Pandare, on morwe whiche that comen was
Unto his nece, gan hir faire to grete,
And seide, " Al this night so reyned it, allas !
That al my drede is, that ye, nece swete,
Have litel leyser hade to slepe and mete:
Al night," quod he, " hath rain so do me wake,
That some of us, I trowe, her hedis ake."

' And nigh he come and seid, " How stant it now?
This Mey morwe, nece, how kunne ye fare?"
Cryseyde answerde, " *Never the bet for yow !*
Fox that ye ben!" '

Here is another familiar turn of speech from the
same poem :—

' God woot I wende, O lady bright Cryseyde,
That every word was gospel that ye seyde !'

Again, in the ' Romaunt of the Rose : '—

' Tho spak Fals-Semblant right anone,
" *Alle is not gospel*, oute of doute,
That men seyn in the towne aboute:" '

and, in the course of the pages which follow, numerous illustrations will be found, not only of the
fact that the ready money of expression in Chaucer's
time was very like what it is in our own, but
of the truth that, given human nature as it is, life
as it is, and the world as it is, the coinage of expression, especially as to its metaphorical coin, must

of necessity prove either quite identical or freely interchangeable. In Chaucer we encounter no stranger : we recognise old familiar faces in his modes of speech ; he is full of the idiom, not only of the English tongue, but of the English character.

CHAPTER II

THE STORY AND THE PILGRIMS.

Concerning the 'fable' (to speak technically) of the
Canterbury Tales, a few of the observations of some of
Chaucer's biographers do not seem to me well founded
or appropriate.   There appears to be no reason for
saying that the work was written in imitation of the
Decameron of Boccaccio, except that critics are rather
too fond of discovering that one author has imitated

another,—as if similar, and often identical thoughts were not certain in the nature of things to occur to different people, whether in the sphere of science proper or imagination proper! It is, indeed, absolutely certain that similar, and as nearly as possible identical combinations of ideas pass through the minds of tens of thousands of human beings every hour of the day. If we suppose any given number of persons of imagination existing in England in the year 1868, the same topics, with similar modes of treatment, will occur to a certain portion of them who most resemble each other. But as there are differences between them as well as resemblances, they will not all of them treat, in public, the same topics in the same way; though it is easy for the critical reader, who knows an idea in profile, or in shadow, as well as in full face or in the light, to discover the similarity of the trains of thought which have been passing through the minds of the similar people. Nor is it beyond the reach of the psychology of literature to trace the sinuosities and breakings off in the treatment by differing yet similar minds of similar topics. Such minds are like travellers setting out upon a journey from nearly adjoining places to other nearly adjoining places. A bird's-eye view shows you whence they come and whither they are going. One takes the highroad, one takes a bridle-road, a third takes a rural short cut through the valleys, while a fourth climbs the hills. But in fact there is no such similarity between the *Decameron* and the *Canterbury Tales* as to call for even *this* kind of criticism. Boccaccio makes a number of ladies and gentlemen run away from the plague to a country house, and there, among arbours, fountains, birds, and other such pretty things, tell tales to each other, in order that they may forget the misery which the very sunshine they are enjoying at peace lights up not far off. The whole conception is evidently mediæval-Italian, — cowardly, romantic, and thin. The treatment is artificial and bald, so far as the framework or ' fable' is concerned. What can be poorer or more theatrical than all this twaddle about the birds, the trees, and the sunshine? It needs not to say that many of the stories have exceeding merit; and some of them, to which Chaucer's tales run parallel, are told with a grace, and above all, with a snaky Italian finesse, which, of course, we do not find in Chaucer. But it is in the framework of his *Canterbury Tales* that Chaucer is by universal consent at his best. In the first place, an English poet of the fourteenth century did not need to travel far for so very obvious and natural an idea as that of making wayfarers amuse each other by the telling of stories. In the second place, Chaucer's 'fable' is thoroughly English, and widely different from that of the *Decameron*. Its Englishness we recognise at a glance,—the inn, the company, the good fellowship, the common purpose (so different from mere running away or retirement), the straightforward look of the pilgrims in the poet's picture,—all this is, I repeat, thoroughly English, and as peculiar to Chaucer as anything English can be. It would be as reasonable to say that Boccaccio imitated the *Arabian Nights,* as it is to say that Chaucer imitated Boccaccio.

II. Whether Chaucer knew the Tabard very intimately or not it is impossible to affirm. Of course, it is probable, to the very verge of certainty, that he did, and that the guests whom he assembled there were portraits in whole or in part. It is idle to be too confident in drawing conclusions from those intimacies of description and narrative which come so naturally to the pen of a man of genius; and Nature may very well have taught Chaucer what she taught Defoe, namely, that the way to make a description truth-like is to introduce touches which an ordinary person would not think of introducing unless they were true and had turned up naturally. Why, in the name of wonder, should Chaucer go out of his way to say that the Wife of Bath was ' gattothed,' unless she was ' gattothed,' and he had seen her? or that the Reeve was a ' sklendre colerik man,' with ' ful longe leggus?' or that the Pardoner had ' glaryng eyghen as an hare,' and a ' voys as smale as eny goot?' or that the Monk had ' eyen steep and rollyng in his heed?' These are a few of the lifelike touches which have helped to make the Prologue to the *Canterbury Tales* one of the best known compositions in the English language, in spite of its antiquated English and the rough, and sometimes worse than rough narratives to which it forms the introduction.

Mr. Wright observes, that no one acquainted with the manners of the Middle Ages could for a moment suppose that people of such diverse social conditions as Chaucer's twenty-nine (in strictness thirty-one) Canterbury pilgrims could all have met at the Tabard on the footing represented in the Prologue, and gone to Canterbury together. Mr. Wright's antiquarian knowledge exceeds beyond comparison any that I can myself pretend to, and the observation is perhaps a just one ; but I do not myself find even that supposition so violent as what I have mentioned in another page, namely, that the Wife of Bath should use the language put into her mouth by the poet in a mixed company. However, the notion of pilgrims so diverse being on such sociable terms was surely not *extravagant.* It seems to me to be one of the most important points soliciting attention in the life of the Middle Ages that social feeling was stronger and more active than caste feeling. It was partly under compulsion to be so ; for when the domestic and civic conveniences and resources of life are not far advanced, human beings must necessarily be thrown *direct* upon each other for much of the help which they can now obtain at second-hand, with the intervention and aid of the ten thousand appliances that make the wheels of civilized life go smoothly. Thus, people of diverse rank and culture would be thrown together in numerous ways, where now they would be apart ; and high and low, layman and clerk, lady and soldier, would be kept in presence of the pri-

mordial facts of life, at no great distance from each other.
The word truckle-bed would alone furnish a text for
a discussion on this subject. The truckle-bed was a
small low bed on truckles, which was placed at the foot
of the great or state-bed of a person of consequence.
In the smaller bed would sleep the esquire of the
knight, or the henchman of the esquire, ready to help
his superior in the night, in rising, or in going to bed.
Now this state of things, though it does not belong to
an age of bell-ropes, gutta-percha tubing, dressing-
rooms, and the like, is much more ' human,' and obviously brought people closer together. It would be easy
to instance, in a similar vein of remark, certain points
in the relation of the lord and the villein under the
feudal system; but it would be inelegant to specify
them.

It must also be noted that, sharply drawn as were
the lines of rank and station in the Middle Ages, the
distinctions were kept up pretty much by superficial
signs, which left the undermost roots of things very
much the same in the consciousness of all persons concerned. What is it makes the gulf between the modern
gentleman and the ' cad?' It lies chiefly in two words,
education and personal refinement: most of all, in the
latter. Now, in Chaucer's day, printing was not in use,
and, of course, there was not that tendency to diversity
at first and equilibrium of culture afterwards, which the
use of printing has brought with it; so that the difference between the lord of the manor and the reeve —

the reeve and the tenant who farmed the land—and
the tenant who farmed the land and the thatcher who
mended the ricks, was not similar in character to what
exists at present. For instance, they would all probably
be inferior to the learned class,—the clerks proper,—to
whom they would alike look up. But as to personal refinement, I think the case is even plainer, though it is
a question impossible to state in detail in a book for
general reading. Still we can easily see that the superiority of the privileged classes was signified and
guarded more by trappings and splendours of attire and
furniture than by fundamental differences in people's
habits. It would be totally impossible for the lowest
' cad' of Chaucer's time to use coarser language than he
sometimes does himself—and that for a very simple reason, namely, that no coarser words do or did exist. I am
now thinking of words which he uses when he is speaking in his own person,—having a specific instance in
my mind. I have also in my mind an incident in one of
the *Canterbury Tales,* in which a young lady is the
actor ; and all I can say is, that it is totally impossible
to conceive that any Audrey whosoever was fundament-
ally less refined in her mode of life than this Rosalind ;
just because this Rosalind was not refined at all.

To these considerations must be added another;
namely, that the frequency of acts of violence in the
Middle Ages, the difficulties of travelling, and the harsh
uncertainties, often making sudden demands upon sociable feeling, which beset daily life, must have pushed

people of different ranks close together, whether they would or not. I cannot convey my own exact impressions into other people's minds, of course, but in reading mediæval literature, I receive a strong impression of ready social feeling, which the frequent intrusion of acts of violence does not lessen. People may fight, and yet be friendly; one need not quote the typical Irishman. It is, I believe, true that the discipline of the camp often turns indifferently good manners into very fine manners; and that very sociable persons are, as a rule, quarrelsome also.

III. Whatever is uncertain about the *Canterbury Tales*, one thing is certain, that they contain, both in the Prologue and the stories, some of the most exact pictures of English life that ever were transmitted at any time in English history by any pen. A very slight experiment, made upon two or three of the pilgrims, say the Miller and the Reeve, will illustrate this at once.

The Miller is a figure which would scarcely turn up at all in the picture, if a modern Chaucer were to paint English life in the nineteenth century. Mr. Tennyson has introduced a miller in one of the most admired, and, if report speaks truly, quite the most fortunate of his poems, and he is a stout person, too, like Chaucer's miller :—

> ' I think I see the miller yet,
>   His double chin, his portly size,
> And who that saw him could forget
>   The busy wrinkles round his eyes ?

> The slow, wise smile, that round about
> His dusty forehead, drily curled,
> Seemed half within and half without,
> And full of dealings with the world.'

This is the image of a stout, healthy, shrewd rustic, but not as remote from the idea of a gentleman as Chaucer's miller is from that of his Squire or Knight, although the lover's mother thought he 'might have looked a little higher' than the lovely miller's daughter. And it is the daughter who is the central and the important figure—nobody cares for the miller.

But, in the old-fashioned song and ballad verse of England and Germany—still more in Germany than in England—the miller is perpetually coming upon the scene, his prominence evidently belonging to a time when the relations of the man who grew the corn, the man who ground it, and the people who ate the bread, were much more direct than they are now; and in fact, in Chaucer's time, the miller was the immediate servant of the lord of the manor, to whom belonged the exclusive right of grinding the corn grown upon his estate. One almost always likes to read of him, too, because he can scarcely be mentioned himself without recalling the picture of the mill itself; ever, to my thinking, one of the prettiest and most fascinating objects in a landscape; though, perhaps, a short stay in Holland might go far to cure one of the fancy. Chaucer's Miller in the *Canterbury Tales* is a very rough, perhaps one might say, brutal figure :—

' The Mellere was a stout carl for the nones,
  Ful big he was of braun, and eek of boones ;
  That prevede wel, for over al ther he cam,
  At wrastlynge he wolde bere awey the ram.
  He was schort schuldred, broode, a thikke knarre,
  Ther nas no dore that he nold heve of harre,
  Or breke it with a rennyng with his heed.
  His berd as ony sowe or fox was reed,
  And therto brood, as though it were a spade.
  Upon the cop right of his nose he hade
  A werte, and theron stood a tuft of heres,
  Reede as the berstles of a souwes eeres.
  His nose-thurles blake were and wyde.
  A swerd and a bocler baar he by his side,
  His mouth as wyde was as a gret forneys.
  He was a jangler, and a golyardeys,
  And that was most of synne and harlotries.
  Wel cowde he stele corn, and tollen thries ;
  And yet he had a thombe of gold pardé.
  A whight cote and blewe hood wered he.
  A baggepipe cowde he blowe and sowne,
  And therwithal he brought us out of towne.'

This is a figure which, as Mr. Carlyle says of Oliver
Cromwell, is decidedly not of the ' man-milliner ' or
' patent digester ' species. He has plenty of bone and
plenty of flesh ; he is a wrestler who could always feel
sure of bearing away the customary prize—a ram ;
short-necked, broad-shouldered, and with, presumably,
short thick legs, for I believe when an ox is said to be
short-shouldered the legs are short. He could heave
up a door with his shoulders, or knock it in with his
head by running at it—the sort of head for the game

of singlestick, or quintin, or any other of the athletic sports which were common in Chaucer's days, and much later. The next touch is very characteristic : you can imagine the red, bristly beard, in shape like a spade. At the top of his nose is a wart, with a tuft of red hair in it, ' red as the bristles of a sow's ears.' His nostrils are dark and spreading. His mouth is as wide as an oven. This is a description to frighten little boys and girls withal ; there is no necessity to add that the miller carried a sword and shield with him. Naturally, he had a white coat, after the manner of millers; and then, for beauty's sake, a blue hood. Besides the usual vice of his trade—the tendency to take excessive toll—he is a noisy gossip and a teller of stories

> ' Of Moll and Meg, and strange experiences
> Unmeet for ladies.'

It is a natural incident of such a character that the man should be noisy ; and we are not surprised to find that he carries a bagpipe, with which he blows the Pilgrims out of town, just, I suppose, as the old mail coach-guards used to blow their horns as the coaches rolled out at Saint Martin's-le-Grand in the evening. This last touch completes the strangeness of the picture ; the bagpipe being mentioned quite as a matter of course, as if it were a common instrument ; which it was in the days of Chaucer, though we are accustomed to think of it as an instrument quite unendurable except on the Scotch hills. Chaucer does not describe the miller's horse, but it must have been a good strong animal to bear the miller. Off go the Pilgrims, then, in the early morning, out of Southwark, towards Deptford, with some clatter of tongue, particularly from the Wife of Bath, who, being deaf, talks of course as if everybody else were deaf; but with much more clatter of horses' hoofs, some jingling of horsebells from the monk's place in the procession, and the wretched ' minstraulxcie' of the Miller, who is on the best of terms with himself, and remains conspicuous in his white coat and blue hood.

Contrasted with the brawny Miller, drunk and unsteady on his horse, and noisy with his unpilgrimlike bellows-pipe, comes the Reeve or Bailiff: —

> ' The Reeve was a sklendre colerik man,
> His berd was schave as neigh as ever he can.
> His heer was by his eres rounde i-schorn.
> His top was dockud lyk a preest biforn.
> Ful longe wern his leggus, and ful lene,
> Al like a staff, ther was no calf y-sene.
> Wel cowde he kepe a gerner and a bynne ;
> Ther was non auditour cowde on him wynne.
> Wel wist he by the drought, and by the reyn,
> The yeeldyng of his seed and of his greyn.
> His lordes scheep, his nete, and his dayerie,
> His swyn, his hors, his stoor, and his pultrie,
> Was holly in this reeves governynge,
> And by his covenaunt gaf the rekenynge,
> Syn that his lord was twenti yeer of age ;
> Ther couthe noman bringe him in arrerage.

Ther nas ballif, ne herde, ne other hyne,
That they ne knewe his sleight and his covyne;
They were adrad of him, as of the deth.
His wonyng was ful fair upon an heth,
With grene trees i-schadewed was his place.
He cowde bettre than his lord purchace.
Ful riche he was i-stored prively,
His lord wel couthe he plese subtilly,
To geve and lene him of his owne good,
And have a thank, a cote, and eek an hood.
In youthe he lerned hadde a good mester;
He was a wel good wright, a carpenter.
This reeve sat upon a wel good stot,
That was a pomely gray, and highte Scot,
A long surcote of pers uppon he hadde,
And by his side he bar a rusty bladde.'

Dropping obvious anachronisms, this is pretty much the sort of figure a modern novelist would paint for a house-agent, or attorney, or tax-gatherer, or exciseman. We have here, upon a grey horse, called Scot (which is said to be invariably the name of a horse in Norfolk), a thin, peppery, close-shaven, close-cut man, with legs that were not only long, but so thin that they were ' like a staff; there was no calf seen,'* says Chaucer. He was a treasure to his lord, whose accounts he had kept under hand since the lord of the manor was twenty years of age. No auditor could bring him in as indebted for arrears ; but he drove sharp bargains with

---

* This is very good ; but not better than Leigh Hunt's description of old Bowyer's leg, ' a balustrade leg.'

other bailiffs and with the herdsmen and others; ' they
knew his sleight and his covin;' and were afraid of him
—'as of the death,' says Chaucer. And no doubt
in earlier times the power of life and death had been
very much in the hands of a reeve who was on terms of
favouritism with his lord; for under the feudal system,
although the lord of the manor was bound to hold a
manorial court, which was usually held in the great
hall of the manor-house, upon offenders, yet, of course,
the power of condemning a serf to death, *fossa* or
furca (*i. e.* the gallows for a man, the pond for a
woman) was very much in the hands of the lord : the
mere fact that any person might in those days be
accused of witchcraft must have given immense power
to bad people who had ends to gain. We are told that
this Reeve was a capital farmer, storekeeper, and stock-
keeper, and that, like other middlemen, he knew how
to enrich himself. He lived in a ' full fair' house
upon a common, with trees around it (a suggestion of a
park evidently), and could even lend to his master;
who would reward him occasionally with a new hood
and cloak, and condescend to thank him. The Reeve
had on a long sky-blue coat, and carried a rusty
sword; being stingy and more accustomed to use the
saw and the hammer than to fight, for Chaucer says he
was a good carpenter—which means, for those times,
much the same thing as a builder, and implies that he
was very useful to his lord in providing or altering the
huts of the tenantry. This sulky little man, who likes

to overlook others and hold himself in reserve, rides *
" the hindmost of the route."

As soon as ever the Knight, who tells his tale first,
the precedence being given by lot, has finished, the
Miller insists on telling his, though he is so drunk he
can hardly sit or speak, and it is part of the joke that
he knows it : —

> ' The Myller that for drunken was al pale,
> So that unnethe upon his hors he sat,
> He wold avale nowther hood ne hat,
> Ne abyde no man for his curtesye,
> But in Pilates voys he gan to crye,†
> And swor by armes and by blood and bones,
> " I can a noble tale for the noones,
> With which I wol now quyte the Knightes tale."
> Oure Hoost saw wel how dronke he was of ale,
> And seyde, " Robyn, abyde, my leve brother,
> Som bettre man schal telle first another ;
> Abyd, and let us worken thriftyly."
> " By Goddes soule ! " quod he, " that wol nat I,

---

* Chaucer's words are, that he rode *ever* the hindmost of
the rout. I have somewhere seen in this connection a mis-
print, so droll that it is worth quoting. The Reeve, said my
author, manifested his unsocial disposition by riding *over* the
hindmost of the rout. Unsocial enough, truly !

† This is a reference to the tone of command assumed by
Pilate in the miracle-plays. It will be noted in the description
of Absolon, the clerk, that he sometimes played Herod, by way
of showing off in the presence of the women ; so we must suppose that also was a part which gave some scope to a performer
fond of d splay. Pilate was, of course, a judicial person, exercis-
ing an authority upon his use of which the issue of the play
turned.

> For I wol speke, or elles go my way."
> Oure Host answered, " Tel on, a devel way !
> Thou art a fool ; thy witt is overcome."
>   " Now herkneth," quod this Myller, " al and some ;
> But first I make a protestacioun,
> That I am dronke, I knowe wel by my soun ;
> And therfore if that I mys-speke or seye,
> Wyte it the ale of Southwerk, I you preye." '

When the Miller has announced that his tale is one which will make a carpenter look ridiculous, the Reeve fires up, and endeavours to stop him : —

> ' The Reve answered and seyde, " Stynt thi clappe.
> It is a synne, and eek a greet folye
> To apeyren eny man, or him defame,
> And eek to brynge wyves in ylle name.
> Thou mayst ynowgh of other thinges seyn." '

Then ' this dronken Miller' begins a speech to ' leve brother Osewold' and persists in telling his story as he had intended. When it is finished, the Reeve shows some displeasure : —

> ' Bycause he was of carpentrye craft,
> A litel ire in his herte is laft ; '

and he now in turn makes a speech, which abounds in images characteristic of his profession as a bailiff; the burden of it being his want of physical vivacity in his old age : —

> ' Gras tyme is doan, my foddin is now forage.   .   .
> In our wil ther stiketh ever a nayl.   .   .
> Syn that my tappe of lyf began to renne,'   .   .

and the like ; great part of the address being unquot-

able here. But the company, or part of them, appear
to take it for a homily :

> ' Whan that oure Host had herd this sermonyng,
> He gan to speke as lordly as a kyng,
> And seyde, " What amounteth al this wit ?
> What ? schul we speke al day of holy wryt ?
> The devyl made a reve for to preche,
> Or of a sowter a schipman or a leche.*
> Sey forth thi tale, and tarye nat the tyme ;
> Lo heer is Depford, and it is passed prime. †
> *　　　*　　　*　　　*　　　*
> It were al tyme thi tale to beguine." '

Pray let us admire Mr. Baily's idea of holy ' wryt' or
' sermonyng ;' and also the fidelity with which Chaucer
reproduces the quarrelsomeness of the stupid, conceited
vulgar, such as the Miller, and the Reeve, who now
replies to the Host :—

> ' " Now, sires," quod this Osewold the Reeve,
> " I pray yow alle, that noon of you him greeve,
> Though I answere, and somwhat sette his howve,
> For leeful is with force force to showve.
> This dronken Myllere hath i-tolde us heer,
> How that bygiled was a carpenter,
> Peraventure in scorn, for I am oon ;
> And by your leve, I schal him quyte anoon.
> Right in his cherles termes wol I speke ;
> I pray to God his nekke mot to-breke !
> He can wel in myn eye see a stalke,
> But in his owne he can nought seen a balke." '

---

* Or of a cobbler, a sailor or a doctor.
† Prime, in the ecclesiastical day, was six o'clock.

After which the Reeve tells his tale: in which a carpenter gets the worst of it. The vindictive indecency of these two inferior animals is almost humorous in itself.

IV. In the fourteenth century, the typical small tenant or labourer of a manor held under a great baron was not what he was or might have been in the twelfth century. It appears to be incontestable, and has been brought out into strong light by Professor Thorold Rogers, that, during the reign of Henry III., long and comparatively peaceful as it was, the English peasant passed out of the condition of serfdom, and became a free tenant of the lord's land, sometimes paying a money rent and sometimes a labour rent (as, to do so much hedging, ditching, thatching, or harvesting per annum), but not liable to the cruel and degrading incidents of absolute serfdom or slavery. Ideas of personal freedom must begin some time or other, and they had risen to a considerable height and diffused themselves widely in the reign of King John. What we chiefly see upon the scene at Runnymede is the baronial congress—the barons asking this, that, or the other concession for themselves and the people. But underneath all this there must have been a vertical diffusion of the spirit of liberty; and, in proportion as the feudal relations of the lords and the people were less and less directed to ends of actual warfare, those relations must have tended to become kindly and respectful towards the tenant. It was impossible, we may well believe, that a feudal tyranny like that which followed the Conquest could endure in England, and the question where it should begin to break up decisively was the only one that events had to solve. When John avowed himself the vassal of the Pope the barons rebelled; the result was Magna Charta—a result so largely disproportionate that one could see, even if proof or hints of proof were wanting, that the dissolution of the feudal tyranny had long before begun, quite irrespectively of the question of England's relations to the see of Rome. It was a long time before Englishmen were as free in practice as the express terms of Magna Charta should have made them; but, after that, the path of liberty in England was upon an inclined plane downwards, and the baronial congress in the reign of King John seems only the natural precursor of the Parliament of Montfort, Earl of Leicester, in the reign of Henry III.

Some of the provisions of Magna Charta are decisive in pointing to the largely improved condition of the English peasantry. For example, the land of a baron was not to be seized by the king for any debt of the baron's so long as the baron had personal property available for the purpose. This provision, with others, was applicable to the relation between the baron and his tenants, as well as to that between the crown and the barons. It was made unlawful to take away instruments of husbandry for a fine, and the right of a free

passage to and from the realm was granted to every
subject.   Here, of course, are some of the most obvious
conditions of freedom ; the last being quite inconsistent with allodial vassalage in the strong sense.   The
insurrection headed by Simon de Montfort (whom Mr.
Rogers calls the Cromwell of the thirteenth century)
would never have been risked if the barons had been in
unfriendly relations with the people on their estates, we
may suppose.   At all events, the spirit of independence
spread both vertically and laterally, and in Richard
II.'s reign, we are face to face with an insurrection of
the peasantry, wide-spread, and perhaps planned all
over the country.   The Black Death has thinned the
population enormously, and, labour being more scarce,
the labourers rise.   The insurrection is quelled, but
the peasantry are better treated after it, and they get
what they want — higher wages and more personal
liberty.   At last we come to a state of things in
which a figure like that of Chaucer's Reeve is
presentable as a true picture of the bailiff or manager
of a manor.   He is a sorry rogue, but he is human and
amenable.

It is impossible to resist the temptation to be indebted to Professor Thorold Rogers for his picture of a
portion of the activity of just such a functionary as this
Reeve.   It relates to the manor of Cuxham, which belonged to Merton College, Oxford, and is an account of
the steps taken by Robert Oldman, the Reeve, to get a
good millstone for the Cuxham mill.   If Mr. Rogers

will pardon the length of the quotation, I am sure the reader will :—

'Robert Oldman, the Cuxham bailiff, was, like his father, who had held the office for many years, a serf of the manor. He must have journeyed on that road to London which passes through Worth, Wycombe, and Uxbridge. The lower route, through Dorchester, Nettlebed, and Henley, had not been made, or, if made, was not frequented, if we may argue from a map of England now preserved in the Bodleian Library, and certainly drawn at about the middle of the fourteenth century, which gives roads and distances. This upper route, lying for a considerable portion of its course on high land, the north slope of which is the Vale of Aylesbury, is one of the most picturesque of highways in the southern part of England. At dawn, in the midsummer of 1331 (for the charges incurred are written at the foot of the roll), bailiff, servant, and horse start on their expedition, and achieve the distance, more than forty miles, in the course of the day, through the beech-woods of Buckinghamshire and the rich pastures of Middlesex. Arrived in London, they take up their lodging at one of the numerous hotels in the city, and according to the fashion of the time, cater for the needs of themselves and their horse. Early next day Oldman sets about the serious business on which he had come, and finds the merchant at the wharf which lay below the southern city wall. Having chosen the stones which suit the two mills, his own, and that at Oxford,

he adjourns to the inn, or to some tavern near, in order
to discuss the terms of his bargain. We may be certain that the chaffering was long and anxious, and that,
in Oldman's opinion, at least, the time and money were
not idly spent, when he aids his bargaining by the
liberal order of five gallons of Gascony. It is not
every day that the merchant finds a customer whose demands are so large, or who has set his heart on the best
articles which can be found in his selda, or warehouse.
These deep potations are at last ended by the merchant
abating something of his morning price, the bargain is
struck, the luck penny is delivered, and there are witnesses to the transaction.   After so unaccustomed a de-
bauch, the bailiff returns next morning by the same
route to his farm and his duties.   But he must journey
again to London, in order to negotiate the terms at
which his goods shall be carried, and to pay for the
millstones.   On this occasion more time is consumed ;
possibly in waiting for such a vessel as would be able to
carry these heavy articles, possibly in another keen bargaining about the amount to be paid for the service.
No doubt other potations were deemed necessary for
the completion of these arrangements ; but in dealing
with sailors and wharfingers, less costly beverages
sufficed, and no special note was made of the consump-
tion.   This contract, however, is settled at last, and
the stones are laid on board, payment being made for
wharfage.   Now comes the toll for the city wall, and,
free at last, the vessel works its way with the tide up

the great river, whose waters were as yet undefiled, through the rich salmon-fishers of Westshene, between the winding banks of the Royal Forest, and beneath the hill not yet crowned with the great palace which the young king would hereafter delight to build. Then on to Maidenhead, where a further murage, due probably, as the former was, to the City of London, whose jurisdiction over the Thames extended at least thus far. And then they traversed the fairest part of the river scenery, the horseshoe, namely, which lies between the wooded hills of Maidenhead, Wycombe, and Marlow, till the boat rested at Henley, then the highest point to which the navigation of the Thames was ordinarily possible. The bailiff is present to receive his goods, and soon gets ready the service which he finds it will be more convenient to employ on the spot, by purchasing iron and steel, by hiring a smith to fashion his steel into picks or awls, and by engaging the services of three men for three days in the labour of boring the stones—a labour of no trifling character, as the smith is perpetually occupied in sharpening the tools.'[*]

After this, we may suppose, perhaps, that Oldman got ' thanks ' from his lord, if not a new ' hood ' or ' cote.'

V. I have given this interesting passage at once,

[*] *A History of Agriculture and Prices in England.* By James E. Thorold Rogers, M.A., Professor of Political Economy in the University of Oxford. Vols. I. and II. Oxford : 1866 Vol. i. pp. 506—508.

because the occasion was convenient; and, indeed, the discursiveness of the present chapter may serve to illustrate at the outset the readiness with which very various topics of English life and history permit themselves to be grouped together around the portraits given by Chaucer in these *Canterbury Tales.* The fable of the poem was, it may be repeated, thoroughly English; and though it would be unmeaning, or at least trivial, to call it democratic in spirit, one may justly say that though the poet frankly calls the churls of the procession by their true name, it was not altogether likely to occur to him to employ a fable which brought together on terms of social equality such very diverse people, unless he had been living and writing in times in which the spirit of freedom was in the atmosphere, and had himself been penetrated by that spirit. It has been said that, whether it will or no, genius is democratic. At all events, the highest genius (of the order which delights in painting life and character) is familiar with the common people, and is fond of dwelling upon them and their ways. Shakespeare was an illustration, and Chaucer is no exception.

One more remark upon the portraits just re-produced. In his unflinching realism of delineation, Chaucer cannot but remind us of Hogarth. But there is realism and realism. If Hogarth had lived and painted in the fourteenth century, a gallery of his pictures would, no doubt, have been a valuable commentary on the text of the poet; but if Hogarth, living when he did, had been set to illustrate Chaucer, he would probably have vulgarised him, even in such pictures as those of the Miller and the Reeve, inevitably as they call up in our minds figures such as we find only in the paintings and designs of the artist of the 'March to Finchley' and the 'Mariage-à-la-Mode.'

CHAPTER III.

CHIVALRY.

THE KNIGHT. The romantic figure, whose large white plume we descry in the dim distance, as it crosses the field of mediæval story, is much more than a soldier — he is a warrior; not only a man who fights, but a man who makes war. And he is still more than a warrior, for he is a warrior with a purpose; a man who makes war for an idea. Nor is this all, he is more even than a warrior with a conscience; for he has knelt at the altar and sworn to a faith, so that he carries a consecrated sword. Once again, as our eye falls upon the scarf which he wears upon his arm, we note that this warrior, besides his will, his purpose, and his faith, has a sentiment, if not a passion too, and pricks over the plain before us, a soldier, a warrior, a believer, and a lover. The energy which comes with a purpose has given him dignity ; the Church has taught him gentleness, and added her chrism ; but woman has taken his troth and given him her badge, and immediately he is beautiful.

In mediæval romance, when the clerk and the knight contend for the priority in love, the romancist makes the clerk victorious. This was a sop to the Church. But, the Church notwithstanding, the knight is the first figure in mediæval life ; and in the *Canterbury Tales*, Chaucer, speaking through Harry Baily, the host and guide of the Pilgrims, has given him the precedence, in order of time, and has put into his mouth the noblest story. This was, indeed, a courtesy due to the chivalric order in general, especially when fresh lustre had been thrown upon it by the splendours with which the new order, that of the Garter, had been just surrounded by Edward III. in the recent festival at Windsor.

The Knight painted by Chaucer is a thoroughly characteristic figure. He had ridden far, a chivalric adventurer, defending truth and the ladies, and fighting in his lord's wars— no man further—both in Christendom and in the Holy Land. He had often been served first at the board, because of his nobleness, and his ran-

som, when he fell into captivity, was high.   He was
wise (or humble and discreet), and, though brave as a
lion, as gentle as a woman.   Nor did he make any display in his person or dress.   He rode a good horse, but
was himself not ' gay ' to look at.   His cassock of fustian was marked by his hauberk, but he had not
changed his clothes on returning late from his travels :
such was his devotion that he had gone straight on pilgrimage : —

  ' A Knight ther was, and that a worthy man,
  That from the tympe that he first bigan
  To ryden out, he lovede chyvalrye,
  Trouthe and honour, fredom and curtesie.
  Ful worthi was he in his lordes werre,
  And thereto hadde he riden, noman ferre,
  As wel in Cristendom as in hethenesse,
  And evere honoured for his worthinesse.
  At Alisandre he was whan it was wonne,
  Ful ofte tyme he hadde the bord bygonne.
  Aboven alle naciouns in Pruce.
  In Lettowe hadde reyced and in Ruce,
  No Cristen man so ofte of his degré.
  In Gernade atte siege hadde he be
  Of Algesir, and riden in Belmarie.
  At Lieys was he, and at Satalie,
  Whan they were wonne; and in the Greete see
  At many a noble arive hadde he be.
  At mortal batailles hadde he ben fiftene,
  And foughten for our feith at Tramassene
  In lystes thries, and ay slayn his foo.
  This ilke worthi knight hadde ben also
  Somtyme with the lord of Palatye,

Ageyn another hethene in Turkye ;
And evermore he hadde a sovereyn prys.
And though that he was worthy he was wys,
And of his port as meke as is a mayde.
He never yit no vilonye ne sayde
In all his lif, unto no maner wight,
He was a verray perfight gentil knight.
But for to telle you of his aray,
His hors was good, but he ne was nought gay,
Of fustyan he wered a gepoun
Al bysmoterud with his haburgeoun.
For he was late comen from his viage,
And wente for to doon his pilgrimage.'

II. Accompanying the Knight, and standing next to him in order of courtesy, stood the Squire, his son.* He has been a good while ' in chivachie;' that is, out of his apprenticeship as a knightly man, expecting sometime to be himself invested. Being strong and brave, he will soon win his spurs ; but at present his prize is ' his lady's grace.' He is courteous, and, according to the chivalric code, full of ready serviceableness. That he carves the meat for his father is a matter of course; it was the duty of an esquire. He curls his hair egregiously. He is exquisitely got up,—' as fresh as the month of May' to look at ; and has so many flowers about him, that he is positively embroidered with white and red roses,—the flowers of love and knighthood. He is strictly in the fashion of the day, with

---

* By the laws of heraldry the eldest sons of knights, and their eldest sons in perpetual succession, are esquires.

the short tunic that the clergy so hotly denounced as
indelicate.   He can joust, of course, and dance well,—
which latter the Clerk cannot do, —and he has the
Clerk's accomplishment besides ; for he can write and
draw an illuminated letter. He is so eager a votarist of
the faith of chivalry, too, that he scarcely sleeps at
all; he is up all night (as the nightingale was *supposed*
to be) composing or singing love-songs.   This young
Squire appears to have a lady of his own, whose favour
he hopes to win ; but ' so hot he loved ' need not, by
itself, imply that ; for a young man might, by the laws
of chivalry, love vaguely : not only a lady whom he had
never seen, which was a common thing ; but he might
simply love . . . . . the universal essence of female
beauty and goodness, if he could, as the metaphysicians
say, posit it, so as to bring it within the range of an
emotion : —

> ' With him ther was his sone, a yong Squyer,
> A lovyer, and a lusty bacheler,
> With lokkes crulle as they were layde in presse.
> Of twenty yeer he was of age I gesse.
> Of his stature he was of evene lengthe,
> And wondurly delyver, and gret of strengthe.
> And he hadde ben sometyme in chivachie,
> In Flaundres, in Artoys, and in Picardie,
> And born him wel, as in so litel space,
> In hope to stonden in his lady grace.
> Embrowdid was he, as it were a mede
> Al ful of fresshe floures, white and reede.
> Syngynge he was, or flowtynge, al the day ;

He was as fressh as is the moneth of May.
Schort was his goune, with sleeves long and wyde.
Wel cowde he sitte on hors, and faire ryde.
He cowde songes wel make and endite,
Justne and eek daunce, and wel purtray and write.
So hote he lovede, that by nightertale
He sleep nomore than doth a nightyngale.
Curteys he was, lowly, and servysable,
And carf byforn his fadur at the table.'

III. After the young Esquire comes the Yeman, in coat and hood of green, with arrows feathered from the peacock, and a close-cropped head :—

'A Yeman had he, and servantes nomoo
At that tyme, for him lust ryde soo ;
And he was clad in coote and hoode of grene.
A shef of pocok arwes bright and kene
Under his belte he bar full thriftily.
Wel cowde he dresse his takel yomanly ;
His arwes drowpud nought with fetheres lowe.
And in his hond he bar a mighty bowe.
A not-heed hadde he, with a broun visage.
Of woode-craft cowde he wel al the usage.
Upon his arme he bar a gay bracer,
And by his side a swerd and a bokeler,
And on that other side a gay daggere,
Harneysed wel, and scharp as poynt of spere
A Cristofre on his brest of silver schene.
An horn he bar, the bawdrik was of grene;
A forster was he sothely, as I gesse.'

The presence of this Yeman, or forester, who was in attendance upon the Knight's Squire, to say nothing of the story of Gamelyn, which some editors or compilers of Chaucer have put into the mouth of the Cook (though it is evidently not Chaucer's composition) suggests an element of English life which was not so prominent in Chaucer's time as it had been a century or so previously, but which still existed.   I mean the number of discontented foresters, or outlaws, or dispossessed persons, who haunted the forests and woodlands and morasses and dark corners of the land.   The Squire's servant or yeoman is, of course, a respectable person, attached to a master, and with no particular quarrel of his own; but Gamelyn, like Robin Hood, with whom he is in one or two ballads associated, was a different type.   Being unjustly dispossessed of his land by his brothers, as thousands of Englishmen were by the forest laws under the Normans, he takes his cause into his own hands, and fights and wins.   The story, as told in the Coke's Tale of Gamelyn, has been taken in part by Shakespeare as the foundation of *As You Like it.* But he omits what is very characteristic in Gamelyn,— the hatred of the monks or religious persons which prevailed among secular, or, in the phrase of the time, " lewd " persons : —

> ' Ther was no lewede man that in the halle stood,
>   That wolde do Gamelyn eny thing but good,
>   But stood besyde, and leet hem bothe werche,
>   For they hadde no rewthe of men of holy cherche ;
>   Abbot or priour, monk or chanoun,
>   That Gamelyn overtok, anon they yeeden doun.'

One reason for this hatred of the priests among the Anglo-Saxons was that the Normans turned out so many of the Saxon abbots and substituted Normans instead. But the common people of England have always a lurking prejudice against the clergy; and, in country districts, where they are often associated with 'lewd' persons as magistrates, we may see, in the dislike which vagabonds and poachers entertain of the clergy, a type of the feeling with which Gamelyn and Adam regarded them. The clergy, however, being usually on the side of constituted authority, of whatever kind, can never have been, and can never be objects of liking to those who, by any means whatever, are forced to take the side of revolt. The ballad of Gamelyn is full of characteristic touches, and well worth reading for its own sake. In Chaucer's century, the peace began to be better kept than it had been; but even so late as that outlaws used to lie in wait in the woods near Alton, for merchants and others visiting or leaving Winchester.

IV. Many things may be doubtful in any comparison of the resources of the fourteenth century and those of our own; but about the difference made in warfare by the introduction and gradually extended use of gunpowder there can be no doubt whatever. Whether it was introduced into Europe by the Saracens, or invented *ab ovo* by Roger Bacon, does not much matter. Cannons were used—a few only—and those,

of course, very clumsy and inefficient, by Edward the
Third at Créçy; but then, and for a long while after,
it is the prowess of the knight with the lance, and of
the foot-soldier with the bow, which decides the fate
of battles, and not cannon or rifles.

As it has never been held, in any age of the world,
that the probability that our descendants will laugh at
us, should prevent our laughing at our ancestors, we
need not allow the reflection, that a short time hence
needle-guns and turret-ships will be found antiquated,
to prevent our smiling at the warlike 'apparel' of
the middle ages, with the ditches and portcullises
which played so large a part in their fortifications.
In the *Romaunt of the Rose*, the Castle of Jealousy is
described in terms sufficiently characteristic of the
period to be worth quoting by way of illustration.
Jealousy, to guard his roses, hired every mason and
quarryman he could find to build him a tower or
castle :—

> ' He hirede hem to make a tour.
>   And first, the roses for to kepe,
>   Aboute hem made he a diche deepe,
>   Right wondir large, and also broode ;
>   Upon the whiche also stode
>   Of squared stoon a sturdy walle,
>   Which on a cragge was founded alle,
>   And right grete thikkenesse eke it bare.
>   Aboute it was founded square
>   An hundred fademe on every side,
>   It was alle liche longe and wide.

Lest only tyme it were assayled;
Ful wel aboute it was batayled ;
And rounde enviroun eke were sette
Ful many a riche and faire tourette.
At every corner of this walle
Was sette a tour fulle pryncipalle ;
And everich hadde, withoute fable,
A portecolys defensable
To kepe of enemyes, and to greve,
That there her force wolde preve.
And eke amydde this purprise
Was maad a tour of gret maistrise ;
A fairer saugh no man with sight,
Large and wide, and of gret myght.
They dredde noon assaut,
Of gynne, gunne, nor skaffaut.
The temprure of the mortere
Was maad of licour wonder dere ;
Of quykke lyme persant and egre,
The which was tempred with vynegre.
The stoon was hard of ademaunt,
Wherof they made the foundement.
The tour was rounde maad in compas;
In alle this world no riccher was,
Ne better ordeiyned therwithalle.
Aboute the tour was maad a walle,
So that betwixt that and the tour,
Roses were sette of swete savour,
With many roses that thei bere.
And eke withynne the castelle were
Spryngoldes, gunnes, bows, archers;
And eke above atte corners
Men seyn over the walle stonde
Grete engynes, who were nygh honde ;

> And in the kernels heere and there,
> Of arblasters grete plente were.
> Noon armure myght her stroke withstonde. . . .
> Withoute the diche were lystes maade,
> With walle batayled large and brade,
> For men and hors shulde not atteyne
> To neighe the dyche over the pleyne.
> Thus Jelousie hath enviroun
> Sette aboute his garnysoun
> With walles rounde, and diche depe,
> Oonly the roser for to kepe.'

Here we have the moat, the round keep, the portcullis, the outer walls, and the turrets. The mortar is made of quicklime tempered with vinegar. There are mangonels, or battering instruments; springolds, or catapults; arbalasters, or machine-crossbows, and guns; and scaffolds, or wooden houses for sheltering soldiers who had to undermine the walls of the enemy. Instruments of offence and defence mingled rather indiscriminately; and 'only the rosery for to keep.'

V. Is it of much importance to draw a *working*, historical distinction between the spirit of chivalry, and what people call the extravagances of the chivalric spirit? The chivalric spirit could only exhibit itself through the conduct of such people as were supposed to be under its influence; and they, being only human, would assuredly run into extravagance. Mr. Hallam enumerates, as the three essential virtues of

a knight, loyalty, courtesy, and munificence. Bravery
is, of course, taken for granted, of a man who is devoted to arms. And all four, bravery, courtesy, loyalty, and munificence, are qualities which easily run
into extravagance. The courtesy, the loyalty, and the
bravery took shapes so tenderly or so splendidly fantastic at times, that we more than forgive the fantasy
for the sake of the splendour or the tenderness. Conceive a monarch, like Edward III., holding at Whitsuntide a high court or festival, at which the Knights
were the typical or predominant figures, and everything that the rude magnificence of the times could
do to glorify the institution of chivalry (though people
in those days did not think much of institutions, and
did think much of living persons) was done: with
pageantry of purple, and gold, and scarlet, and noise
of trumpets, and congregations of fair women, and
strange vows sworn upon the bodies of peacocks and
pheasants!

Hallam quotes St. Palaye (tome i. p. 191) for a
festival of this kind, celebrated by Philip of Bur-
gundy, in the year 1453. A show, or pageant, ' representing the calamitous state of religion in consequence of the recent capture of Constantinople . . .
was followed by the appearance of a pheasant, which
was laid before the Duke, and to which the Knights
present addressed their vows to undertake a crusade
in these words:—" I swear before God, my Creator, in
the first place, and the glorious Virgin, his mother;

and, next, before the ladies and the pheasant." '* But nothing in this kind is so curious as the story of the Vows of the Heron; a ballad which dates from the middle of Chaucer's century, and the middle, also, of the wars with France. It is not an English ballad, but it relates, in a very quaint and characteristic manner, to the birth, then remotely expected, of that Prince Lionel, of whom something has been already said; and a brief hint of the machinery of the poem may not be unacceptable to the reader. The heron, as is well known, was a symbol of cowardice.

The Romance opens by a reference to the time of year and the aspect of nature:—

> ' Ens el mois de Septembre qu' estés va à declin,
> Que cil oisillon gay ont perdu lou latin,
> Et si sekent les vignes ; '

and so forth.

---

* One of Praed's pretty charades turns upon the part filled by that splendid bird in the ceremonial of chivalry. I rather think it begins : —

> ' I graced Don Pedro's revelry
> All dressed in fire and feather,'

and concludes : —

> 'He flung the slave who raised the lid,'

[which covered the peacock]

> ' A purse of maravedis ;
> And this that gallant Spaniard did,
> For me and for the ladies.'

' In the month of September, when summer declines,
And the gay little birds lose their note, and the vines
Grow dry, and the grapes are full ripe; and the trees
Are stripped of their leaves, which cover the road,
  In the year thirteen hundred and thirty and eight ;
I pledge you my word, in his marble abode
  At London was Edward, in pomp and state :
And with him were courtiers, and dukes, and great earls,
And ladies, and virgins, and various girls. . . .
The king sat at table ; no mischief he planned ;
He was thinking of love with his head on his hand . .'

He was thinking kindly, indeed, of his gentle cousin of France, and bearing him no ill-will whatever. But chance and change happen to all men ; and by a gentle vassal, who was of a glorious line, namely, as the courtiers affirm, Robert of Artois, chance and change happened to Edward on that occasion. It was Robert who began it,—

' Chie comencha la guerre et l'orrible hustin,'

all through which many a brave Knight was cast down in death, many a lady made a widow, and many [a child] a poor orphan, and many a good sailor cut short of his life, and many an honest woman thrust into a diverse fate, and many a beautiful church burnt down and razed.

' Et encore sera se Jhesus n' i' met fin ; '

' and the like will happen again, unless Jesus puts a stop to it,' says the poet.

All this comes of the circumstance that the great

Robert of Artois, who was a banished man 'from France, the noble country,' was that day at London; and, being suddenly pricked by remembrances of France, the ' *très gentil pais,*' resolved to go out hunting. So, taking with him a muskadin falcon, he went forth with his people, fowling along the bank of the Thames till he caught a heron. An idea struck him. He was observed to turn red! He resolved to present this wretched bird to Edward, and make the company take upon its roasted carcase deadly vows of vengeance against France. He hurried home with his underlings—' *ses soubgis'*—and went to the kitchen himself to see the heron stuffed, and direct the cooking. It was roasted and ' seated' (*assis*), between two plates of silver. Then Count Robert laid violent hands on two fiddlers, and one performer on the guitar; and he summoned two virgins of noble birth, and they carried the heron into the vaulted palace, the two girls singing, and Count Robert uttering loud cries, and calling upon the ' wicked and dirty' people present to make room for the procession: ' Here is food for craven gentlemen, and amorous ladies, with dainty skins! Lords, my falcons have taken this heron. I have here the most cowardly of all birds (I am sure there are no cowards in the present company), for the heron will cry and bray (*s'escrie et brait*), as if it were being killed, merely at the sight of its own shadow.

' Now, I propose,' continued Count Robert, ' to

present this heron to the greatest coward now living, or that ever lived—namely, Edward—who is the rightful heir of France; and yet, because his heart fails him, will, out of cowardice, die disseised of his inheritance. So, I will trouble him to give us his views in the form of a vow upon the heron.'

When the king heard this, he, not unnaturally, turned red in the face, while his heart shook with rage and mortification. 'You call me a coward,' said he, ' but one of my views is that I am worth more than this pusillanimous heron; and the deed will show it if I live long enough! Nay, I will die rather than not fulfil the vow which I am about to make. I vow and promise to God in paradise, and to his sweet mother by whom he was nursed,—

' Et à sa douche mere de qui il fu nouris,'

that before this year be passed I will . . . cross the sea, and my people with me, and defy the king of St. Denis, and fires shall be set burning throughout all the land, and I will fight Philip of Valois, who bears the *fleur-de-lis*. I will fight him, of that let him be sure! even though I had only one man against ten. Does he imagine he may with impunity rob me of my lands and my country? If I ever did him homage—and really I am surprised to think of it!—I was so young of years that the act of fealty was not worth two ears of corn.' The king then becomes classic in his allusions, and swears by St. George and St. Denis, that since the time of Hector, Achilles, Paris, and Alexander the Great, no such truce as he will cause to be made before the year 1346 was ever yet made. 'With my oath,' concludes the king, 'I have undertaken this vow!'

At this Count Robert chuckles, and whispers to himself that 'by God in paradise, we ought well to have joy that we happened to catch this heron to-day. Now we shall have great war according to my desire. I was wrongfully banished from France and the good king, my brother-in-law, and he has put my wife, my daughter, and my children in prison. But by the faith which I owe to my sons and daughters, if it please Jesus Christ, I will, before I die the death, have a lodging in France, for I have friends there,—

'Me logeray en Franche car jou i ai des amis.'

I am descended from Monseigneur St. Loys . . . . and by that God who was fixed upon the cross I will go to France! I am not in the least frightened at the notion,—

. . . . 'ne'n suis mie esbahis.'

and I will fight before I will leave it. This I have undertaken and vowed.'

'When this Robert of Artois had made that vow of his will, he took the two dishes (which were all of silver) and the heron in them, of which he made a present to the king.'

' And the two minstrels fiddle so sweetly away,
    In equal accord with the soft guitar-play,
    And, hard by, the damsels sung sweetly, " I go,—
    I go to the greenwood, for love taught me so." '

And there you might with much pleasure behold
great enjoyment of game and solace,'—hot cockles perhaps, played by some of the court ladies and gentlemen, or blind man's buff, or both,—' which after that
day turned to great disaster, and will again, unless God
take pity. And this Robert of Artois did not stop
there,—

' La table tressali tost et apertement.'

To the Earl of Salisbury he went first, who sat by
his darling, who was gentle and courteous and of fair
bearing, being daughter of the Earl of Derby, and
loving him loyally. And to him spake Robert very
graciously,—

' Fair sir, who art so full of great bravery, in the
name of Jesus Christ, to whom the world belongs, I
humbly beseech you without delay to make upon this
our heron a vow of right devotion.'

To this the Earl of Salisbury made answer :—

' And why should I not be ready to put in risk my*
whole body so highly that I might be sure I should

* I cannot help thinking that there is here a slight error in
the text given by Mr. Wright in the *Political Poems and
Songs*,—at all events, I make in the reading of this passage a
change upon that assumption.

perfectly achieve my vow?   Seeing that I serve a
maiden of such perfect beauty, that if the Virgin Mary
were here present, and only her deity were taken away
from her, I should not be able to make any dissever-
ment of the two.   I have asked her for her love, but
she stands at guard, yet gives me gracious hopes that
I shall yet receive mercy at her hands, if I live long
enough.   Therefore I pray this maiden from my heart
devoutly that she would lend me but one finger of her
hand, and put it entirely over my right eye.'

This is, indeed, a small favour for a brave knight
to ask of a fair lady, and mademoiselle does not refuse
it.

'By my faith!' says she; 'a lady who expected of
her lover to have the whole force of his body, would
act basely if she denied him the touch of one of her
own fingers: indeed I will lend him two.'

Immediately, continues the ballad, she placed her
two fingers upon his right eye, and firmly closed it.
Then he asked her very tenderly,—

'Beautiful lady, is my eye quite shut?'

And the lady said, 'Yes, certainly.'

Then he spake with his mouth the thought of his
heart: 'And I vow and promise to God omnipotent,
and to His sweet mother (who is of resplendent beauty)
that my eye shall never be opened again, neither on
account of weather or wind . . . . till I shall have
been in France, where there are good people, and I
shall have set fire everywhere, and fought with great

force against the people of Philip. And if I am, by
good chance, not taken in battle, I will aid Edward to
accomplish his design. Now happen what may happen,
it shall not be otherwise !'

Then the maiden with the elegant body (*la pu-
chelle au cors gent*) took away her finger, and the eye
remained closed in the sight of all the people. This
astonishing phenomenon excites Count Robert extremely; 'And when Robert understands this, much joy
takes hold upon him.'

After this ' the noble Robert of Artois did not
in the least relax (*ne s'est mie alentis*), but made
his appeal unto the maiden, the daughter of the Earl
of Derby.

' Damozel,' said he, ' in the name of Jesus
Christ, will you now vow upon the heron the right
of this country ?'

' Sir,' said the maiden, ' it shall be all at your
will; for I vow and promise to the God of Paradise
that I will not have for a husband any man who is
now alive—duke, earl, sovereign, prince, or marquis—
before this vassal shall have accomplished the vow
which, for my love, he has so loftily undertaken.
And when he shall return, if he escapes alive ———'
what a kind ' if !'—' I give him my body heartily
and for ever.'

When the vassal heard this, says the ballad, his
heart was overcome; and, indeed, in his bosom he was
more joyful and more courageous.

To make a long story short, this precious heron—
getting cold all the time—is carried right round the
circuit of the guests by the ferocious count; and the
noble personages present, one after another, make
vows upon it—savage vows, full of fire, and murder,
and desire to knock foreign people off their horses—
' so that he shall be clean thrown to the ground, and
I will have his horse,—I don't know if he will give
it to me.' The two maidens go on with the singing,
and the three minstrels with the fiddling and tinkling.
The song of the girls must have been rather monotonous :—

> · Loyal loves do lead us on,
>   Which have this enchantment done ; '

but then the swearing was monotonous also. The
Earl of Suffolk observes, that ' lovers for love's sake
ought to exert themselves. `He who loves for love
must labour in word and deed :—

> · And each one will do it when comes the attack,
>   But the hardest of all will be to get back,'—

an almost inhuman allusion to the chances of war.
Perhaps Robert of Artois feared its effect upon the
company might be rather relaxing, for he immediately
began to make the minstrels *labour* on the fiddle,
and set the ladies to dance, *in order to entrap the
prey.* So the swearing proceeds, diversified by a
little quarrelling. Jean de Faukemont vows that he

will spare neither woman, child, nor sucking baby that he can find; but John de Beaumont, upon taking *his* little vow, observes that he is surprised at so much talk and boasting. ' When we are in taverns, drinking of the strong wines,' says he, ' and the ladies look on, with their resplendent grey eyes, smiling with beauty, nature provokes us to have in our hearts desire to contend, expecting mercy in the end. And then we conquer Yaumont and Aguilant, and some of us conquer Olivier and Roland. But,' continues this considerate person, ' when we are in the fields, on our swift warhorses, with our shields at our necks, and our lances lowered, and the great coldness of the weather is freezing us all up, then our members fail us both before and behind, when our enemies are approaching us. Then we would rather be in such a great cellar that we should never make any vows whatever. I wouldn't give a bezant for such boasting as this.' However, he proceeds to explain that those comments are not intended as a prelude to his backing out of the confederation, and then goes on to make a longer vow than any of the others, engaging to stand by the good King Edward, and lead his people in this war.

' When Jean de Beaumont had said what he thought,' Robert of Artois approached the Queen herself, and, kneeling down before her, stated that when she had done her vow upon the heron's body, he intended to have it cut up and eaten.

' Vassal,' said her majesty, with some scorn, ' now

talk to me no more! A lady cannot vow, because she has a lord; or if she does vow anything, her husband has power to recall that which she vows.* And shame be to my body if I should think of such a thing, until my dear lord shall have commanded it.'

Then said the King,—

' Swear away, my body shall acquit it. My body shall labour in order to bring it to an end. Vow boldly, so help you God!' To this the Queen replies in words which must be given in the original:—

> . . . ' Je sais bien que piecha
> Que sui grosse d'enfant, que mon corps senti la,
> Encore n'a il gaires qu' en mon corps se tourna ;
> Et je voue et promette à Dieu qui me crea,
> Que nasqui de la vierge, que ses corps n'enpira,
> Et que mourut en crois, on le crucifia,
> Que jà li fruis de moi de mon corps n'istera,
> Si me n'arés * menée ou pais par delà,
> Pour avauchier le veu que vo corps voué a,
> Et s' il en voellh isir, quant besoins n'en sera,
> D'un grand coutel d' achier li mien corps s' ochira,
> Serai m' asme perdue et li fruis perira.'

This outrageous and outrageously expressed view of the Queen's amounts, as far as it can here be given in plain English, to this:—' I shall, before very long, in the course of nature, become a mother. But I

---

* See Numbers, xxx. 6–8.

† Is not this correct ? Can ' si m'en arés,' which is the text before me, be right ?

vow and promise to God, who created me, and who
was born of the Virgin . . . . and crucified, that
until you, the king, have led me over to France, where
you shall fulfil the vow you have sworn, I *will* not
be the mother of a living child.' There is something
about ' a great knife of steel,' which I omit. The
ballad continues :—

> ' And when the king heard how her majesty swore,
> He looked grave, and said, " Certainly, none could vow
> more," '—

an opinion in which the reader will coincide with the
monarch. ' Then the heron was divided, the Queen
ate of it, and when this had been done, the King
made ready and prepared the ships, and the Queen
entered into them, and he took many a free knight
with him. From there into Antwerp the King made
no halting. And when they have come across the sea :—

> . . . . . ' la dame delivra ;
> D'un biau fils gracieux la dame s'acouka.'

' Lion of Antwerp he was called when they baptized
him :'—

> ' And thus the fair lady acquitted her vow,' (*Le sien
> veu aquitta*),
> ' But before the remainder are quitted also,
> Full many a good man will for it lie low,
> And many a good knight will clamour with woe,

And many good women tired of it will grow.
Then the court of the English across there did go.'
[*Here end the Vows of the Heron.*

' *Chi finent leus veus du hairon.*'

Prince Lionel was born at Antwerp in 1338; but this is almost the only bit of pure fact there is in the ballad. Mr. Wright says he ' should not be surprised if documents were still found to prove that the persons introduced in it could not have been assembled together in London at any one time. The date,' he adds, ' is of course wrong, as in September, 1338, Edward had already been on the Continent two months.' It is, nevertheless, possible that there was a foundation in fact for what is certainly a very characteristic story. The Earl of Salisbury had lost the sight of one eye in the Scottish wars of the reign of Edward III., and the passage in Froissart, where he describes certain ' bachelors' from England as having each one eye covered with red cloth, is familiar to most of us: ' And it was said that these had vowed to certain ladies of their country that they would never again see with both eyes until they had done some prowess with their bodies in the kingdom of France: the which they would in no wise tell to such as inquired of them; so that there was great wonder made at it by every body.'

Whether the poem was founded upon circumstances which did actually occur or not is, however,

immaterial to us; to whom it is sufficient that such
a ballad was possible. The vows of monks, friars, and
nuns, kept the idea of vowing difficult things, and
the obligation of loyalty to such vows, before the minds
of persons, not religious, ' such as ben seculare,'—if
that were necessary; and the world of action and passion outside of the Church had its vowed orders also,
who, not content with the general oath or obligation
of their estate, seem to have been ready enough with
those fantasies of unnecessary loyalty which made such
a poem as the Vows of the Heron *vraisemblable.* As
we shall have occasion to notice again, hard swearing, sometimes profane, but often not profane, was
part of the regimen of the middle ages, and the
belief of our forefathers in the efficacy of oaths is
truly astonishing. Two things must, of course, have
been salient in such times — a wayward strength
of personal will, and a form of the religious spirit
which we should now call superstition or feti-
chism. These are both boyish or juvenile characteristics, and the former needed the chastisement
which it in some degree received among knightly
persons from the knightly grace or virtue of courtesy.
But this had its limitations. Hallam reckons among
the more obvious disadvantages of chivalry, that ' it
widened the separation between the different classes of
society, and confirmed that aristocratical spirit of high
birth by which the large mass of mankind were kept
in undue degradation. Compare,' he continues, ' the

generosity of Edward III. towards Eustace de Rib-
aumont at the siege of Calais with the harshness of his
conduct towards the *citizens.*' And then he proceeds
to give a story from Joinville, ' who was himself im-
bued with the full spirit of chivalry, and felt like the
best and bravest of his age.' Certainly the story is
very *naïve.* Henry, Count of Champagne, acquired,
and deservedly, the surname of Liberal or Munificent ;
and of his munificence Joinville quotes what he
evidently considers a striking and satisfactory example.
A poor knight begged him on his knees to give him as
much money as would enable him to marry his two
daughters. A rich burgess, named Arthault de Nogent,
desiring, in the simple goodnature of his citizen sto-
lidity, to get rid of the petitioner, said to him,— .

' My lord has already given away so much that he
has nothing left !'

This was, no doubt, saying that the Count was
poor, and, as he the citizen was wealthy, it was not a
pretty thing to say. But the Count was equal to the
occasion. "Sir William,' said he to the burgess, ' you
do not speak truth in saying that I have nothing left
to give away. Why, I have got *you!* Here, Sir
Knight, I give you this man, and warrant your possession of him !'

Upon this, the poor knight seized the burgess by
the collar, and informed him that he was a prisoner
until he had paid a fitting ransom ; and indeed, says
Joinville, he was compelled to pay four hundred pounds

for the marriage-portions of the young ladies of the poor knight. After that, we need not wonder at any treatment rich Jews received. The soldier and the priest have been exacting persons in all ages. The priest, whether as individual or institution, saying implicitly, ' I am entitled to lay hands freely on your substance because I am the intermediary by whom you will have to get to heaven, if you escape the other place, and surely you cannot grudge me anything I ask for services so important.' The soldier saying implicitly, ' I am entitled to rations out of your substance because it is I who fight for you, and at any risk to myself draw a cordon of protecting force around your lives.' It is true the poor country curate and the happy soldier who lives on his pay and spends half-a-crown out of sixpence a-day, do not draw prizes; but then, as Paley so adroitly puts it, ' we sow many seeds to raise one flower.' At all events, we see plainly enough what a privileged person the soldier of gentle blood was in the time of Chaucer. From the age of seven the sons of gentlemen were usually nurtured in the castles of the greater barons. They were called pages or varlets until fourteen years old : at fourteen they were called esquires. They waited upon the knights and learnt the use of arms ; they served the lords and ladies in hall and court-yard, and at times of festival. Thus they caught the spirit and gathered the traditions of a knightly career. In due time, perhaps, the young esquire became a knight himself.

Then he wore a helmet with a crest, and gilt spurs.
Scarlet was a colour that belonged to him, as purple
to kings. He could himself confer the order of knighthood on any esquire, and once free of the chivalric
order, he was free of it all over the world wherever
knighthood was known ; besides being certain that the
hospitality of princes and barons was at his command
go whither he would. ' Knight-errantry as a profession,'
Mr. Hallam thinks, ' can hardly be considered to have
had any existence beyond the precincts of romance.'
Yet he goes on to recognise the possibility of the
' errantry ' when the knight was travelling : for example,
on his way to the Holy Land, or on his way back from
it ; and, indeed, though the existence of a *profession*
of knight-errantry among any large number of men may
be inconceivable, yet when an order of heroic persons
pledged to the succcur of the weak was a living fact,
it is easy to see that extravagant persons must have
been among its members, and to conclude that the
extravagant persons would naturally have done extravagant things. It does not much matter, however,
whether Chaucer was ridiculing a class of real persons
or the sort of figure which the romance-writers made
of the knight of the period, when he told the burlesque
story of Sir Thopas :—

> ' Sir Thopas wax a doughty swayn ;
> Whyt was his face as payndemayn,
>   His lippes reed as rose ;

His rode is lik scarlet en grayn,
And I yow telle, in good certayn,
   He had a semly nose.
His heer, his berd, was lik safroun,
That to his girdil raught adoun ;
   His schoon of cordewane;
Of Brigges were his hosen broun.'

Besides being personable and well dressed, he had all the accomplishments:—

' He couthe hunt at wilde deer,
And ride on haukyng for ryver
   With gray goshauk on honde ;
Therto he was a good archeer,
Of wrastelyng was noon his peer.'

And many fair ladies languished and pined for him, even by night, when, says Chaucer, frankly, they had better have been fast asleep :—

' Ful many mayde bright in bour
That mourne for him, *par amour*,
   Whan hem were bet te slepe :
But he was chast and no lecchour,
And sweet as is the brembre flour
   That bereth the reede heepe.'

He wanted adventure, however :—

' And so it fel upon a day,
For soth as I yow telle may,
   Sir Thopas wold out ryde ;
He worth upon his steede gray,
And in his hond a launcegay,
   A long sword by his syde.
He priketh thurgh a fair forest.'

While he was in the forest, a 'love-longing' came
over him in a dream. Love-longing was a sort of
chivalric mania that came upon your knight or dame
without warning. Sir Thopas longed for an elfin
wife :—

> ' An elf queen schal my lemman be,
>   And slepe under my gore.
> An elf queen wol I have, I wis,
> For in this world no woman is
>   Worthy to be my make
>   In toune ;
> Alle othir wommen I forsake,
> And to an elf queen I me take
>   By dale and eek by doune.
> Into his sadil he clomb anoon,
> And priked over stile and stoon
>   An elf queen for to spye.'

He came upon the castle of the three-headed giant,
Sir Olifaunt (elephant?), who informed him that the
fairy queen was staying there, but was not for Sir
Thopas :—

> ' Heer is the queen of fayerie,
>   With harp, and lute, and symphonye,
>   Dwellyng in this place.'

Very good, said Sir Thopas; wait till I get my
armour on to-morrow; to which Olifaunt made answer
by casting stones out of a sling at 'Child Thopas,' who,
beating a retreat,—

' Is come ageyn to toune.
His mery men commaunded he,
To make him bothe game and gle,
    For needes most he fight
With a geaunt with heedes thre,
For paramours and jolite
    Of oon that schon ful bright.
" Do come," he sayde, " my mynstrales
And gestours for to telle tales
    Anoon in myn armynge,
Of romaunces that ben reales,*
Of popes and of cardinales,
    And eek of love-longyng." '

Then they make him a draught of sweet wine,
and dress him for the combat. Among other articles
of dress under his armour he has ' a brech and eke a
schert :'—

' His steede was al dappul gray,
    It goth an ambel in the way
        Ful softely and rounde
    Upon his crest he bar a tour,
    And therin stiked a lily flour :—
        God schilde his corps fro schonde ! '

And then Harry Baily, the host, as we all remember,
interrupts the narrative with imprecations :—

' " Now such a rym the devel I byteche !
    This may wel be rym dogerel," quoth he.'

Chaucer pathetically inquires why he is to be in-

* Reales, royal.

terrupted any more than the others, when he is only doing his best :—

> ' " Why so ? " quod I, " why wilt thou lette me
> More of my tale than another man,
> Syn that it is the beste rym that I can ? " '

But the host is obstinate, and becomes grossly indecent in his phrases of contempt, so that Chaucer has to begin again and ' tel a litel thing in prose.' From this we learn at least that knight-errantry was not in favour with the licensed victuallers of the fourteenth century. But I cannot help noticing that the precise point at which the host interrupts the narrative is one in which Sir Thopas is represented as a man of habits uncongenial to the views of licensed victuallers in all centuries whatsoever. For example, he always slept in the open air :—

> ' He nolde slepen in noon hous,
> But liggen in his hood.'

And, to add insult to injury :—

> ' Him self drank water of the welle,
> As dede the knight sir Percivelle
> So worthy under wede,
> Til on a day —— '

A water-drinker, too ! And here the man whose ' ale of Southwerke ' had turned the Miller's head so soon, will hear no more—

' " No mor' of this, for Goddes dignite ! "
Quod our hoste.'

But it was not ridicule that put down the knight, errant
or attached. It was gunpowder, the indirect result
of which was to give more importance, not only to the
infantry of an army, but to precision of movement and
solidity of attack, as distinguished from anything that
the mere personal prowess of the lancer could do. As
soon as war could get on without him, as an institution
at the service of the promoters of war, he began to
feel the influence of that breath of the people's thought
or feeling which was beginning to make rust-marks,
even in Chaucer's time, on privilege of so many kinds.
The institution of knighthood gave us some noble types
—the Black Prince and Sir Philip Sidney—and it
bequeathed to us certain elements in the sentiment of
progress. But, though it was in its glory in the reign
of Edward III., the full orb was a little turning
towards the wane before Chaucer wrote ' Sir Thopas.'

CHAPTER IV.

THE GAY SCIENCE.

WE do not know, and—as I do not believe in a science
of history—I think we never shall know, the laws of
Schwärmerei, or the enthusiasm of multitudes. The
space from the eleventh to the fifteenth century was
crowded with events more or less involved or coiled up
in such enthusiasms; and, looking back from this

distance of time, it is as if we could discern, through the mist of our wonder,

> ‘ The prophetic soul
> Of the great world, dreaming on things to come.’

First, we are astonished at it; then we scrutinise it. And then again, dissatisfied with our unprofitable inspection, we find, as soon as ever we are a little familiar with the few hard facts we can see clearly, that the glamour of wonder returns. Once more, we see and feel, but do not understand. The mystery of human life is as great as ever, and the entangling of the threads of good and evil, of fatality and will, of conscious intent and (what I do not know how to call anything but) dreaming intent, as complicated and mysterious as ever. We cannot take up into our thoughts this Romantic movement : the burthen is too great for us. But if I had to name the conditions under which such a movement would be proved natural to human nature, I really think I should name those imposed upon society by the Mediæval Church. It was totally impossible for the communities of the West to take shape without a large infusion of the strong heroic virtues; and, whatever the Church may have done towards mitigating pure secular ferocity, it never disowned the sword which helped or seemed to help it. It would never have done for a Church which ultimately rested on force to discredit the military virtues ; and we have seen that the consecration of a knight to his functions was almost a sacrament. Now, under any circumstances, the spirit of adventure, by which I mean the spirit that is apt to question the unknown or the future in any shape—the spirit of adventure, I say, which is another name for the love of mystery, is naturally akin to love and reverence for women. And if we give to the daring soldier—the *huntsman* of danger and wrong—a faith which apotheosizes a woman, and so tends to make the gentle virtues prominent in his thoughts, we inevitably go far to make a woman-worshipper. Such a man, with such a faith, was the mediæval knight, and music—a festive and social accomplishment—was a natural part of the education of a gentleman; so that we frequently find the knight a singer and a harper as well as a swordsman and a good rider. But it is not to be supposed that he would be allowed to keep so easy a faculty as that of the singer or musician all to himself. Richard Cœur de Lion was a troubadour, and a thousand brave soldiers beside; but the soldier and the poet are types which are not *commonly* found united in one person; and, accordingly, knightly deeds and ladies' love were not left to be sung of by knights alone. The minstrel-romancist, or troubadour, appears upon the scene; a whole literature of loving and fighting springs up in Europe, the minstrel-romancist doing impartial honour to knights and ladies; the Courts of Love are established; and, almost at a bound, we have before us erotic parodies of the faith of the Church, the subtleties of the Schoolmen, and the discipline of the Feud. The mediæval Church, while it often acted *so as to* protect woman for the time—for example, in forbidding a wanton divorce— did, after all, very much degrade woman in other ways, proclaiming her inferiority and uncleanness, and so often identifying and connecting her with foul and abominable fancies. But it placed the Virgin on the steps of the divine throne and crowned her with stars. Then, after centuries of noise and turbidity, destroying much and threatening much, but leaving untouched the deeper idiosyncracies of races, it befell that,—just at the moment when, quickened by the breath of an intellectual revival, the currents of Teutonic and Celtic sentiment met,—in a happy hour the image of the celestial maiden was reflected in the confluent waters, and the prepared vision saw, through the disturbing ripples, not the figure which the Church had painted, but another; and from that hour the knight and the poet thought no shame to praise God and his lady in the same hymn. Indeed, it is scarcely too much to say that, at this epoch, the knight and the poet have two gods and two heavens. Almost is the phraseology of psalm and prayer, chant and canticle, used indiscriminately. Half-sincere people, who prefer inventing opinions to knowing or thinking the truth, may profess to find allegorical meanings in all this, but it is superabundantly plain that it is fantasy that we have, not allegory. May is the month.

dedicated to the Blessed Virgin by the Church, and May is accordingly the month of Love, in which the Courts of Love are held, under the lindens. The birds are the choristers of the heaven of the God of Love, and the councillors of His court. There is, indeed, something quite conventional in the use to which the birds, the trees, the flowers, and the leaves, are put by all the mediæval poets and romancists. They drop into the verse or the story almost as mechanically as the Flora and Phœbus, and vernal meads, and feathered warblers of a later period. It would be too much to say that all this sentiment or teaching of the romance-literature is conventional in itself, though it may all have been the subject of convention. No degree of use and wont or artificiality of statement can remove the charm of sentiment such as this, which is put into the mouth of the lover in the *Franklin's Tale*, when he has come back to his mistress, Dorigen, wife of Arviragus, to tell her that he has been enabled to do her bidding, and that the rocks of the Breton coast are now removed :—

> ' And whan he saugh his tyme, anoon right he
> With dredful hert and with ful humble cheere
> Salued hath his owne lady deere.
> " My soverayne lady," quod this woful man,
> " Whom I most drede, and love, as I can,
> And lothest were of al this world displese,
> Nere it that I for you have such desese,
> That I most deye her at youre foot anoon,
> Nought wold I telle how me is wo bygoon,

But certes outher most I dye or pleyne ;
Ye sleen me gulteles for verrey peyne.
But of my deth though that ye have no routhe,
Avyseth yow, or that ye breke your trouthe ;
Repenteth yow for thilke God above,
Or ye me sleen, bycause that I you love.
For, madame, wel ye woot what ye han hight ;
Nat that I chalenge eny thing of right
Of yow, my soverayn lady, but youre grace ;
But in a gardyn yonde, at such a place,
Ye wot right wel what ye byhighte me,
And in myn hond your trouthe plighte ye,
To love me best ; God woot ye sayde so,
Al be that I unworthy am thereto ;
Madame, I speke it for thonour of yow,
More than to save myn hertes lif right now ;
I have do so as ye comaunded me.
And if ye vouchesauf, ye may go se.
Doth as you list, have youre byheste in mynde,
For quyk or deed, right ther ye schul me fynde ;
In yow lith al to do me lyve or deye ;
But wel I wot the rokkes ben aweye." '

Or this, from the statutes—Chaucer's statutes, which
are of his own invention—of the realm of Love : —

'The tenth statute was Egally to discerne
Betwene the lady and thine abilite,
And thinke thyself art never like to yerne,
By right, her mercy not her equite,
But of her grace and womanly pite :
For though thy self be noble in thy strene,
A thousand fold more noble is thy quene.'

Whether the brief hints I have just given of the

exalted fantasy which was brought by the Romantic
poetry of the age to the description of the dignity
of Love and the service done to him are at all exaggerated, the reader will judge from the passages
which I am about to quote from Chaucer's *Court of
Love.* It is not only unnecessary, it is pedantically
idle, to discuss the question, raised by Tyrwhitt and
wisely begged by Warton, whether or not Chaucer
had ever seen, or did in any of his poems imitate
Provençal poems. Chaucer was a man of letters and
of the world. He must have been acquainted with
troubadour poetry. He translated the *Romaunt of
the Rose.* And, apart from all this, being a man
of letters and of the world—above all, a poet—he
could no more have escaped the romantic-erotic spirit
of the day than one of a range of hills could keep
its grassy summit dry while all the rest were dewy.
Here, then, are a few verses from the *Court of Love,*
in which it will be observed he calls the lovers who
have suffered for love 'saints,' or holy ones :—

> ' For there nis god in Heaven or Hel, ywis,
>   But he hath been right subject unto Love :
>   Jove, Pluto, or whatsoever he is,
>   Ne creature in earth, or yet above;
> *   *   *   *   *
>   There saints have their comming and resort,
>   To seen the king so ryally besein,*
>   In purple clad, and eke the queen in sort :

---

* Compare Isaiah, xxiii. 7.

And on their hedes saw I crownes twein,
With stones fret, so that it was no pain,
Withouten meat and drink, to stand and se
The kinges honour and the ryallty.
* * * * *
" Ye shall wel see how rough and angry face
The King of Love will show, whan ye him se :
By mine advice kneel down and ask him grace,
* * * * * *
Why wille ye than the King of Love displese ?"
" O mercy, God," quoth iche, " I me repent,
Caittf and wretch in herte, in wille and thought!
And after this shall be mine whole intent
To serve and plese, how dere that love be bought :
Yet sith I have mine own penaunce ysought,
With humble spirite shal I it receive,
Though that the King of Love my life bereve.
And though that fervent loves qualite
In me did never worke truly, yet I
With al obeisaunce and humilite,
And benign herte, shall serve him til I die :
And he that Lord of might is, grete and highe,
Right as him list me chastise and correcte,
And punishe me, with trespasse thus infecte."

This is pretty strong language,—with a few slight
alterations it might be transferred bodily into Quarles,
or some other writer of the same spiritual-erotic
school. But these illustrations would be incomplete if
I did not produce part of the triumphal canticle which
is appended to the poem, and which represents the
birds,—choristers of the Court of Love,—as parodying
the office for Trinity Sunday :—

' On May day, whan the lark began to rise,
To matins went the lusty nightingale
Within a temple shapen hawthorn-wise;
He might not slepe in al the nightertale,
But " *Domine labia*," gan he cry and gale,
" My lippes open, Lord of Love, I crye,
And let my mouth thy praising now bewrye."
The eagle sang "*Venite* bodies alle,
And let us joye to love that is our health."
And to the deske anon they gan to falle,
And who came late he pressed in by stealth :
Than said the faucon, our own hertes wealthe,
" *Domine Dominus noster* I wot,
Ye be the God that done us brenne thus hote."
" *Cœli enarrant*," said the popingay,
" Your might is told in Heaven and firmament."
And than came in the goldfinch fresh and gay,
And said this psalm with hertily glad intent,
" *Domini est terra ;* " this latin intent,
The God of Love hath yerth in governaunce :
And then the wren gan skippen and to daunce.
" *Jube Domne*, O Lord of Love, I praye
Command me wel this lesson for to rede ;
This legend is of alle that wolden deye
Martyrs for love ; God yet their soules spede !
And to thee Venus singe we, out of drede "

And there is much more of the same sort ; the
robin, the turtle-dove, the thrush, the peacock, the
linnet, the owl, the lark, and the kite, taking part in
the service. The cuckoo ends it ' with *Benedictus*,'
and bursts out laughing, thanking God that it is his
good fortune to ' end the song, And all the service
which hath been so long.'

If to this we add that the lover, for love's sake, was often supposed to add dignity to his passion and honour to his mistress by an asceticism which parodied that of the cloister — an asceticism which included fasting, vigils, and exposure to extremes of weather — we see how completely this love-cult was *calqué* upon that of the mediæval Church.

II. There is nothing really absurd in making a serious affair of love-longing. The Scotch minister, when he had been engaged to the girl for some years, said timidly one day, 'D'ye think, lassie, we might tak' a kiss?' The damsel looking as if she thought he might, the minister folded his hands, and asked a blessing. He then took the kiss, and gave thanks. But soon his love-longing returned upon him, and he whispered, ' Eh, lassie, but it's verra guid; d'ye think we might tak' anither?' In our own day it is well known that Auguste Comte has proposed to restore the worship of Woman. *A Dieu ne plaise* that I should laugh at the idea, though I do at his naïve way of trying to formulate it. I was once told, with perfect gravity and simplicity, by a Positivist gentleman, that another Positivist gentleman, although to his grief there were no public opportunities of realising the worship of woman, faithfully carried out the cult in his own family. It is to be feared that few marrying men lay much stress upon the words in the marriage-service, With my body I thee worship ;' but Auguste Comte is very explicit about the matter. He says it was Feudalism which introduced for the first time the worship of Woman; but Chivalry in this respect, he continues, ' was constantly opposed by the Catholic system, which was so austere and anti-social that it could not sanction marriage, except as an infirmity, which it was necessary to tolerate, but which was hazardous to personal salvation. . . . . . . Notwithstanding all the noble and long-continued efforts of our mediæval ancestors, the institution of the worship of woman was very imperfectly effected, especially in its relations to public life.' The mediæval Knight, he says, was divided in his worship between God and his Ladye; but ' in those days'—those days being the days ' when the influence of chimerical beliefs will have passed away !'—' Man will kneel to Woman, and to Woman alone. . . . The worship of Woman, when it has assumed a more systematic shape, will be valued for its own sake as a new instrument of happiness and moral growth. . . . Prayer would be of little value unless the mind could form a clear conception of its object. The worship of Woman satisfies this condition, and is so far of greater efficacy than the worship of God. . . . The worship of Woman, begun in private, and afterwards publicly celebrated, is necessary in man's case to prepare him for any effectual worship of Humanity. . . . Without personal experience of love a public service in honour of Woman would be nothing but a repetition of unmeaning formulas.' The last proposition every one will accept at once ; but that Man can, or ever will, form a clear conception of Woman is much more questionable. However, Comte proceeds to make this astounding observation : ' The subject of the worship of Woman by Man raises a question of much delicacy ;—how to satisfy analogous feelings in the other sex. . . . Theory indicates a blank hitherto unnoticed, but does not enable me to fill it.' It certainly seems to me that the Pickwick Papers contain nothing more savagely humorous than these passages. But, if in the cold grey light of the age in which our lot is cast, a man could deliberately propose that men and women should meet in public and worship each other—for all the ' delicacy' in the world cannot escape that consummation of the scheme—it is hardly incredible, or even improbable, that in days of pageantry and caste there should have been assemblies of some kind or other in which lords and ladies met and held love-courts. In the Middle Ages the women did not exactly worship the men ; but the ladies waited on the knights, bathed and dressed their wounds, held their stirrups, and allowed them to dictate reciprocities of homage. The well-known story of the lady who, having bidden her lover go and fight in his shirt as a proof of his bravery and devotion, was obliged, when he had won, to sit at table in the blood-stained garment, is a case in point.

III. In a poem which, though it is far above

praise of mine, I may be allowed to call one of the
sweetest of the century, Mr. Coventry Patmore calls
Love the 'nursling of civility :'—

> ' Lo, how the woman once was wooed ;
>   Forth leapt the savage from his lair,
> And felled her, and to nuptials rude
>   He dragged her, bleeding, by the hair.
> From that to Chloe's dainty wiles,
>   And Portia's dignified consent,
> What distance !   But these Pagan styles,
>   How far below Time's fair intent !
> Siegfried sued Kriemhild.   Sweeter life
>   Could Love's self covet ?   Ballads teach
> In what rough sort he chid his wife
>   For want of curb upon her speech !
> Shall Love, where last I leave him, halt?
>   Nay ; none can fancy or foresee,
> To how strange bliss may time exalt
>   This nursling of civility.'

All this is forcible enough ; but it refers only, or
chiefly, to that unconscious softening of the forms
and terms of love between man and woman which is
implicit in civilization.   But it is conceivable,— it is
not only conceivable, it has entered into the heads of
speculators to conceive and actually suggest that this
' nursling of civility,' or the love of cities, should,
like some other nurslings of the same, be at last
nursed out of sight, or improved off the face of the
earth.   Godwin thought it not impossible that the
crowning race of men and women should be a race

which would no longer enter into the relation in
which the continuance of every race whatever is bound
up. True, the love which the Troubadour sang was,
according to *la haute école*, love for love's sake;
amour par amour; and was not supposed to have
anything to do with marriage, or even to be the
business of the husband any more than what passed
in the confessional. But, in practice, what was, and
is, implicit in love tended to become explicit; it was
not easy to arrest at the flower the *essor*, as the
French would say, which naturally tended to pass
onwards to the fruit; and the worship of beauty and
tenderness took on colour, eagerness, and fire: which
do not belong to *worship* of any kind. All this was
natural and inevitable ; but the mediæval idea was
distinctly that of a cultus, not a pursuit; the worship,
not the wooing of woman, though the wooing un-
derwent some change in consequence of the worship.
Whatever a woman may grant, or be compelled to
yield, there is always something which she can with-
hold; and, in proportion as men are worthy, they
find their chief account in that something. Here
is the third heaven of a woman's power; the sphere
in which she can command worship, as well as wish-
ing. And, as far as the man is concerned, here,
also, is the third heaven of his delight. There is
nothing noble, beautiful, or pleasant in refraining,
in dropping pursuit, when the motive is fear of
consequences, or even deference to rule; but it is

noble, beautiful, and pleasant to refrain in the name and for the sake of love; to say, ' I worship so much, that the love which fuses my worship into an absorbing sentiment has no will of its own, and is rapturously content with the will of my ladye, whatever it is." Is there a living man who, fancying he has been in love, has not yet learnt this?

> ' If yours you seek, not her delight,
> Surely a dragon and strong tower
> Guard the fair lady in her bower.'

If there be such a man, he has a secret of joy yet to learn.

In the Middle Ages there was no necessary discrepancy between the idea of a wife and the idea of a virgin—for the idea of a virgin-mother even was familiar to men's minds. Hence there was nothing absurd or unreal to the fantasy of the times in the idea of a married woman giving virgin love to a man who was not her husband. But, apart from this, wherever vows are plentiful, casuistry begins (because life is a problem, not a theorem, and obligations cannot be infallibly chalked out beforehand); and wherever, as in the mediæval love-cultus, vows cross each other's paths perpetually, the casuistry needs to become a science.

Accordingly, we have, in the literature of mediæval love, a jurisprudence of *amour par amour;* codes of laws for vowed knights and ladies; and courts of love, in which questions are debated and decided. We are not bound to believe the chronicler who tells us that the ladies who sat in these courts were always dressed in green (which, indeed, was the colour of jealousy), and wore golden necklaces or collars ; much less that they were so highly perfumed that people who came too close were thrown into violent sneezing-fits. But, reviewing the literature of the subject, even Sir Charles Coldstream could hardly help admitting that there was something in it. A learned Frenchman, Reynouard, maintained, as is well known, that the Courts of Love did actually exist; while Professor Diez, of Bonn, maintained that they did not. I incline to think that they did. It is not essential to believe, for example, that our own Richard I. was ever the judge of such a court, or that the thing itself was at all commensurate with its literature, or that more than a fraction of the ' cases ' had any existence out of the brains of the recorders of them. But, if we admit the existence of this love-cult, which we cannot help admitting, we find it hard to shut out anything so natural as the Court of Love ; it seems to belong to the spirit of the time. The court may have been originally instituted as a pastime, but so is a game at forfeits, in which penalties are pronounced ; we cannot doubt that the kiss which is commanded in fun at the Christmas frolic has frequently been given and taken in sufficient earnest ; and we can well fancy a half-serious element sliding into even a round game of this kind, with knights and ladies for the players. And, indeed, there is no reason in the nature of things why love-courts should not have had as much power as good society has now. They might have passed awful sentences of excommunication—curses which would have shocked my Uncle Toby. It would have been a serious thing to condemn a Knight or a Troubadour to go unkissed of honourable ladies for the term of his natural life; or even to 'suspend' him for a term of years, as a bishop does a clergyman. It is true a Knight could go elsewhere and get kissed; the world is wide, and sweet lips are as common as daisies. It is also true that honourable ladies cannot be overlooked at all hours; that kisses may be stolen, and that one kiss stolen might count for five unstolen; but it is impossible but that a knight or a poet should feel abashed and melancholy upon being told by a bevy of fair women — say sixty, all in blue, with collars of gold—that he was disgraced by his own act, and out of the pale of sacred love for a time, or for ever. The majority of ladies would feel an *arrêt* very keenly, if we may draw an inference from the emotion with which a modern lady finds herself shut out from So-and-So's 'set.'

IV. The cases in the love-courts have been so often made the subjects of popular writing that it is almost impossible to present any of them with the

least air of newness. But, fortunately, whatever relates to sweethearts and sweethearting keeps pretty
fresh from age to age, and scarcely goes a-begging for
readers yet. It is true Mr. Mill thinks the question
discussed between Delight and his antagonist in
Chaucer's poem, one of which the importance is over-
rated ;* and some estimable writers have been trying
to frighten men into better behaviour by announcing
that women intend shortly to decline marriage; but
it may be observed, by people with eyes, that the
intercourse of young couples still exhibits certain phe-
nomena which no more present the appearance of
being worn out than did the buttercups and daisies
of last June.

A little toleration is bespoken for a few specimens
of mediæval casuistry in love matters.

To begin at random. A knight is in love with
a fair creature whom he is rarely able to see himself;
and, like Miles Standish, and some other incautious
suitors, he employs an inferior person, namely, his
secretary, to fetch and carry for him : probably
thinking that a knight was too great a man to
be supplanted by a secretary. But he suffers for
his folly. The secretary says one word for his
master, and two for himself, and the lady falls in
love with him. The indignant cavalier summons
the clerk and his mistress before the Comtesse de
Champagne, and her sixty ladies, then sitting, or

* Political Economy, Book iv., chap. vii., § 3, last sentence.

ready to sit, in full court of love, and demands justice.
The court hear the arguments, and pronounce judgment to this effect:—That the secretary is a gay de-
ceiver, and the lady another; so that they are well
matched, and their bliss is their bane. But that the
young man, having broken the faith of chivalry, has
placed himself without its pale, and is therefore out-
lawed of all courts of love and knighthood; while the
lady is, in like manner, excommunicated, because
she has 'bemeaned' herself to a gentleman's secretary,
when she might have had a knight. No punishment
appears to have been inflicted upon the knight himself, though the Court of Ladies might well have been
expected to snub a man and a soldier, who was such
a fool as not to know that *go, and do not send,* is
ladies' law in love-matters.

A troubadour fell in love-longing for a damsel of
very tender age; a child, in fact, like Dante's Beatrice.
As soon as she had grown a little older, the troubadour made a declaration of his passion in the pre-
scribed form, and the girl promised him a kiss—some
day. The troubadour remained constant in his love,
and eventually claimed the kiss. But his mistress,
now grown to woman's estate, declined to kiss him;
alleging that when she made the promise she was too
young to know what it was to which she pledged
herself. The judgment of the court was that the
troubadour should have the kiss; but, only on condition that he immediately restored it.

This is one of a large number of cases, which, by the evident playfulness and no-meaning of the decision, suggest that these courts might *possibly* have had no existence out of the fancy of the book-makers. The jest of taking a kiss, on condition that it be returned, is an obvious one ; familiar in a dozen places, of which one is the well-known May-pole song :—

> ' Then after an hour, they went to a bower,
>   And played for ale and cakes ;
> And kisses, too ; — until they were due,
>   The lasses kept the stakes :
> The girls did then begin
>   To quarrel with the men ;
> And bid 'em take their kisses back,
>   And give them their own again.'

A lover sues a lady for pricking him with a pin while she was kissing him—which was certainly a very mean action. The lady respondent 'pleads first, that the kiss was forced from her; and, second, that the pricking was done by accident, if at all. But all her artfulness does not avail her. A medical inspection is prayed on the part of the plaintiff, and the wound proved. The Court accept his evidence, and condemn the lady to kiss the place, when required, until it is well.

A knight loved a lady, long and well, and she returned his passion. By and bye the knight had to go out in the wars, where, after a time, he fell sick of desire to behold his lady. He was unable to go

to her, as, in like case, Lord Lovel did to Lady Nancy
Belle—for the fever of his desire laid him on a bed
of sickness.   A troubadour carried to his lady the
news that her knight was ill, and that the physician
declared his life forfeit unless she went and allowed
him to see her.   During the knight's absence, however, the lady had been betrothed and married.   The
brute of a husband—Danger is the name of the
husband in these romances—objects.   Ordered, by
the Court, that his objection be overruled, and that
the lady go and console her knight.   The husband,
it is presumed, might follow her, but that is
affair.   All he is entitled to is her person ; and
he is not where she is—whose fault is it ?

' Mon Dieu !' said the Frenchman, amazed at
English manners and morals, ' ces messieurs Anglais
aiment leurs femmes !'

But Love, as understood by the troubadour mind,
could not exist between married couples.   Of all
the points of law, discussed and settled in the Courts
of Love, this is, perhaps, the clearest.   A brave
knight fell in love-longing for a young lady who was
already betrothed.   There is an obvious logical in-
consistency in what follows next ; but it seems the
girl promised him her love, if ever she *lost* the love
of her then suitor.   In due time she and her betrothed were married.   Confident in his reading of
the law of the case, the knight immediately claimed
the fulfilment of the lady's promise : holding that,

by winning a husband, she had lost her lover. This case is reported as having been decided by Eleanor of Aquitaine, who afterwards became the wife of our Henry II.; but this lady only claimed for herself the work of affirming an indisputable precedent applicable to all such questions:—' We presume not to vary from the decision of the Comtesse de Champagne, who, by an *arrêt* of the most solemn character, has pronounced that between husband and wife true love can never be. The judgment of the court, therefore, is, that the lady fulfil her promise by giving her love to the knight.'

This, if it were serious, would be admirable. ' John,' said the good wife, irritably, ' don't kiss me —people will think we are not married.' This was the way in which they looked at the matter in those days, and it served the mediæval Church quite right.

A knight loved a lady; and one night she kissed him in the dark, receiving from him a vow of eternal fidelity, and giving him a red scarf by which to remember her. But it seems there was another lady, who was sick, almost to death, for the love of this knight. One day he received by a page a message calling upon him to meet his ladye in the same place as that where he had received the scarf and given the pledge. Here, in darkness again, the second lady met him; and, as her voice was much like that of the first, passages of love once more passed, with more kissing, and a fresh vow of fidelity on the part of the knight, who again received a scarf—the scarf, however, being this time blue.

After an interval, each of these ladies laid claim to the love of the knight, and summoned him before the Court. The knight asserted that he had only *intended* to vow allegiance to one lady—the lady of the red scarf. The lady of the blue scarf, however, alleged that he had plighted his troth to her on a former occasion, and broken it, and that she had then resorted to the stratagem of which we have spoken. With this conflict of testimony before it, the ladies being equally beautiful, and the knight himself either confused in his mind, or pretending to be so (because he sighed for a change), the Court decreed that the knight and the two ladies should be led by discreet persons into a dark room; that the knight should be made to turn round three times, and then take one of the ladies by the hand and kiss her, and that that one should have all his love and faith.

V. It may be conjectured that all this kind of fantastic fuss was too often, to quote Lady Booby, ' the prologue to a play.' A knight might be, like Joseph, own brother to Pamela, and yet find himself very much puzzled to discriminate between Venus Urania and Venus Pandemos, when he was introduced into this strange world of greenery, and nightingales, and minstrels, and fair ladies. Chaucer, in the 'Court of Love,' appears deliberately to confuse the issue between this Venus and that. He, indeed, introduces Delight, and his coarse antagonist, discussing the question; and he puts—as a poet could do no other—the sweetest words in the mouth of Delight; but, after all, it is only as if he told us he was present at a dispute between Ninon de l'Enclos and Madame de Guion :—

> ' And there beside, within a bay window,
>   Stood one in grene, ful large of brede and length,
>   His beard as black as feathers of the crow ;
>   His name was Lust, of wonder might and strength ;
>   And with Delight to argue there he thenkth,
>   For this was alle his opinion,
>   That love was sinne : and so he hath begun
>   To resone fast, and ledge auctorite :
>   " Nay," quoth Delight, " love is a virtue clere,*
>   And from the soul his progres holdeth he :
>   Blind apetite of lust doth often stere,
>   And that is sinne.   .   .   .   .
>   Yet think it wel that love may not be sinne ;
>   For God, and saint, they love right verily,
>   Void of all sinne and vice."   .   .   .   .
>   " Now stint," quoth Lust, " thou speketh not worth a
>   pinne."
>   And there I left them in their arguing.'

This is all very well ; but what are we to make out of one (at least) of the twenty statutes of the ' Court of Love'—nay, of two, which cannot be

---

* ' No passion, but a virtue 'tis.'
>   Coventry Patmore. *Angel in the House.*

quoted? What of the complaint, which Mr. Swinburne, with his peculiar humour, terms ' appalling '— of the monks and nuns, which immediately follows upon this unfinished debate between Love and Longing? There is a bewildering crowd of people in the different courts of the palace :—

> ' " Lo ! yonder folk," quoth she, " that kneele in blew,
> They weare the colour aye and ever shalle,
> In sign they ever were and wille be trew
> Withouten chaunge." '

These are the true lovers, all in blue. And this is the song of praise :—

> ' Yet eft again, a thousand million,
> Rejoysing, love, leading their life in blis :
> They said, " Venus, redresse of al division,
> Goddesse eternal, thy name yheried is !
> By loves bond is knit al thing, ywis,
> Beast unto beast, the earth to water wan,
> Bird unto bird, and woman unto man ;
>
> This is the life of joy that we ben in,
> Resembling life of heavenly paradise ! " '

But now Philogenet comes to those who are vowed to what was called the ' religious' life, and their lamentations, if not ' appalling,' are certainly uncomfortable. If I were as fond of ' tracing' things in literature as some people, I might suggest that Milton had these passages in his mind when he wrote the soliloquy of

Satan, looking on at Adam and Eve 'imparadised in one another's arms;' but as the suggestion would be wrong, I omit it. It is, however, quite possible that William Blake, in the poem beginning (I quote from memory):—

' I went to the Garden of Love,'

and which contains some such lines as these:—

> ' And priests in black gowns were walking their rounds,
> And binding with briars my joys and desires,'

had in his mind, or rather, under his mind, some of the lines, which run as follows:—

> ' This is the court of lusty folk and gladde,
> And wel becometh their habit and arraye:
> O why be some so sorry and so sadde,
> Complaining thus in blacke and white and graye?
> Freres they ben, and monkes, in good faye:
> Alas, for routh! great dole it is to seen,
> To see them thus bewaile and sorry been.
> See how they cry and wring their handes white,
> For they so soon went to religion!
> And eke the nonnes with veile and wimple plight,
> Their thought is, they ben in confusion;
> " Alas," they sain, " we feigne perfeccion,
> In clothes wide, and lack our liberte;
> But al the sin mot on our friendes be.
> For, Venus wot, we woulde as faine as ye,
> That ben attired here and wel besene,
> Desiren man and love in our degre,
> Firm and faithful right as would the quene;
> Our frendes wick, in tender youth and grene,

Against our wille made us religious;
That is the cause we mourne and wailen thus."
Than saide the monks and freres in the tide,
" Wel may we curse our abbeyes and our place,
Our statutes sharpe to singe in copes wide."
* * * * * *
" We serve and honoure, sore against our wille,
Of chastity the goddes and the quene;
Us leefer were with Venus biden stille,
And have reward for love, and subject been
Unto these women courtely, freshe, and shene.
Fortune, we curse thy wheel of variaunce!
There we were welle thou rievest our plesaunce."
Thus leave I them, with voice of plaint and care,
In raging wo crying ful pitously.'

All this is consistent; or may, without more
straining than is by courtesy allowed to commentators
on sacred and profane writings in general, be made
consistent with the doctrine of Delight; that Love
' holdeth his progress from the soul'—a true and
beautiful doctrine—but it will by no means hang
with the doctrine that ' his progres' ends there; which,
indeed, is false. Still less will it cohere with Chaucer's
account of his Lady Rosial, at whose feet he falls in
the ' Court of Love.' Her head was ' round by compass [the compasses] of nature;' her hair was golden;
the brows were ' lively;' her nose was ' even as a
line;' her eyes were ' orient;' her cheeks of ' lovely
red and white :' —

' Her mouth is short, and shut in little space,
Flaming somedele, not over red, I mene,

With pregnant lippes, and thicke to kisse, percase ;
(For lippes thin, not fat, but ever lene,
They serve of naught, they be not worth a bene).
*　　*　　*　　*　　*　　*
　　　　　　　　　　White as snow
Ben all her teeth, and in order they stond
Of one stature ; and eke her breath, I trow,
Surmounteth alle odours that ever I found
In swetenes ; and her body, face, and hond
Ben sharply slender, so that from the hede
Unto the foot, all is but womanhede.
I hold my peace of other thinges hidde
Here shal my soul, and not my tongue, bewraye.'

This is a beautiful description, and full of the elements of ' Delight.' Compared with a hundred descriptions of female beauty in the poets (say, some contained in William Browne's *Britannia's Pastorals*), it is reticent, a draped contrasted with an undraped figure; but it is distinctly erotic. Yet it well-nigh ceases to have that character, if we leave out the touch about the lips—so much depends upon a single circumstance in a multifarious description !

There is no doubt, upon the face of the facts, that this confused love-cult was made the vehicle of much triviality, much dangerous dalliance, and some downright licentiousness. But it is useless talking of its influence on the morals of the time; for one cannot contemplate it as a thing apart, descending like an aerolite, and impinging upon what it found. To England, indeed, it was foreign ; a sort of liqueur, it appears to have been, which found a transient place among native drinks. The Chivalric or Romance ideal of womanhood, and what is due from manhood to womanhood, was natural in its time and place, and, if its extravagances had been ten times greater than they seem to have been, we should hardly be able to help thinking that it was a good thing, in the absence of a better. But it was for knights and dames; not for burgesses, much less for the common people. What is coming upon the world now, who shall say? But the common people seem to me thus far to have been always much the same as they are now in their ways of thinking of woman. It would, no doubt, be, in some small measure, true to say that because Dante and Petrarch loved and sang, there is a grace the more in the loves of every errand-boy and maid-of-all-work that now keep company—it *must* be true, one would say. Yet it is difficult to look steadily at the lives led by the masses of the people, without being struck almost dumb with the thought, how very little these finer fluctuations of human feeling, which move and colour the upper currents of literature, and leave these striking deposits in history—how very little, I say, they appear to have to do with that great body of men and women, who, if numbers fix nomenclature, must be called the human race. The literature of Chivalry and Romance is one of the most *arresting* facts in modern history. But what effect did the Romance spirit have upon the toiling swarms that the

Black Death carried off by millions in mediæval Europe? The Lay of the Last Minstrel was

> '   . . .   not framed for village churls,
> But for high dames and mighty earls ; '

and so was Chivalry. All this pageant of bravery and tenderness looks like a thing painted in the air, far over the heads of the multitude.

CHAPTER V.

FEMALE TYPES IN CHAUCER.

THE difference between the 'accomplishments' of a lady of the time of Chaucer and of the time of Mr. Tennyson, is an amusing thing to reflect upon. When Othello, buffeted to and fro between reminiscences of his wife's attractions and the recurring suggestions of his own supposed wrongs, is enumerating, by snatches, the things for which he had loved and admired her, he mentions, among other things, her skill with her nee-

dle :—' The world hath not a sweeter creature . . . . .
So delicate with her needle.' A man of distinction
would not think, in modern times, of his wife's needle-
work whilst he was torn with jealousy, or on any high
occasion whatever, not only because the accomplishment of the needle is cheap and common and quasi-
menial, but because the products of skill with the needle
seldom come before us now in such connexions as Mr.
Matthew Arnold calls ' grandiose.' In an earlier day it
was obviously different. The art of the embroideress
was in requisition for the adornment of high places of
all kinds — altars, thrones, footstools, chairs of state,
and the hangings of castles and palaces. When the
lady of a castle, with the help of her maidens, protégées,
daughters of retainers, foster-children, poor sisters,
girl cousins, or what not, embroidered the story of
Theseus and Ariadne for the arras that kept the wind
out in the hall of state of her husband's castle, or for
the king's chamber, perhaps, by way of tribute, it was
natural enough to speak of the art of the needle as a
high accomplishment. In a day when high-born lady
abbesses worked samplers, it was something to say of a
charming wife, that she was ' so delicate with her needle ;' but now-a-days when walls and doors and windows
are air-tight, and the decorator and the painter have
parted company, and house-ornament is easy to be had,
and pictures are plentiful, we do not think of the white
hands of ladies in bower or nunnery using their needles
to beautify our homes and brighten their walls with

heroic story in coloured thread-work. This single
change is so significant that it may stand for a thousand, in approaching some of the types of women
given us by Chaucer.

II. It is noticeable that Chaucer has never painted
the common housewife in her place. The Wife of
Bath is scarcely a housewife; we do not see her in
that capacity at all events; and of the wife of the
merchant, nothing kindly and home-like is said by
the poet. The virtuous wife is quite another figure,
—her, we find in, perhaps, every poet that has painted
character; but the *house*-wife, the figure so familiar
to us all in chap. xxxi. of the Book of Proverbs, is
nowhere to be seen in Chaucer. For this there may
have been a hundred reasons besides the obvious and
sufficient ones which lie upon the surface. In the
first place, the modern style of painting life,—the
Dutch manner applied to interior details,—was not
then regnant; and, in the second, a house-wife was
scarcely a figure that could be made heroic in the days
of the Romaunt of the Rose. A wife might be brought
upon the scene, like Griselda, to exhibit the woman, in
the shameful spirit of the age and of other ages, as
the appendage and feudatory of the man; or, in contrast with the mistress, present on the canvas, or presumed to be there, as in the Franklin's Tale, where a
question fit for the Courts of Love is raised by the
fidelity of the lady and the preposterous ' chivalry' of her

husband. But, realist as Chaucer was, it did not occur to him to paint a house-wife.

If, however, we have not in Chaucer a house-wife painted with loving, domestic touches, we have a maiden, painted in such colours, that all she wanted was a husband to make her such a housewife. There are no words which a little attention will not make out in the description of the damsel Virginia, in the Doctor's Tale; and it is truly beautiful, closing with a domestic reference which, if not very high pitched, is sufficient : —

> ' This mayde was of age twelf yer and tway,
> In which that nature hath suche delite.
> For right as sche can peynte a lili white
> And rody a rose, right with such peynture
> Sche peynted hath this noble creature
> Er sche was born, upon her limes fre,
> Wheras by right such colours schulde be ;
> And Phebus deyed hadde hire tresses grete,
> I-lyk to the stremes of his borned hete.
> And if that excellent was hir beaute,
> A thousand-fold more vertuous was sche.
> In hire ne lakketh no condicioun,
> That is to preyse, as by discrecioun.
> As wel in body as goost chaste was sche ;
> For which sche floured in virginite,
> With alle humilite and abstinence,
> With alle attemperaunce and pacience,
> With mesure eek of beryng and array.
> Discret sche was in answeryng alway,
> Though sche were wis as Pallas, dar I sayn.
> Her facound eek ful wommanly and playn ;

Noon countrefeted termes hadde sche
To seme wys ; but after hir degre
Sche spak, and alle hire wordes more or lesse
Sounyng in vertu and in gentilesse.
Schamefast sche was in maydenes schamfastnesse,
Constant in hert, and ever in besynesse,
To dryve hire out of idel slogardye.'

Against this lovely child-woman of fourteen years
old, the Prioress, who may be taken as the nearest
picture in Chaucer of the gentlewoman of his day,
shows very poorly. Instead of the simplicity of Virginia, we have affectation and self-consciousness — the
Prioress is ' of her smiling full simple and coy.'
She talks indifferent French : she knows how to behave
at table, keeping her fingers dry, and not dropping
her meat from her knife — because forks, of course,
were unknown. She affected courtly manners ; and had
the usual false sentiment of over-accomplished women
in any age : she would weep if she saw a mouse in a
trap, *if it were dead or wounded,* otherwise it would
serve for a pet, like a bird in a cage. She had her pet
dogs with her, which she fed with morsels from the
table. If one of them happened to get hit by somebody's
walking-stick, she cried. Her wimple covers
her head, and hides her hair, but she has a well-marked
forehead. Of her dress we are told little, because there
was not much to tell of the attire of a religious person ;
but the lady had taken care to have her cloak well
made. She wears a chaplet (called ' a pair ') of beads

round her wrist, and her golden brooch bears a motto
of the order in which the religion and the chivalry of
the day may be said to have met and kissed each other;
' Love conquers all things,'—at the best an ambiguous
motto for a religious fine lady. Some of the commentators object to the singing through the *nose*, and want
to make ' voice' of it; but it is a touch we can by no
means part with. In every one of these pictures it is
probable Chaucer had a real person in his eye, and he
would not have made a lady prioress sing through her
nose for nothing : —

> ' Ther was also a Nonne, a Prioresse,
>   That of hire smylyng was ful symple and coy,
>   Hire grettesh ooth nas but by seynt Loy;
>   And sche was clept madame Englentyne.
>   Ful wel sche sang the servise devyne,
>   Entuned in hire nose ful semyly;
>   And Frensch sche spak ful faire and fetysly,
>   Aftur the scole of Stratford atte Bowe,
>   For Frensch of Parys was to hire unknowe.
>   At mete wel i-taught was sche withalle;
>   Sche leet no morsel from hire lippes falle,
>   Ne wette hire fyngres in hire sauce deepe.
>   Wel cowde sche carie a morsel, and wel keepe,
>   That no drope fil uppon hire brest.   .   .
>   In curtesie was sett al hire lest.
>   Hire overlippe wypud sche so clene,
>   That in hire cuppe was no ferthing sene
>   Of grees, when sche dronken hadde hire draught.
>   Ful semely aftur hire mete sche raught.
>   And sikurly sche was of gret disport,
>   And ful plesant, and amyable of port,

And peyned hire to counterfete cheere
Of court, and ben estatlich of manere,
And to ben holden digne of reverence.
But for to speken of hire conscience,
She was so charitable and so pitous,
Sche wolde weepe if that sche sawe a mous
Caught in a trappe, if it were deed or bledde.
Of small houndes hadde sche, that sche fedde
With rostud fleissh and mylk and wastel breed.
But sore wepte sche if oon of hem were deed.
Or if men smot it with a yerde smerte :
And al was conscience and tendre herte.
Ful semely hire wymple i-pynched was ;
Hire nose streight ; hire eyen grey as glas ;
Hire mouth ful smal, and therto softe and reed ;
But sikurly sche hadde a fair forheed.
It was almost a spanne brood, I trowe ;
For hardily sche was not undurgrowe.
Ful fetys was hire cloke, as I was waar.
Of smal coral aboute hire arme sche baar
A peire of bedes gaudid al with grene;
And theron heng a broch of gold ful schene,
On which was first i-writen a crowned A,
And after that, *Amor vincit omnia.*" '

A different portrait, but equally the portrait of a *conventional* woman, is that of the Wife of Bath. This coarse creature, who cannot be reproduced entire upon a modern page, is simply the rude, sensual opposite of the Abbess; and she is, like the Abbess, an inferior person, one of the tens of thousands who are pretty much what their opportunities give them leave to be. She has much more animal energy than the

Prioress, and a different set of tendencies, but, such as they are, she gives them swing, under all the superficial disadvantages of a culture much inferior to that of the Lady-prioress, and the result is her 'character':—

> ' A good Wif was ther of byside Bathe,
> But sche was somdel deef, and that was skathe.
> Of cloth-makyng she hadde such an haunt,
> She passed hem of Ypris and of Gaunt.
> In al the parisshe wyf ne was ther noon
> That to the offryng byforn hire schulde goon,
> And if ther dide, certeyn so wroth was she,
> That sche was thanne out of alle charité.
> Hire keverchefs weren ful fyne of grounde ;
> I durste swere they weyghede ten pounde
> That on the Sonday were upon hire heed.
> Hir hosen were of fyn scarlett reed,
> Ful streyte y-teyed, and schoos ful moyste and newe
> Bold was hir face, and fair, and reed of hewe.
> Sche was a worthy womman al hire lyfe,
> Housbondes atte chirche dore hadde sche fyfe,
> Withouten othur companye in youthe ;
> But thereof needeth nought to speke as nouthe.
> And thries hadde sche ben at Jerusalem ;
> She hadde passed many a straunge streem ;
> At Rome sche hadde ben, and at Boloyne,
> In Galice at seynt Jame, and at Coloyne.
> Sche cowde moche of wandryng by the weye.
> Gattothud was sche, sothly for to seye.
> Uppon an amblere esely sche sat,
> Wymplid ful wel, and on hire heed an hat
> As brood as is a bocler or a targe ;
> A foot-mantel aboute hire hupes large,

And on hire feet a paire of spores scharpe.
In felawschipe wel cowde lawghe and carpe.
Of remedyes of love sche knew parchaunce,
For of that art sche knew the olde daunce.'

This is the portrait of a vulgar rich *bourgeoise* of the west of England, where they made good cloth. She would allow no one to go up the aisle to the altar to deposit her offering or to kiss the sacred relics before her. Her head-dress, heavy with many folds, according to the fashion of the times (so that the neck was often invisible), might have weighed ten pounds — on Sundays! She has scarlet stockings and well-greased shoes. Her red bold face and her talk together tell us enough of her story to enable us to understand why she had been sent on so many pilgrimages, and was now going on another. She sits well upon her pony, with a pretty veil or wimple, and has a hat as large as a shield. She wears spurs — perhaps she rides across — and has a cloth around her wide hips. She is a free talker, and free laugher, and we scarcely need listen to her prologue and story to guess that she is a shrew.

III. And she is not the only shrew that Chaucer has drawn. The host Harry Baily had a vixen for his wife; when he beats his servant lads she brings out the thickest sticks, and urges him to break their bones out of hand — a pretty picture of the rights of a master and mistress in the days of Richard II. If people are not polite to the lady at church — St. Mary Overy's, of

course, is the church she went to — and if her husband,
Mr. Baily, does not resent the slight in what she considers a becoming manner, she attacks him on his
return home, and 'lui dit des injures'—calls him a
milksop, and proposes to exchange her spinning-wheel
for his dagger. From morning till night she tells
him he never willst and up for his wife ; and, unless
he chooses to be always fighting he has to run away
from home to get a little peace. Thus we have his
readiness to accompany the pilgrims to Canterbury accounted for. But the poor man winds up with a boast :
' Some day she will enrage me so that I shall be
sticking one of my neighbours. I am afraid of her,
because she is such a large woman, and capable of
using her hands (as you will find out if you meddle
with her), but when I have my dagger drawn, I'm a
dreadful man to tackle. However, let us pass away
from this matter : '

> ' Whan ended was my tale of Melibé,
> And of Prudence and hire benignité,
> Our hoste sayde, " As I am faithful man,
> And by the precious corpus Madryan !
> I hadde lever then a barel ale
> That gode leef my wyf had herd this tale.
> For sche is no thing of such pacience
> As was this Melibeus wyf dame Prudence.
> By Goddes boones ! whan I bete my knaves,
> Sche bringeth me forth the grete clobbet staves,
> And crieth, ' Slee the dogges everychon !
> And breke of hem bothe bak and bon !'

And if that eny neghebour of myne
Wol nought to my wyf in chirche enclyne,
Or be so hardy to hir to trespace,
Whan sche comth hom, sche rampeth in my face,
And crieth, ' False coward, wreke thy wyf!
By corpes bonés! I wil have thy knyf,
And thou schalt have my distaf and go spynne.'
Fro day to night right thus sche wil bygynne ;
' Allas !' sche saith, ' that ever I was i-schape,
To wedde a mylk-sop or a coward ape,
That wil be over-lad with every wight !
Thou darst nought stonde by thy wyves right.'
This is my lif, but if that I wil fight ;
And out atte dore anoon I most me dight,
And ellis I am lost, but if that I
Be lik a wilde leoun fool-hardy.
I wot wel sche wol do me sle som day
Som neighebor, and thanne renne away.
For I am perilous with knyf in honde,
Al be it that I dar not hir withstonde.
For sche is big in armes, by my faith !
That schal he fynde that hire mysdoth or saith.
But let us passe away fro this matiere.'

The shrew belongs to all ages, from Socrates downwards, and all countries from the Peloponnesus to
Southwark ; but the ' knife' of the good man, worn as
a matter of course, and the ' clobbet staves' to beat
the servants, also as a matter of course, are touches
characteristic of the special time and place.

IV. Again, a pretty wife—once more she is not
a *housewife*—belongs to nearly all times and countries

(excluding, we may say, the Stone age and aboriginal Australia); but the charming picture Chaucer gives of the miserly old Carpenter's wife, aged eighteen, will be found to contain some special features worthy of notice :—

> ' Fair was the yonge wyf, and therwithal
> As eny wesil hir body gent and smal.
> A seynt sche wered, barred al of silk ;
> A barm-cloth eek as whit as morne mylk
> Upon hir lendes, ful of many a gore.
> Whit was hir smok, and browdid al byfore
> And eek byhynde on hir coler aboute,
> Of cole-blak silk, withinne and eek withoute.
> The tapes of hir white voluper
> Weren of the same sute of hire coler ;
> Hir filet brood of silk y-set ful heye.
> * * * * * * *
> Ful smal y-pulled weren hir browes two,
> And tho were bent, as blak as is a slo.
> Sche was wel more blisful on to see
> Than is the newe perjonette tree ;
> And softer than the wol is of a wethir.
> And by hir gurdil hyng a purs of lethir,
> Tassid with silk, and perled with latoun.
> In al this world to seken up and doun
> Ther nys no man so wys, that couthe thenche
> So gay a popillot, or such a wenche.
> For brighter was the schynyng of hir hewe,
> Than in the Tour the noble i-forged newe.
> But of hir song, it was as lowde and yerne
> As eny swalwe chiteryng on a berne.
> Therto sche cowde skippe, and make game
> As eny kyde or calf folwyng his dame.

> Her mouth was sweete as bragat is or meth,
> Or hoord of apples, layd in hay or heth.
> Wynsyng sche was, as is a joly colt ;
> Long as a mast, and upright as a bolt.
> A broch sche bar upon hir loue coleer,
> As brod as is the bos of a bocleer.
> Hir schos were laced on hir legges heyghe ;
> Sche was a primerole, a piggesneyghe.'

This young creature, being just eighteen years old, is
'genteel' and slender.   Her jacket is bordered or
barred with silk.   Her apron is white, and broad,
being gored about her loins.   Her 'smok' open at the
sides, and hanging by her shoulders like a pinafore, is
'embroidered' with black silk, outside and underneath,
where it shows.   The strings of her white cap are of
the same colour.   She has a fillet of silk over her
forehead, confining in front the peplum she wears over
her hair.   Her eyebrows are arched, and black.   At
her girdle hangs a leathern purse, ornamented with
brass and silk.   Her collar is low, so that her bosom
has a chance of being seen, and it is fastened with a
brooch as large as the boss of a shield.   Her shoes are
laced high up on her legs.   She is as fresh as a primrose, and as dainty as a sucking-pig !

I have a little curtailed the comment, but as
Chaucer sometimes says things even more 'unnecessary' than Lear's 'age,' the picture is complete.   No
man will read it without a feeling that the fourteenth
century was very like the nineteenth — in certain
respects which 'make the world go round.'

This young creature may have combed her hair opposite a metal mirror, or over a tub of clean water; she was innocent of tooth-brushes, fed high, and drank beer in huge draughts. But the beer of those days was, perhaps, seldom strong; and she had no tea, coffee, or other hot drinks to spoil her teeth or relax her system. The sweet, breezy healthfulness of Chaucer's picture is probably not at all in excess of the facts. Chaucer says she was prettier to look at than a pear-tree in spring,—'than is the newe perjonette tree,'—and an orchard on a fine morning, with a fresh wind tossing the boughs a little, is just what such a pretty young creature reminds you of. By-the-bye, Chaucer's expression is not prettier to look at, but 'more blissful to see;' that is, more capable of communicating joy than a flowering pear-tree. After this, that she was brighter of complexion than a new-minted noble, and softer than wool, and that she made the air around her body pleasanter than do apples laid up in heather, are touches that we could almost spare, charming as they are. The whole picture is a striking exemplification of the lightsomeness of the poet, and of the prominent part which the spring plays in his, as in other old English poetry. It might not be uninteresting, in the proper place, to compare some of our older and some of our more recent poets with special reference to the tendency to make spring on the one hand, or autumn on the other, a prominent symbol, or source of symbols, in their poetry. At all events, in Chaucer, we have not passed the time when the spring of the year is in the ascendant.

It may be noted, in passing, that the line,—

'Long as a mast and upright as a bolt,'—

has been quoted, I think by Dryden among others, as an instance of a perfect ten-syllable iambic line : the inference from its perfection being that if in any case Chaucer's lines do not scan, it is the fault of the modern ear which misses some disused feature in the accentuation, or the fault of a copyist who has left out a word.

But, to pass on to some general considerations about the ordinary life of women in the times of the Edwards.

V. The language of the common people in regard to women and the relations of men with women appears always to have been pretty much the same in this country. In a previous page we have been noting the fact that the Chivalric or Romantic influence was a thing which was visibly confined to certain layers or strata of the social atmsophere ; and it is certainly a great change of air to come down from the Court of Love to a song like this : —

> ' Herfor, and therfor, and therfor I came,
> And for to preysse this praty woman.
> Ther wer iij wylly, 3. wyly ther wer,
> A fox, a fryyr, and a woman.'

The minstrel who sings this song announces that he has come on purpose to praise a pretty woman, and proceeds to say, in the first place, that she was as cunning as a fox, or a friar.   He then adds: —

> ' Ther wer 3 angry, 3 angry ther wer;
>   A wasp, a wesyll, and a woman.'

The pretty woman had the temper of a wasp.

> ' Ther wer 3 cheteryng, iij cheteryng ther wer:
>   A peye, a jaye, and a woman.'

The pretty woman had the tongue of a jay or a magpie.

> ' Ther wer 3 wold be betyn, 3 wold be betyn ther wer:
>   A wyll, a stokefysche, and a woman.'

This pretty woman wanted a thrashing: but in some of the songs it is the wife who does the thrashing, and the husband who receives it: —

> ' All that I may swynk or swet,
>   My wyfe it will both drynk and ete,
>   And I say ought she wyl me bete.
>   If I say ought of hyr but good
>   She loke on me as she was wod (mad)
>   And wyll me clout about the hod.'

If she goes to the ale-house,—which appears to be a common thing,—she makes her husband walk at her horse's side, while she rides at her ease, and she makes him wait while she drinks her fill: —

> ' If I say it shal be thus,
> She sey, Thou lyyst, churl, I wous,
> Wenest thou to overcom me thus ? '

Naturally enough, the minstrel adds : —

> ' If ony man have such a wyfe to lede,
> He shall know how *judicare* cam in the cred
> Of his penans God do hym med ! '

The song from which I am about to quote makes
pictures, in its own coarse way, of female manners;
and they are not agreeable pictures.   It has a
motto : —

> ' How, gossip myn, gossipe myn,
> When wyll ye go to the wyn ? '

And then the minstrel goes on to tell us in confidence
how men's wives are in the habit of carrying on : —

> ' I will yow tell a full good sport
> How gossyps gather them on a sort,
> Theyre syk bodes (sick bodies) for to comfort,
>   When thei mett in a lane ore stret. .   .   .
> .   .   .   .   .   .
> Good gossipe myn, where have ye be ?
> It is so long syth I yow see,
> Where is the best wyn ? tell you me.'

The lady, thus appealed to, makes answer : —

> ' I know a drawght off mery-go-downe,
> The best it is in all thys towne ;
> But yet I wold not, for my gowne
>   My husband it wyst.' .   .   .   .

Half-a-dozen other 'gossips' are then summoned to be
of the party, 'for they will come, both all and some.'
Their names are prettier than their ways: Eleanor,
Joan, Marjorie, Margaret, Alice, and Cicely. Each
of them brings some provision from home: goose,
pig, capon, pigeon-pasty, 'ore sum other thyng,' and
then they walk discreetly, and not in a band, to the
tavern: —

> 'Go befoore by tweyn and tweyn,
> Wysly, that ye be not seen. . . .
> A strype ore ij God myght send me,
> If my husband myght her se me.'

Seated at 'the borde,' they fill 'pots of muscadell,'
and the talk sets in: —

> 'How look ye, gossip, at the borde's end?
> Not mery, gossip? God it amend. . . .
> Wold God I had done after your counsell!
> Fore my husband is so fell
> He betyth me lyk the devill off hell;
> And the more I cry, the lesse mercy.
> Alys with a loud voyce spak them,
> I-wis, she seid, lytyll good he can,
> That betyth or strykyth ony woman,
> And specially his wyff. . . .
> Margaret mek seid, So mot I thryff,
> I knew no man that is alyffe,
> That gyve me ij strokes, but he shal have fyffe!'

Two things at least are manifest in this song; one,
that it was not unusual for a man to beat a woman;
and, another, that it was not considered right, however

usual it may have been. But the sentiment which is, perhaps generally, assumed to be of immemorial date upon this subject is really modern. We should not bear to hear, in our own day, of the flogging of women in prison even, whatever had been their offences ; but our forefathers were familiar enough with the idea. The ill-favoured man holding the cane over the shoulders of the wretched woman in one of the ' Harlot's Progress ' series, is familiar to our memories, and so is the well-known appeal of the women in Bridewell, ' Pray, Sir Robert, knock ! '—the descent of the hammer being the signal for the cessation of the whipping. It is plain that, in Shakespeare's time, it was considered unchivalrous to strike a woman under ordinary circumstances ; for when Iago is about to stab his wife, Gratiano interposes with, ' Fie ! your sword upon a woman ! ' It is true, the case here is one of stabbing rather than striking ; but when Othello hits Desdemona, he very much astonishes the ' gentleman from Cyprus.' Lodovico says :—

> ' My lord, this would not be believed in Venice,
> Though I should swear I saw it ; 'tis very much ;
> Make her amends.' . . . .

And yet, afterwards, he asks Iago a question which reads rather curiously : —

> ' What, strike his wife ! . . . *Is it his use ?*
> Or did the letters work upon his blood
> And new create this fault ? '

That Lady Jane Grey was beaten by her parents when she was a grown woman we know from her own testimony. They treated her so harshly, yea, presently sometimes with pinches, nips, and bobs, and in other ways which the sweet, noble creature would not name, for the honour she bare them (I am quoting her from memory), that she often thought she was in hell; and then, presently, said she, comes good Mr. Aylmer (her tutor), and treats her so kindly that she thinks nothing while she is with him, and only begins to be unhappy when he goes away. Perhaps we shall get as near the truth as, in a question of obsolete or nearly obsolete manners, as we are likely to get, if we say that probably the judicial flogging of women was approved and not regarded with horror; at all events it was done. King Lear says : —

> ' Thou rascal beadle, hold thy *bloody* hand !
> Why dost thou lash that whore ? '

And beating by a parent, and among the common people beating by a husband, would be considered quasi-judicial. The practice of the Romish Church in respect of penitentiary flagellation, making no distinction of sex, and generally familiarising the mind with the idea of scourging, had something to do with it. But, in practice, women were never whipped on a large scale in the north-west of Europe. ' Nature teaches that air,' as Sam Slick says. For the modern sentiment upon this subject Nature has at least laid this foundation, that the moments of tenderness between a man and a woman leave sufficient trace in the memory of the stronger of the two to make him, in practice, slow to entertain the idea of striking what he has only just now been caressing. Religious intolerance, kindled into religious hatred, appears to have been a very *recent* offender in regard to the flogging of women. Young and beautiful Quakeresses were once scourged in Massachusetts for the offence of proselytizing.

This is, in part, a digression; but it may help unaccustomed readers to conceive, by an *a fortiori* process, how very rough in the days of the Edwards must have been the current relations of average men and women—chivalry notwithstanding. Nobody can even glance at Shakspeare without being struck by the frequency with which shrews and shrewishness are referred to. It is just the same in the ballads from which I have been quoting;* and the 'common scold,' with her appropriated punishments of the gag and the ducking-stool, is a frequently recurring figure down to much later than the fifteenth century. The point, of course, lies in the word 'common;' a common, or public shrew, so loud of tongue, and so accustomed to make it an instrument of attack, and to disturb whole neighbourhoods with it, that she had to be taken account of by beadles and peace-officers, and ducked or gagged now and then in the name of

* " Songs and Carols of the Fifteenth Century." Edited by T. Wright, Esq. Percy Society, vol. xxiii.

the public peace. The type still exists, and may occasionally be heard of, and even heard, in remote country districts or the low neighbourhoods of towns. But the indoors life of our own time tends to improve this precise specimen off the face of the earth. The modern scold is rarely a *common* scold : the husband has her all to himself, or, at least, has the worst of her all to himself. Of the two types of the shrew given us by Chaucer, one is a full-length portrait—the Wife of Bath—a jolly, rosy vixen, whom he evidently enjoyed the painting of; the other, Mrs. Harry Baily, is a mere consequential vixen, who nags at her husband, and thrashes her servants all round. But both figures belong to a time of rough, out-of-door life, when it looks very much as if women moved more independently of their husbands, though the doctrine of their inferiority was more rigorously held and preached than it is now.

VI. In some respects the culture of well-bred women was in the centuries which followed the first Renascence higher than it is now : at all events, it included a large number of what would now be called masculine accomplishments. The book-culture, for example, of Lady Jane Grey and Queen Elizabeth, was of the highest—was what most men would now call unfeminine. What remains we possess of the correspondence of cultivated Englishwomen in those fresh energetic days show a freedom and vigour of mental movement which might well make a modern fine lady envious, if she were capable of understanding it. Unquestionably, one reason for the greater uniformity in those earlier days of the book-culture of men and women, who were cultivated at all, was that the means or subjects of culture were themselves more uniform. There were the classics, there was geometry, there were dialectics, and there was music taught as a science. Of physics, as we now understand it, there was scarcely a trace. Applied science—and it is very much its applications which determine the rank or place a study shall take—there was none. Culture was culture; it meant Greek and Latin, and a few other things; and if women were cultivated, they were cultivated much as men were. That they learned Latin as a matter of course is not to be wondered at, for as late at least as Bacon we note the astonishing place it held in the thoughts of the educated classes. He translates his Essays into English, but believes that the Latin edition will last the longest, being written in the universal language!

This uniformity of culture, along with two other circumstances, first, that the gentle or high-bred class was more habitually self-conscious of its unity as a class than it is now (when, indeed, it can hardly be conceived as a class at all); and, secondly, that in days of violence, intrigue, and social uncertainty, women had so often to act side by side with their husbands, or act *for* them in matters of defence, negotiation, and the like—these circumstances, I say, contributed to make women of position and culture the apparent equals of their husbands, whatever the theory was.

Of course all this does not apply to women of lower grades. Here, however, other circumstances come into play. The men were more frequently from home than they are now. Housekeeping was more of a craft and a mystery than it is at present. When we look at the astonishing cookery of our ancestors—when we note the intrepid manner in which they put, or told you to put, fifty different ingredients into a dish or a drink—we wonder where they found time to do it all. Turn to an old receipt-book, and observe the easy indifference with which you are told, if you want a tansy-pudding, or a basin of gruel, to 'Take' a score of the most impossible things in the world. *This*, too, is to be gathered when the moon is at the full, and *that* when the dew is on the grass; the witch-broth recipe in 'Macbeth' is nothing to it. The ladies must always have been getting up at daybreak, or watching for eclipses of the moon, or catching salamanders, or tying up marjoram, sassafras, borage, or mint; getting in benzoin, zedoary, gum this and gum the other—or else how did they produce those astounding boluses and electuaries? Consider next their baking, their brewing, their pickling, their preserving, their spinning, their embroidering, their knitting, their sheep-shearing, their midwifery, and other leechcraft. And then think of all this as a mystery communicable by

tradition and otherwise among women, but constituting
a world of its own, in which women were the queens.
The Danes introduced into England a law or regulation
of the Scandinavians, which made the wife really and
truly a domestic queen.   To her belonged the keys of
the household, the key of her board or store-room, the
key of her linen-chest, and the key of her cupboard or
corner of conveniences and household implements.   If
the husband did not give her these, and allow her to
retain them, she could claim and take them by force of
law.   To this day the wife is, we are told, to be
wholly supreme in the department of the household.
In happy homes this supremacy is of little or no
meaning; but in some cases, if literally asserted and
allowed, it must prove very inconvenient to the husband.   A wife might, for example, persist that linen
was dry when it was damp, or make bad tea and
coffee, or lock up the wine just when it was wanted. In
the time of Chaucer there is no doubt that the line of
separation between the function of the husband and
the function of the wife was much more strictly drawn
than it is now.   The domestic society, as a nucleus
for other social activities or functions, did not occupy a
prominent place, nor could it, in times when every
house was almost as often a herberge or hostel for the
stranger as a home, to say nothing of other matters.
Hence we have the man living much abroad with his
compeers, while the wife, in a world of her own,
consorts with her gossips, who constitute her court, or

army of supporters, and they find the ale-house convenient as a banqueting place.

The tendency of men and women to consort in
separate herds was, unquestionably, encouraged by the
mediæval Church, whether designedly or not ; and the
tendency exists now in Roman Catholic countries.   As
near home as Ireland we may see it.   Roman Catholic
dignitaries, who have interested themselves in the
question of intemperance among the poor, will tell you
that Irishmen get together and drink at the ale-house
or whisky-shop, but that domestic conviviality is a
much rarer thing.   I cannot, of course, here pursue
the subject, or attempt to adjust the proportions of
cause and effect in these concomitant things ; but the
mind at once fixes upon the spirit of caste which
belongs to Roman Catholic organization, the doctrine
of the inferiority of woman and of the married to the
' virgin' life, and upon the influence of the priest—
neither man nor woman himself, but an isolator by
necessity of function—as striking ingredients in this
matter.   No moral culture can be perfect which does
not place and keep the man and woman side by side
on terms of equality (equality *ad hoc*, to say the
least).   By the accident that she was the guardian of
learning, and that the learning of the time was more
uniform than ours, the mediæval Church may be said
to have indirectly helped to keep the culture of cultivated women at a very great height as compared with

that of the conventional modern standard.*   But now
that a wide culture for women includes science, because
science is thrusting its way into all education whatever, the Roman Catholic Church looks with no favourable eye upon the idea of an enlarged intellectual
curriculum for women.   In all that relates to women,
the power of the mediæval Church began to break in
the time of Chaucer's great contemporary Wycliffe;
there are signs in our own day that the power of the
Roman Catholic Church is increasing in the same
direction.   One comfort we have, that that Church can
no longer be supposed to keep the keys of culture.

* Heloise, for example, was a very learned woman, in some
important respects (I believe, in knowledge of Greek) the superior
of Abelard.

CHAPTER VI.

MERRY ENGLAND.

Some of the students of Chaucer appear to have been so puzzled by his use of the word *merry* in the Nun Priest's Tale, where he says that the voice of the widow's Cock was like ' the mery orgon,' as actually to go about to modify the meaning of the word merry, as used in the fourteenth century, But, in the first place, Chaucer says in his ' Goodly Ballade :'—

> ' God wote on musike I can not, but I gesse,
> Alas why so, that I might saie or syng.'

so that he probably did not know much about the ' orgon ;' and in the second place, he would naturally apply the word ' merry' to the organ, because it was an instrument employed in the praise of God.   ' Is any merry ? let him sing psalms.'   And, by the bye, after Chaucer's own frank confession that he was not musical, we need not trouble ourselves much about his description of the musical accomplishments of Nicholas in the Miller's Tale.   We are informed that he sang the ' Kynges note,' but nobody seems to know what the ' Kynges note' was.   What if Chaucer, accurate in detail as he usually is, did not himself know ?   Perhaps it was one of the ballads of King Edward's wars.   At all events, the word ' merry' has been used from time immemorial with the same flexibility of application as the words good, fair, free, and the like.   Nicholas had ' a mery throte,' and Absolon was ' a mery child.'   It is true he sang and strummed as much as Nicholas, but the poet's proximate reason for calling him a ' mery child ' is that —

> ' .   .   .   .   He had a gay surplys,
> As whyt as is the blosme upon the rys.'

A gay white surplice !   All words of this order were used by our forefathers with a freedom, the loss of which, where we have lost it, is matter of regret.   It is not pleasant, for example, to find a modern hymnist stumbling at the word ' gallant,' applied by an older writer to the bowers of the Jerusalem the Golden, and substituting another adjective, because he was really

afraid of that fine old word. Meanwhile we may
amuse ourselves with the question—Is it true that
England is now less of a merry England than it once
was?

We look back through the mist of centuries as
well as we can, and, taking Jack-in-the-green on
the way, permit our eyes to rest upon a heteroge-
neous picture of gabled houses, splendid shows,
glancing colours, and rapid movement, with plenty
of music. The Midsummer watch is set, and the
watchmen, with their cressets, walk the streets. Or
the garland is stretched overhead, and the girls are
dancing. Or the butts are fixed, and the lads are out in
the meadow with their bows and arrows. Or the fool,
in motley, shakes his bells and plays his pranks in some
gay procession. Or the young cockneys are up and
abroad early in the first of May, to fetch in the sweet-
smelling boughs. And somewhere in the air is the
sound of the timbrel, shaken, as we guess, by a healthy
maiden, and the ringing of bells, and even the horn of
the huntsman, for, perhaps, the chase is up in Epping
Forest. Was there then more ' *gaieté de cœur* ' in this
England, or in a still younger England, than in the
England that we all know to-day?

II. It will not seem paradoxical to thoughtful readers
to remark that though the growth of personal freedom
promotes happiness, it need not promote obtrusive,
visible gaiety, or merriment in a people. Nor does it.

That external gaiety, that loud-voiced muscular mirth, that zest in pleasure, as distinguished from business or duty, which we think we notice in the merry England of our ancestors, is in fact the gaiety of half-cultivated creatures, who love noise and bluster, just as savages do ; but in part it is the gaiety of a common people who were not free.   It is the characteristic of the slave to make a noise over his pleasures when the hour of relaxation has struck.   In the time of Chaucer Englishmen had ceased to be slaves, the lowest and meanest of them ; but the condition of the common people was of the kind in which the burden is felt, though the chain is away. It was a time of privilege and stern authority, when such words as king, lord, master, parent, 'prentice, labourer, had an oppressiveness of meaning in them which we must make an effort to realize, if we realize it at all. William of Wykeham impressed labourers for the new works at Windsor Castle.   Mothers inflicted the *chatiment de l'enfance, qui commence par alarmer la pudeur* on marriageable daughters.   Two such facts are as good as a thousand.   In days like those, task-work of every kind must have weighed like a yoke upon the worker, even when it was in itself light,—the weight lying not in the quantity of labour given, but in the spirit in which it had to be yielded.   Everywhere there was *privilege*, rising stair on stair, from the lowest social levels to the highest : and a fair bargain, upon equal terms, between him who stood on the lower stair and him who stood a stair higher, was impossible, because the *spirit* of exaction was rife on one side, and the instinct of submission, not to say servility, was rife on the other. We get some idea of this state of things from what we now see in remote agricultural districts, or in schools where fagging is the custom. The merriment of men and women in whom a sense of inferior position is nourished by a system of social privilege, is apt to be explosive. In an age when an architect could impress workmen and pay them whatever he chose, to have a holiday, to be set free from work, was to be set free from much more than work. It was to be out of an atmosphere of serfdom. Uproarious joy while it lasted was a sort of defiance to privilege; and yet, notwithstanding, how often do we find an element of snobbishness in it. Often, indeed, when the holiday joy finds a tongue in ballad or song, it is a mendicant joy. The holiday-maker is a beggar, too : he wants largess in some shape, beer, perhaps, or small coin, but certainly something. Take, as a sample of a spirit of snobbish subordination, the well-known harvest song : —

> ' Here's a health unto our master,
>   The founder of the feast !
> I wish, with all my heart and soul,
>   In heaven he may find rest.
> I hope all things may prosper,
>   That ever he takes in hand ;
> For we are all his servants,
>   And all at his command.
> Drink, boys, drink, and see you do not spill,
> For if you do, you must drink two,—it is your master's will.'

It is in no spirit of churlishness, read the word how you will, that I am making these remarks. But to him who has eyes to see, it is plain that the loud merriment, public and obtrusive, of the times which we mostly think of when we call England merry, had a ' note ' of the feudal spirit about it, which puts it out of our power to compare modern with ancient England, and ask, to any good purpose, which was the merrier.

I am sorry, then, that I cannot follow those writers who go into raptures over the feudal spirit, as if it had a natural tendency to make life joyful. Interpreted in action by noble, loving, forbearing natures, the feudal spirit might have worked well, just as the modern spirit of independence and *laisser-faire* would work well if interpreted in action by such natures. But I side with those who think the feudal spirit was only a step upwards on the road from slavery ; and that the modern spirit, however ill expressed in life, is another step on the same road, and a step from which there can be no return, let the reactionists write and do what they please.

III. To pass on. One striking difference, of course, occurs in the pleasure-taking of the old times and the new. The old-world holidays were more conversant with nature, like the ordinary work-day life of the same world, and this may have been a great point in their favour. Even if the people that went out for May-

boughs were often clamorous beggars, it was not such
a bad idea, that, of going out to fetch in the spring to
the town, and plant the green banners where they could.
I confess I take but little interest in what is called
tracing the origin of old games and customs, when the
customs themselves have an obvious smack of nature
with them, because I always feel sure they would have
been introduced somehow, if the ' origin' had been untraceable. The Midsummer watch and the Midsummer
bonfires *may* not come into this category ; but the custom of maying seems almost as natural as kissing ; and
so of dancing round the may-pole. I do not in the least
doubt or undervalue what the antiquaries have told us
of such matters, but surely to bring in the may, and
set up a garlanded pole for a dance is as obvious as a
child's gathering buttercups and daisies, and skipping
about for joy.

All literature idealises ; not necessarily in the sense
of heightening in the way of bettering or worsening,
but inevitably, in the sense of selection ; hence a recurring difficulty with regard to the degree of reliance
to be placed upon the pictures of any time contained in
its literature. To this difficulty is, of course, always to
be added this other one, that literature, like the rest of
the furniture and expression of human life, conven-
tionalizes.

In our own day a spirit of minute realism, often
mere copying, has taken possession of the most accepted
art whether in literature or out of it. This has been

accounted for in various ways, but one obvious fact in the case seems to have been disregarded. Life is now so large, and civilisation so full of enclosure, that one half the world does not know how the other half lives. We have foreign countries at our right hand and our left. Bermondsey is so little known to Mayfair that Mayfair reads a book about Bermondsey with as much sense of novelty as our immediate predecessors felt in reading Bruce or Mungo Park : and, for another instance, all the world that is not in good society reads about good society with a similar sense of novelty. Hence, the realism of our existing literature will bequeath to our successors trustworthy pictures of our life, in spite of some selection and heightening. I need not mention the newspaper, too,—that makes all the difference, in the checks it affords the student of life in the less ephemeral literature of a time.

But in the time of Chaucer there was reigning in literature, a spirit, not of realism but of conventionalism, and, of course, there was no newspaper. Now, even with all our modern advantages we may possibly succeed in conveying to our successors a good many false impressions. Look, for example, at the prominence which the topic of mountaineering assumes in newspapers and magazines ! If an antiquary of five hundred years hence were to say that mountaineering was a common pastime of the English people he would not make such a very bad hit for an antiquarian, but what nonsense it would be ! How many Englishmen go up the Alps in a year ? The question should rather be, how few ? and so it is sufficiently answered.

We are on safe ground when we affirm that the English in the time of the Plantagenets loved gardens ; for the English always did, and always will. The Englishman, too, not only loves to adorn the homestead; but, by impulse, attaches and shuts in and cultivates, for use and beauty, a portion of the soil round where the homestead stands. There is no paradox here ; a civilised people is a people that live in cities ; but a city need not be like Cheapside or St. Giles's. Let Holland speak for that. The instinct of garden-getting and garden-keeping is an instinct which belongs to nations that love the permanent, and that make the homestead their symbol. " God Almighty," says Bacon, " first planted a garden ; and indeed it is the purest of human pleasures." We may all have our likings for the open common and the wind-swept meadow. I prefer them myself to every form of what an American called Nature with her hair cut and combed ; but nobody ever saw a broken and trampled garden without a feeling that the home had been violated, as nobody ever came across a garden flower in a wild spot without a ' homelike ' emotion. Briefly, once more, the English love a garden, and when we find the garden a signal feature in the literature of five centuries back, we need not fear to accept as truth the natural inference ; namely, that the garden formed a signal portion of the pleasures of English men and women in that century.

IV. Yet there is, unquestionably, a conventional
element in the garden-writing of Chaucer and his contemporaries. Although in rude times, when the baron,
the knight, the esquire, and the fair ladies, lived much
in castles, and going abroad was not safe or not convenient, the garden, considered as a pleasaunce or place
of much resort, held a place which it does not now
hold; and although the badness of the accommodation,
which even the best castles and mansions afforded, must
have made the green and many-coloured hospitalities of
Nature very inviting soon after the cuckoo had come,—
true as this is, I say, we cannot fail to discern an artificial, an imported note in this garden-writing. Obviously, it comes from France and Italy, from Vall'om-
brosa and the Loire. The poetry of the time is—

> ' Tasting of Flora and the country green,
>   Dance, and Provençal song and sunburnt mirth.'

It is gay with the birds, and the gardens, and the sunshine; but the landscape is not characteristically
English; the references to nature are general, and
mostly artificial. Chaucer himself, in the best passages
of his poetry, is an exception; he uses his eyes and describes what he sees (as, for example, where he describes
the descending autumn sun as being of the colour of
latoun or brass); but it is not till the time of Elizabeth
that the English landscape breaks, like a fresh picture,
through the written page. Then, instead of flowers
merely, we have specified by name the well-known

flowers of England, and, though we have more of the
meadow and the river, we have less of the garden.

Thus, there is little, if anything, that is not conventional and Italian or Provençal rather than English
in that passage in the Franklin's Tale, in which we
are told that Dorigen being inconsolable (for her husband's absence) while she stayed by the sea, her friends
carried her into ' a gardeyn' because it was ' a place
delitable' :—

> ' Hire frendes sawe that it nas no disport
> To romen by the see, but discomfort,
> And schope hem for to pleien somwhere elles.
> They leden hire by rivers and by welles,
> And eke in other places delitables ;
> They dauncen and they pley at ches and tables.
> So on a day, right in the morwe tide,
> Unto a gardeyn that was ther beside,
> In which that they had made her ordinance
> Of vitaile, and of other purveance,
> They gon and plaie hem al the longe day ;
> And this was on the sixte morwe of May,
> Which May had peinted with his softe schoures
> This gardeyn ful of leves and floures :
> And craft of mannes hond so curiously
> Arrayed had this gardeyn trewely,
> That never was ther gardeyn of suche pris,
> But if it were the verray paradis.
> The odour of floures and the fresshe siht,
> Wold han y-maked any herte light
> That ever was born.'

Here, indeed, the scene is laid in Brittany, and the

poet is following an original; but Chaucer did not
stick at an anachronism or care greatly about the *genius
loci;* and, if he had been much in the habit of making
real to himself the landscapes or gardens of England,
he might naturally enough have allowed some touches
of reality to drop from his pen about particular flowers
or particular trees. A fine description of a garden in the
poet's time was evidently supposed to consist in the
piling up of conventional features, romantic and
classic. In the Merchant's Tale, we have a description of the garden which the 'noble knight January'
kept so jealously that he would not let his wife have the
key of it. Here, again, it should be observed, the
scene is laid in Lombardy :—

> ' This noble January, with al his might
> In honest wise as longith to a knight,
> Schop him to lyve ful deliciously.
> His housyng, his array, as honestly
> To his degré was maked as a kynges.
> Amonges other of his honest thinges
> He had a gardyn walled al with stoon,
> So fair a gardyn wot I no wher noon,
> For out of doute I verrely suppose,
> That he that wroot the Romauns of the Rose,
> Ne couthe of it the beauté wel devyse ;
> . . . . . . For to telle
> The beauté of the gardyn, and the welle,
> That stood under a laurer alway greene.
> Ful ofte tyme he Pluto and his queene
> Preserpina, and al the fayerie,
> Desporten hem and maken melodye

Aboute that welle, and daunced, as men tolde.
This noble knight, this January the olde,
Such deynté hath in it to walk and pleye,
That he wold no wight suffre bere the keye,
Save he himself, for of the smale wyket
He bar alway of silver a smal cliket,
With which whan that him list he it unschette.'

This, then, is the way in which the garden appears in Chaucer—an adjunct 'for pleasaunce' of the castle or the mansion. Thus, in the 'Knight's Tale :'—

'This passeth yeer by yeer, and day by day,
Till it fel oones in a morwe of May
That Emelie, that fairer was to seene
Than is the lilie on hire stalkes grene,
And fresscher than the May with floures newe—
For with the rose colour strof hire hewe,
I not which was the fyner of hem two—
Er it was day, as sche was wont to do,
Sche was arisen, and al redy dight.
For May wole have no sloggardye a night ;
The sesoun priketh every gentil herte,
And maketh him out of his sleepe sterte,
And seith, ' Arys, and do thin observance."
This maked Emelye han remembrance
To do honour to May, and for to ryse.
I-clothed was sche fressh for to devyse.
Hire yolwe heer was browdid in a tresse,
Byhynde hire bak, a yerde long I gesse.
And in the gardyn at the sonne upriste
Sche walketh up and doun wher as hire liste.
Sche gardereth floures, partye whyte and reede,
To make a certeyn gerland for hire heede,

And as an aungel hevenly sche song.
The grete tour, that was so thikke and strong,
Which of the castel was the cheef dongeoun.
(Ther as this knightes weren in prisoun,
Of which I tolde yow, and telle schal)
Was evene joynyng to the gardeyn wal,
Ther as this Emely hadde hire pleyyng.
Bright was the sonne, and cleer that morwenynge,
And Palamon, this woful prisoner,
As was his wone, by leue of his gayler
Was risen, and romed in a chambre on heigh,
In which he al the noble cité seigh,
And eek the gardeyn, ful of braunches grene,
Ther as the fresshe Emelye the scheene
Was in hire walk, and romed up and doun.

Here we have the lady Emily doing customary honour
to May by gathering and wearing garlands ; and a little
later on in the story, Arcite, in order ' to doon his observance ' to May, goes forth to make himself a
garland :

' The busy larke, messager of day,
Salueth in hire song the morwe gray ;
And fyry Phebus ryseth up so bright,
That al the orient laugheth of the light,
And with his stremes dryeth in the greves
The silver dropes, hongyng on the leeves.
And Arcite, that is in the court ryal
With Theseus, squyer principal,
Is risen, and loketh on the mery day.
And for to doon his observance to May.
Remembryng of the poynt of his desire,
He on his courser, stertyng as the fire,

Is riden into feeldes him to pleye,
Out of the court, were it a myle or tweye.
And to the grove, of which that I yow tolde,
By aventure his wey he gan to holde,
To make him a garland of the greves,
Were it of woodewynde or hawthorn leves.'

V. There is no doubt whatever that Mayday rites,
with the majority of our predecessors in the time of
Chaucer, and much later, had a quasi-religious character,
like other observances of times and seasons. That they
were occasions of sweethearting and merry-making also
there can be no doubt. Who does not remember, in
" A Midsummer Night's Dream," Lysander's appoint-
ment with Helena ?

' If thou lovest me, then,
Steal from thy father's house to-morrow night ;
And in the wood, a league without the town,
Where I did meet thee once, with Helena,
To do observance to a morn of May,
There will I stay for thee.'

But what a different England it must have been when
to miss the maying would have been as unlucky in the
eyes of a matron and her daughters as it would now be
to miss the pudding on Christmas day ! Until more
than two centuries later than the time of Chaucer, indeed, maying was a quasi-religious ceremony in this
country. The Puritan Stubbs, in his ' Anatomy of
Abuses,' says that ' against May, every parish, town,
and village, assembled themselves together, both men,

women, and children, old and young, even all indifferently, and either going all together, or dividing themselves into companies, they go, some to the woods and groves, some to the hills and mountains, some to one place, some to another, where they spend all the night in pastimes and in the morning they return, bringing with them birch boughs and branches of trees, to deck their assembly withal.' His description of the bringing home of the May-pole itself is still more striking. The youths and maidens, he tells us, bring home this ' stinking idol with great veneration. They have twenty or forty yoke of oxen, every ox having a sweet nosegay of flowers tied to the tip of his horns ; and these oxen draw home the May-pole, covered all over with flowers and herbs, bound round with strings from the top to the bottom ; and sometimes painted with variable colours, having two or three hundred men, women, and children, following it with *great devotion.*' No doubt the decorations of the pole were often in bad taste, and homely to excess. Stubbs informs us that the May-pole was set up ' with handkerchiefs and flags streaming on the top. They strew the ground around it ; they bind green boughs about it ; they set up summer halls, lawns, and arbours, hard by it ; and then fall to banqueting and feasting, to leaping and dancing about it.'

In this description of Maying and May-pole customs in England—which has, I fear, been excessively quoted ?— there appears to me to be more exagge-

ration than zest : it is evidently the object of Stubbs
to make out a case of paganism against the Mayers :
and, apart from all question of the origin of the custom
(what *is* the good of quoting Ovid's Fasti about such a
very simple natural matter ?), there can be no doubt
that Puritanism was logical in condemning it. Be-
lievers of certain particulars in the creed which is
called Puritan (though the Manichæan taint is, of
course, earlier than Puritanism, and, in one shape or
another, as old as religious thought) have often de-
lighted in nature ; and sung, painted, or written their
delight. But it has been at the expense of their logic.
Wordsworth's poem, entitled, ' Nutting,' is quite as
' pagan' as Maying, if the Puritan point of view is accurately fixed ; nor is it possible to reconcile Wordsworth's nature-worship with the creed which peeps out
here and there in the Ecclesiastical Sonnets. It is
almost too much to attribute a religious faith of any
kind to the multitude in any age or country—they
have, taken in the mass, only a superstition, which
might be made to take any colour at the will of a sufficiently ingenious person who chose to lay himself out
for the purpose. But it is very plain the Mayers, in a
clumsy, stupid way, endeavoured to give a simple,
natural observance—as easy as kissing and just as
likely—a Christian colouring. The Hitchin May-day
song is to the purpose here; and, often as it has been
quoted, I fear it must now be quoted once more :

' Remember us poor Mayers all!
 And thus do we begin
To lead our lives in righteousness,
 Or else we die in sin.

We have been rambling all the night,
 And almost all the day :
And now returned back again,
 We have brought you a branch of May.

A branch of May we have brought you
And at your door it stands ;
 It is but a sprout,
 But it's well budded out
By the work of our Lord's hands.

The hedges and trees they are so green,
 As green as any leek ;
Our heavenly Father he watered them
 With his heavenly dew so sweet.

The heavenly gates are open wide,
 Our paths are beaten plain ;
And if a man be not too far gone,
 He may return again.

The life of man is but a span,
 It flourishes like a flower ;
We are here to-day, and gone to-morrow,
 And we are dead in an hour.

The moon shines bright, and the stars give a light,
 A little before it is day ;
So God bless you all, both great and small,
 And send you a joyful May!

This song has all the usual characteristics of such poetry—the frankest incoherence and the wildest irregularity, for example—but the manner in which religious ideas are thrust in, head and shoulders, along with the moralising, is the characteristic which I would now signalise. Whatever may be the date of the song, it exactly expresses the popular way of jumbling up religious ideas with others supposed not to be religious, as if they wanted sprinkling with holy water before they could be considered clean and proper— a trick belonging to habits of thought which were much more intense and influential in the fourteenth century than they could ever have been afterwards, because the influence of the notions which tend to compel such habits has been declining ever since.

All I should have to say upon the subject would be this. If modern habits and modern self-consciousness would permit it, the Maying customs would be as beautiful and appropriate as they could ever have been; but then they should be held religious only as all other things should be held religious, and no attempt should be made to adulterate Maying-songs with homily.

VI. There is probably as much time spent in amusement of one kind or another by the Englishman of to-day, as ever was spent in amusement by the Englishman of the days of the Edwards. Some points of difference in the way in which pleasures are provided and taken now and the way in which they were provided and taken then, lie quite upon the surface of the subject. For example, more of the commercial element,—at all events, more of the systematized commercial element,—enters into popular amusements in our own times. The theatre and the concert, as we now know them, had of course no existence in the time of Chaucer. On the other hand, we have lost the wandering minstrel, juggler, or merryman; except as a beggar. All this belongs to the growth of cities; and so does the decline of emulative sports. Large as may be the space which, for example, cricket fills in the eyes of a special public, it is a thing by itself; and there is nothing in modern times which appears to take any place so generally representative as an archery bout, or a May-pole dance, or a morris dance, or fool's dance. But, after all, there is such a great gulf between the two periods of 1350 and 1870, that particular conclusions are as hazardous as general conclusions are sterile. It certainly looks a little odd to find proclamations or statutory enactments in the reign of Edward III., forbidding the subjects of his Majesty to spend so much time in cards, dice, bull-baiting, cock-fighting, foot-ball, and the like, because they took up the time which might be better spent in military games, and especially in archery; and, again, forbidding the boys to play at the 'jue à barres,' or ' chaperon-des-gentz,' within the purlieux of the king's palace at Westminster during the sitting of Parliament.

Conceive boys playing at tip-cat in Palace Yard, and an act of Parliament passed to prevent it!

One of the most obvious particulars in which the old days and the new days differ is that of display or pageantry,—it is common-place to speak of it. We have infinitely less colour, movement, and clangour in our amusements; our public processions or shows are very few, and those few have a hard struggle to live. To what a miserable skeleton, for example, is the poor old Lord Mayor's show cut down! The splendour of what is shown to us for money is incalculably greater of course,—what would Chaucer say to a transformation scene by Beverley?—but Odd Fellows and Foresters are the kind of people to whom it is almost wholly left to keep up the tradition of massive processions, with flags and gay dresses. One could scarcely think of a more striking exemplification of the difference between the old and the new ways of doing such matters than the Garibaldi demonstration (to employ the usual word) of a few years back. The procession itself was the most miserable tag-rag and bob-tail affair in the world; but the spectacle within the Crystal Palace at Sydenham upon his reception day was splendid enough,—it was a cumulative display, with a commercial mainspring, and the lowest charge for admission was half-a-crown!

Again, take dancing. It would be an idle question, whether in comparison with the number of people there is more or less dancing in England than there used to be, but it is very certain that just as there is less free spontaneous display, there is also much less spontaneous movement under the name of dancing. This is, partly of course, a result of the growth of culture, bringing with it increased self-consciousness, and partly also what keeps pace with this, the growth of Art as a thing by itself. We do not quite imitate the Oriental satrap, who is astounded that the Frank should not get all his dancing done for him and relegate it all to paid performers ; but the damsels of the city of London do not dance in public till moonrise, *usque imminente lunâ,* as Fitzstephen has it ; nor is it customary now, as it was in the time of Stow, for the serving maidens to dance, *after evening prayers,* in the presence of their masters or mistresses, in the street, while one of the number plays the timbrel : the prizes consisting of garlands, being hung ' athwart the street.' Nor can we understand, except by a considerable effort in realising the childish simplicity of our forefathers and foremothers, a scene like this, in Chaucer's ' House of Fame ' : —

> ' . . . Al maner of mynstralles,
> And gestours, that tellen tales
> Both of wepinge and of game. . . .
> There herd I pleyen upon an harpe,
> That souneth bothe wel and sharpe,
> And other harpers many oon. . . .
> And smale harpers with her glees,
> Saten under hym in sees ;
> And gonne on hym upwarde to gape,

And countrefet hym as an ape,
Or as craft countrefeteth kynde.
    Thoro saugh I stondem hym behynde,
A fre fro hem, alle be hemselve,
Many thousand tymes twelve,
That maden lowde menstralcies
In cornemuse and shalmyes,
And many other maner pipe,
That craftely begunne to pipe,
Both in doucet and in riede,
That ben at festes with the bride.   .   .   .
    There saugh I pleyen jugelours,
Magiciens, and tregetours,
And phitonisses, charmeresses,
Old witches, sorceresses,
That use exorsisaciouns,
And eke thes fumygaciouns ;
And clerkes eke, which konne wel
All this magike naturel.'   .   .   .

It is true this jumble of ' minstraulcie ' juggling
and mimicry is represented as part of a dream, and
it is also true that it occurs in the House of Fame,—
a busy, public, and blatant place ; but there is undoubtedly in the passage some fair representation of
the rude and noisy mirth-making of our forerunners
We have all manner of minstrels, or people who sang
stories and sang songs to music to entertain the guests ;
then jesters who tell stories both of game and weeping,
both serious and sad ; harpers, with other harpers
underneath, making mock of the first ; then, innu-
merable players upon the bagpipe, the shawm, the
dulcimer (doucet), and the flageolet or fife (riede, or

reed); such music as you had at weddings. Then came jugglers, witches, incense-makers, and professors of natural magic. In fact, we have here the whole tribe, or nearly the whole tribe, of professional mirth-makers. And here, as in a hundred places, the thing that chiefly strikes us is that the mirth-making is professional, and that it is very noisy. The presence of these jesters or story - tellers, and minstrels in the House of Fame, reminds one, in passing, of the power which that class of persons possessed, or was supposed to possess, in the middle ages, in affixing and fixing characters. One readily remembers here what Hamlet said to Polonius, 'Good my lord, will you see the players well bestowed? Do you hear, let them be well used, for they are the abstract and brief character of the time : after your death you were better have a bad epitaph than their ill-report while you live.' A curious illustration of the power possessed by such vagabonds in times when amusement had to be hired and brought into the households of the great. The times are changed. Society consolidates itself. We usually go abroad for such entertainments as gestours, jogeleurs, and glee-men can give us; and instead of the minstrel, jester, or amusement-man having the entry of the lord's castle, and the power of making or marring his character, my lord and my lady divide the 'professionals' from the rest of the company by a rope, when they give a little music. At least, the thing *has* been done in the reign of Victoria.

VII. The subject of popular amusements in England during the Middle Ages has, in most of its picturesque details, been fairly run down to rinsings. We have read, till we are weary, of bull-baiting, bear-baiting, running at the quintain, wrestling, morris-dancing, hobby-horsing, and other such matters, which are now familiar to every child that has seen a pantomime, and read a few notices of obsolete manners in England. If we may trust some records examined by Mr. Thorold Rogers, or rather, if we may draw general conclusions from them, the number of hours devoted to labour in the course of a week by our ancestors was quite as great as it is now, if not greater. There is, indeed, much ground to think that the reason why the amusements of the people in the Middle Ages stand out so sharply in the general pictures we form to ourselves of those times is that they were more massed together in separate pieces, apart from the rest of life, than our own amusements. A well-to-do Englishman of the time of Victoria glides quietly from his work to his dinner, and from dinner to the theatre or concert-room ; he does not go with much pomp to a joust or tourney, or miracle-play, on the feast of Whitsuntide, while the serving-men and the burgesses and burgesses' wives, for whom tournaments and hawking are not fit sports, go to see cocks fight, or bears baited, or clowns break each other's heads at single-stick. All this easily lends itself to display ; but it is obvious that the life in which amusement has to find excuse for itself is not necessarily the merriest life.

The idea of recreation pure and simple, as we now know it, is not so obvious in the boyhood or adolescence of English history as that of amusement obtained by giving free play to some of the wilder impulses. Of hunting there is enough, and to spare, though it is, of course, unscientific. Edward III., if Froissart may be credited, took about six hundred hunting-dogs to France with him when he carried war into that fair land. While there were wolves and boars in the forests, as there certainly were later than the time of Chaucer by a good deal, the chase was a necessary as well as an amusing pursuit. But of all the forms in which the chase was pursued in the Middle Ages, that of hawking is the one around which the most pleasant associations gather themselves at the mere echo of a word. Chaucer, with his usual frank anachronism, not only makes the people hold a lych-wake (or corpse-vigil) over Arcite, but places Duke Theseus in the hall of an English noble, and makes him give an entertainment *on Sunday night* to a hundred lords ; in which the hunting element plays a very prominent part. I do not mean that the gentlemen hunted in the dining-hall, but that they had their dogs and hawks with them :—

‘ The mynstralcye, the servyce at the feste,
The grete giftes to the most and leste,

> The rich array of Theseus paleys,
> Ne who sat first ne last upon the deys,
> What ladies fayrest ben or best daunsyng,
> Or which of hem can daunce best or sing,
> Ne who most felyngly speketh of love,
> *What haukes sitten on the perche above,*
> *What houndes lyen in the floor adoun :*
> Of al this make I now no mencioun.'

Assuredly the dogs and the birds together must have made a pleasant smell in the place; to say nothing of vermin, and the inevitable noises. But the hawk, like all birds, except the vulture, which is mean, as well as foul, and the penguin which is stupid, is pleasant to think of and read about. Perhaps the very airiest and most buoyant idea in the world is this of hunting on horseback with the hawk. Of course I am thinking only of such ideas of airy buoyancy as are immediately poetic ; for being up in a balloon is, speaking absolutely, a more airy and a more buoyant thing. But think of my lady in green and gold, with her hair tossed and tangled by the wind in the morning sun, riding her pretty palfrey at a conscious *allegretto,* with the bells of the birds making music, and the excitement when the quarry is well in sight and the hawks go free from my lady's hand; there is, surely, only one form of pleasure-taking which contains so many latent impulses and suggestions of what is elastic, open, and gallant,— of course I mean yachting.

That my lord and my lady loved falcons, then, who can wonder ? In Mr. Henry Taylor's play of ' The Virgin

Widow,' the serving maiden, Mariana, enters to Fior-
deliza, saying, ' Please you, my lady, the falconer sends
his duty, and Alathiella has not touched her food for
three days.   He is fearful she will die, and he says
the Count gave a thousand crowns for her.'   Rosalba
makes answer, ' Poor bird! she doted on her master,
and has never held up her head since she missed him.
I fear she will die, like some of her betters, of a
broken heart.'   To which Mariana replies, ' He says
he knows but of one thing to do with her; which is,
to take her to the conjurer at the farm,'—the conjurer
being a man in high repute for magico-medical skill.
There is no exaggeration in the notion which such a
passage conveys to readers who are not already well
informed upon the subject of the estimation in which
the noble birds were held in the Middle Ages.   People
took their hawks into church, and even to the altar.
They took them to battle, and would not sell them
even by way of ransom.   Who does not know the
charming story of the lady and the knight and the
hawk in Boccaccio ?   Froissart says that Edward III.
took no end of hawks to France, or, at all events, had in
France with him thirty mounted falconers, and that he
went to the river-side almost every day to fly his birds
at the water-fowl.   This is, no doubt, an exaggeration.
King Edward was a very energetic person, but he
could scarcely have found time even for such attention
as he did devote to his army,—there were complaints
which survive in the ballads of the time, that while the

king was carrying on an amour the commissariat languished,—if he added daily hunting and hawking to his other pursuits. Still, the stringency of the laws relating to hawking in the reign of this king sufficiently suggests that his majesty loved to amuse himself with the spirited little creatures. Any one finding a hawk that had lost its way from its proper place was bound to carry it to the sheriff. The sheriff was then bound to have the hawk proclaimed all over the county, and its owner might recover it upon payment of the sheriff's expenses. If within a given time—(I think it was three months!)—nobody came forward to claim the precious little bird, the man who had first found it might have it—provided he were a gentleman or entitled by the heraldry of the sport to the possession of any such noble creature as a hawk. For concealing or appropriating a lost hawk there were heavy fines and terms of imprisonment. Though ecclesiastics had no business to hunt with either hawk or hound, they constantly did so. Cowper, we know, would not permit a clergyman to play the violin.

> ' Oh, laugh, or mourn with me the rueful jest,
> A cassock'd huntsman and a fiddling priest!'—

says he: but neither in George's days nor in Richard the Second's could satire keep clergymen from hunting, if they loved the sport. If satire could have done it, a sense of the reflex humour of what he was doing would have restrained that Bishop of Ely who, in the fourteenth century, excommunicated for sacrilege the thieves who actually stole a hawk from her perch in the cloisters at Bermondsey — *the hawk being the Bishop's own,* and the theft being committed while some religious service was going on.   I am not learned enough in the Romish regimen to know whether or not there is excommunication major and excommunication minor; but, if not, my uncle Toby would have thought the punishment exceeded the offence.   But, besides the *really* representative quotation which I have given from the 'Virgin Widow,' exhibiting the solemn anxiety of the falconer to assuage the sufferings of Alathiella, I may add that there were appropriate forms of thanksgiving dictated, in books devoted to the art of hawking, for the recovery of a hawk from any sickness. The first time you went out hunting with your hawk after its convalescence, you were to say, ' The Lord of the fowls of the air hath preserved thee, hallelujah, amen ! ' or words to that effect.

It was not likely that, during the times when sumptuary laws or conventions, or both, were considerably operative in moulding the life of Englishmen and marking gradations of rank, the hawk should escape being taken into account.   Some hint of this I have just given; and ultimately the heraldry of sport was carried so far that hawks were classified according to their own real or imaginary rank and appropriated in their order, as different social types.   For an emperor there was the eagle, for a yeoman the goshawk, for a cleric the sparrow-hawk, for a knave the kestrel. But these were the refinements of an art in its climax, and no such distribution existed in the early days of the sport. Chaucer's Knight, Sir Thopas, carried a gos-hawk; and the sparrow-hawk that angered Geraint was not a priest. The prettiest part of the hawk lore was, undoubtedly, that which related to the bells with which their legs were hung. Whether you could buy the best hawk-bells at Milan or at Dordrecht was, for instance, a nice question; and, whether the bell on the right leg ought to be a semitone or a whole tone above the bell on the left, was another. We may well imagine a bevy of ladies out hawking on a sweet, fresh morning — it was said they hunted with hawks better than men, and I can well believe it — finding plenty to occupy their charming little tongues in discussing such questions.

It was the gun, of course, that at last put an end to hawking. No doubt shooting with the fowling-piece is a less cruel method of catching birds than catching them by setting birds of prey at them; but it is hard not to regret the charming sport —

> ' Only a page that carols unseen,
> Fitting your hawks their jesses.'*

Was there ever a brighter, freer, more musical suggestion put into a couplet? For two things I have many a time sat in a waking dream and wished myself

* Robert Browning, ' Pippa Passes.'

for a short space in the Middle Ages. I should like to have the mediæval Christian faith for a day ; to sit in a cathedral, join in the service, thrill at the Dies Iræ, listen to the tread of the passing worshipper as if he were walking in the very aisles of everlasting fate, and watch, with fear and passion, the face of my dear lady as the light through the painted window slanted over her brow. And I should like to go out hawking, with my dear lady, for a morning also. True, my love and I would need to be much more hard-hearted than men and women of gentle nurture in the days of Victoria ; but let that pass, for a day only. And let me go forth with her into the open, and trot to the river-side, with the falconers at such a distance that they cannot hear our talk, which is, I need not say, of Lancelot, Sir Isumbras, the Tale of Troy, the last tourney (at which I won with my lady's colours on my shoulder), and my own undying passion. Up sweeps the wind, charged with the soft odours of many a travelled mile, and gently buffets my lady's cheek till it is like an apple, ' the side that's next the sun.' We see the river a little ahead. A kingfisher darts up from among the tall rushes. There is a heron, and we mean to have him. Take off the hood, let go the jesses, up springs the falcon, his bells jingling, and the real sport of the day is begun. If this is not better than going out blazing away with a gun at once noisome and noisy (instead of musical), I have no taste. It is a poor excuse to say that you kill more

game with one gun than you could with a whole stand
of falcons, and in half the time. There speaks the
greedy stomach. Give me the poetry, and you may
take the victuals. But it is useless complaining. The
argument from cruelty is a good one, and not even for
the pleasure of missing Mr. Coles's shop (which so
annoys Mr. Matthew Arnold) at the corner, and the
pleasure of feeling that I might go out hawking to-
morrow, would I wish the king's mews back to Charing
Cross.

There are, after all, two or three particulars, if no
more, in which we may find a suggestion that the
England of to-day really and truly *is* less merry than
the England of the Middle Ages. One obvious consideration is that the population in general have not
the same simple religious faith that they had then.
It is easier for a man with a superstition to be merry,
than for a man with a half faith. There is thus a
sense in which a poor Italian peasant may be merrier
than a well-to-do Englishman. He can devolve his
sins on his confessor, his troubles on his patron saint,
and so lay down his cares. Undoubtedly merriment
of this order does not accompany a general sense of
responsibility, such as it is our aim to cultivate in
England now ; though, in the time of Chaucer, responsibility was not for churls any more than falconry
was. Another obvious point is that the squalid *contrasts* of great towns are not favourable to merriment ;

though they are to drunkenness. And yet another point is that England is not now a conquering country. War brings mourning, but it brings elation also. The meanest man in the population partakes of the sense of power which a victory brings to a country. Once more, we must take into account, perhaps, the gradual civification of the surface of the land, and the removal of the country to a distance from the eyes of so large a number of the people. The return of the Spring, the sight of the near meadows, 'painted with delight,' as Shakespeare says, the sights and sounds of harvest-home, were all occasions of common joy to the people in a thousand places where they now miss any such excitements, sweet and wholesome as they were. It may be said, even now, that when the fine days begin, the town pours out its wholesome merriment into the green suburbs, whoever stays within the stony bounds for amusement. The sweethearts, and the boys and girls,—all whose hearts overflow with natural gladness, —go off into the fields to romp and be gay. If they want any pleasure *made* for them, it is of a very simple character,—a merry-go-round is enough ; but better is the pleasure they make for themselves at kiss-in-the-ring or leap-frog. It is scarcely possible to doubt that there was more of this spontaneous pleasure-making in the England of the Edwards than there is now. But of course the change in this particular is part of a larger change which lies, we hope, in the path to a greater good. The lightsomeness, of which I spoke as a main characteristic, of Chaucer's writings, is long ago gone from our literature, and the other forms of our art do not help us as they ought. When our religion and our art have overtaken the problems set them by the changing conditions of our history, we shall have no reason, even if we now had any reason, to regret Merry England.

CHAPTER VII.

THE HEART OF ENGLAND.

THERE was once a magistrate who, acting impromptu,
in every case of wrong-doing that came before him,
upon an old maxim which is well known, used to ask
at once, ' Well, who is she? '— so convinced was he that
there was a woman at the bottom of all human mis-
feasance. But there is no real humour in this; because woman, being half the human race, is at the

bottom of everything, good, bad, and indifferent. We cannot escape her, turn which way we please; and the reader of these pages will have to put up with a good deal more of her, before I have done. 'What did I have for dinner yesterday, John?' said the doubting gentleman. 'Yesterday? a chop and a steak, sir!' To which the gentleman made answer, meekly, 'Oh, then let me have a steak and a chop to-day.' We must return, for a few paragraphs, to the subject of the part played by women in mediæval life because we must try somewhat more seriously than we have as yet done, to get at the heart of England in the days of Chaucer; but I hope not to weary the reader by mere repetitions and transpositions of certain ideas as elementary in their way as any simples of modern eating.

I. In the Middle Ages the Church had taken possession of all the critical periods of life. It had said, 'There is nothing sacred but what we make sacred.' Everything was, so to speak, excised and made to pay toll, in money or in sentiment, to the Church. It seized the human being at birth, and said, 'We must christen him or he will be lost.' It took him up again at marriage, and said, 'The instinct which underlies the attraction of sex is deadly sin, but we will do what we can for you, and by a sacramental process we will convert this foul, corrupt, and damnable thing into something venial.' It pursued the human being to his

death-bed, and sent him out of the world with the
tolling of a sprinkled bell (necessary for frightening
away evil spirits) and the 'sacrament' of extreme
unction. From first to last it took possession of
humanity; would neither let it come into the world,
increase the world, or go out of the world without its
authoritative interference,—in the sense, not of a willing helper, but of one who had property in a vassal or
villein, and could pronounce him and all his possibili-
ties unclean and damnable, if without ecclesiastical
sanction for his very existence and all his functions.

Pleasure or delight was the especial hatred of an
asceticizing Church ; and, above all, the delight which
we habitually roof over in our thoughts with the words
'a happy home.' As many people of both sexes as it
could possibly induce to celibate it did, and upon the
married state itself it placed every restriction it could
think of. There was not a corner of conjugal life that
it did not invade with its petty inquisitiveness and its
noisome adjectives. When it could do no more, it
could at least call names. It married men and women
at the church door,* and did its best to prevent a

* The Wife of Bath says,—

    ' I thank it God, that is eterne on lyve,
    Housbandes *atte chirch dore* I have had fyve.'

I think it is at Norwich Cathedral that there is a sculptured representation yet existing of a marriage at the church door. After
the marriage, the priest used to go up to the altar and there
celebrate the mass, at which the bride and bridegroom ' assisted.'

second perpetration of anything so abominable as the ancient rite of Paradise. Here, indeed, a natural emotion of the human heart, which is something much better than jealousy, springs to meet the Church half way, and it is with only partial displeasure (and that a displeasure founded chiefly upon questions of social expediency) that we find her inviting the vow of a widow who assumes the ring and mantle, in token of everlasting fidelity to the husband she has lost.

But though our sympathy with the widow or the widower who assumed such a vow may be complete, we look with suspicion upon the part played by the Church in the matter. The widow may be supposed to have said in her heart when she presented herself before the bishop to ask the consecration of the Church upon the perpetuity of her espousals,—' I have loved, and love my husband so entirely that the mutual spiritual possession which exists between him and me would make a second marriage an outrage committed upon what is most sacred in our lives, as well as an injustice to a second husband.' This we all understand and honour,* and Auguste Comte undoubtedly took hold of one of the deepest parts of our nature when he made perpetual monogamy a portion of his scheme of ethics. But

---

* The greatest burlesque of this that I know of was furnished by the Duchess of Marlborough, who, after the death of her favourite, Congreve the dramatist, had an image made of him, with which she used to ' converse ' (!), we are told, in the most ' polite ' manner.

the Church had only a hatred more or less masked (in a general very little masked), for that part of the widow's emotion which was strictly conjugal—what it wanted to do was to cut down human delight to its lowest, and it greedily seized the occasion.

While, however, the Church meant one thing, and the vowed lady meant another, or, perhaps, did not know what she meant, human feeling, among those who had time for sentiment, was making something else of the whole transaction. The Church might throw ugly epithets at the crisis of emotion which ends in marriage ; but this way of treating the subject, however it might suit some men (especially men who, having deteriorated their moral vision by a bad life, had fled to the cloister in a fright to get it mended), would never suit the majority of women, or men of artistic sensibility, in whom the feminine element is naturally strong. In most women 'passion' is so lost in emotion that the two things can as little be dissociated as the flower and the perfume of the flower. This may be discerned at either end of a woman's moods, when she loves, or has loved, or is longing to love ; you may see it in the immortal exclamation of Heloise,* and in the flesh-coloured embroidery of the aspirations of Madame de Guion. The mediæval Church wronged woman in this respect—it made ' a vile trans-

---

* 'Carius mihi et dignius videretur tua dici meretrix quam illius imperatrix.' Cruel injustice is done to Heloise if we do not allow its full force to the *dici* here.

lation' of her love—and its influence survives to our own day in precisely the same sense. Woman, on the one hand, in her utter innocence, misunderstood the Church, and threw herself into its arms. But man said, *distinguo*. He remembered, when his wits were a little shaken up by the revival of letters, that there was such a thing as being in love ; he knew that love was the foster-mother of all the virtues ; and felt the absurd injustice of the nasty adjectives. But all this at first vague and obscurely ; criticism and action not proceeding step by step. The spirit of the time said to itself, ' We will take the Church at its word ;' and yet it had a half-unconscious reserve of feeling which whispered, ' We shall, out of the path on which we are now starting, find bye-paths into which the Church will scarcely follow us.' The beginnings of change are always vague ; full of logical confusions and moral casuistries ; and the reviving human sentiment of the middle ages scarcely knew, or rather did not know, the way in which it was going when it found itself borne along upon the roseate billowy clouds of the new romantic movement, in which the troubadours swarmed, and thrummed, and sang, and the Courts of Love set up in fact, or in fantasy, the formula of the new social progression. If we will only realize deliberately for a moment what human nature is, and, among other things, how impossible it is for a man to divest the image of a woman of its appropriate human atmosphere (rarefied and purified as that atmosphere is in chaste minds), we shall recognise, what we are too apt to forget, how cognate to paganism was the homage or worship vowed to the Virgin Mary in the middle ages. To a sensitive youthful imagination she was not a Jewess of Galilee, but a lovely, tender queen of heaven. The figure of the Mater Dolorosa could have little meaning to a youth of nineteen; and immediately upon the revival of letters, the image of Mary was, so to speak, *calquée* upon the image of Venus Urania, and which came uppermost at a particular juncture was determined by the poetry of the situation, whatever it was. 'It is possible, is it,' said, or intended to say, the dreaming spirit of the time ; 'it is possible, then, for a woman to be at once a virgin and a vowed sacred bride ? It was possible for St. Catherine to marry her Saviour ? It is possible to come a step nearer to the solid earth, and yet keep hold on heaven? It is possible, and admirable, is it, for a woman who has been wed, to love her lord when he has passed beyond her reach ? There is a distinction, is there, between the claim of the body and the claim of the soul ? Be it so. We had felt as much, men have always felt as much, when in love; always felt that that alone is perfect love which asks nothing of the beloved, or which can at least burn on when nothing can be given or taken, as in love unrequited, or love forbid. We will set up, then, in the name of the heart and the spirit, a *cultus* of Love. As to the marriage bond, the Church shall have its own way—the bond shall continue inviolable, but by the Church's own law, base, a mere excuse for "venial sin." We entirely acquiesce, and shall proceed to celebrate the tender rites of Love.' Thus, the young imagination of Europe, starting from the human side, commenced what was in truth a revolution in the ecclesiastically accepted view of the relations between men and women, but sheltered itself under the thought that if its line of movement were simply pushed to its logical termination, it would meet the line which from the opposite side the Church had drawn to the same point.

II. When the poet looks at the love of beauty in woman, with all its concomitants of self-devotion, and its mysterious issues of ever-new being, with still new concomitants of self-devotion again,—he sees in it what is strictly divine and worshippable. He sees, that is to say, an outbreak or disclosure of the great inscrutable central fire of life which shoots up to the surface of Nature universally. He looks upon it without judging, without criticising, without moralising, making only one demand (and *that* he makes unconsciously as a skylark sings, or a daisy flowers), namely, that what has an infinite source and has infinite issues, shall always have the infinite of symmetry in its individual forms. It is precisely the same with bravery in man. This, too, he looks upon with uncriticising joy, as an outbreak, in counterpart, of the same great central fire. If the poetical imagination be driven out

of paradise and forced by pain to put on self-consciousness and keep awake to criticise, it still knows the
worship of sorrow only as founded on a conflict of joys,
to be some day reconciled in a higher joy. It
knows nothing, cannot by possibility have anything
to say, of a worship of sorrow founded on an extraneous
curse. This is, however, what the mediæval Church
endeavoured to force upon the poetical imagination
of the time. With the natural consequence,—dislocation and confusion. Beginning at the lower or more
tangible end of the problem, the mediæval Church endeavoured to manipulate daily life upon the principle
that there was nothing in it that was *natural* but
what ought to be taxed; with, again, the inevitable result,—dislocation and confusion. It endeavoured to take possession of love, and make something
impossible of it. It endeavoured to take possession of
valour, and use it exclusively for its own purposes,—
valour formally consolidated as secular power to burn
heretics; valour at large with the sword drawn, as
enterprise, to kill extraneous infidels and conquer ter-
ritory for the Church. Now the *essor* of valour and
the *essor* of love are the beginnings of the social
state; and I hope we shall not grow tired, even at
the cost of some reiteration, of considering the manner
in which the policy of the mediæval Church acted upon
the heart of life in Europe, and especially in England.

III. It seems to me obvious that the mediæval Church

did an unwise thing for herself in taking the virtue of
manhood, or courage, with the sentiment of tenderness to women in any shape whatever under her protection. Everything which tended, as the institution of
chivalry certainly did, to the elevation of individual
honour, and the consolidation of individual self-
reliance, was unfavourable to the interests of an institution which depended for so much of its power and
success upon the merging of the individual in the cor-
porate body of the Church. The elevation of woman
to a pedestal upon which she sat to be admired for
what she was in herself alone (however colourably
that view might have been disguised), was the natural
complement of the consecration of manhood, forming,
as it did, a consecration of womanhood at the hands of
manhood. Consistently with herself, the Church of Rome
—I might, perhaps, extend the area of the proposition,
and include, if they were frank, some other institutions
—could not possibly consecrate womanhood, as womanhood. She was not only inferior, and under a special
curse, she was ' unclean,' and ' defiling.' But the matter
was taken out of the hands of the Church; and very
soon, God, and Love, and Venus, and the Virgin Mary,
were conjoined in the phrases of chivalric literature in
manner the very last which the Church had contemplated, though it was natural enough; for the consecration of beauty would hardly stay long behind the
consecration of valour: and that the ladies understood their share of the matter, is plain from the fact

that they were often found playing the parts of esquires to the Knights who fought in their service, tending their horses, and buckling, or unbuckling, their armour.

Something like knighthood, as an institution, was, perhaps, known among the Teutonic or Western nations at an incalculably early date : at all events, the investiture of a young man with arms was accompanied by ceremonies of some gravity. If it be true that, in the institution under Charlemagne, of a separate order of feudal warriors, bound to fight on horseback, dressed in a coat of mail, and called Caballarii (Chevaliers), we obtain our first glimpse of the figure we now call a Knight, we are not carried much farther on towards Chivalry. But when we come to the time of the Crusades, and find Knights by the thousand taking service under lords who were bound for the Holy Land, we perceive that the Knight may now naturally assume a more sacred character. The man who fought to recover the Sepulchre of Christ from the hands of the infidels was a very different person from the mere cavalier, feudally pledged to fight for a particular baron. And it is obvious to add,—what has not, however, I think, been noticed,—that the lady-love, who gave such a Knight his *congé*, or accolade, or Godspeed, upon such an errand, was a different person from a mere sweetheart. But the Crusaders brought back with them to the north certain things which they did not carry out with them ; and, among these, a tinge of southern sentiment. In the camp, they must have had frequent intercourse with Troubadours and Trouveres by profession; to say nothing of the fact, that hundreds of Knights were themselves Troubadours: and in this way, those who had not yet learned the lore of love would learn it during their campaigns.

It would often happen, as befell, for an example, in the case of the Good Knight Bayard, who belongs to a later date, that the lady who gave the Knight his badge, or accolade, in the name of God, on parting for the wars, would be a married lady; and here arose at once an allegiance of sentiment, or emotion, that lay parallel with that of the marriage law: the allegiance, indeed, of a second and concurrent marriage, which often left the husband nothing but the allegiance of the ' bond' (which, by the natural gravitation of feeling and circumstance, too often became no allegiance at all under such circumstances). The Church might complain of all this as a perversion, but she could not deny that the spirit of her legends gave a colourable excuse for it. From the marriage of St. Catherine with her Saviour, to the ideal marriage of a brave Knight and a fair lady, was no great step for the imagination to take. We must always remember what sort of man the typical Knight was. He was a man who drew his sword and held it before him when the Gospel was read in church (probably bearing a pet falcon on his other wrist at the same time) in token that he was always ready to defend the faith of Christ; he had bathed, or received a chivalric baptism, fasted, taken the holy communion, and watched his arms in prayer, all night in church, upon his being invested with his arms. Hence, to love him was like loving an angel from heaven; and the Church had no right to quarrel with chivalry for simply carrying out its own teaching upon the subject of the relation between men and women: namely, that the crisis of that relation was sin—mortal in folks unwed, venial in the wedded, but still sin.

Very good, said the chivalric sentiment of the day, unconsciously penetrated with that beauty of life which the Church denied, let wedlock take the chaff, we will have the wheat. The bond, the servitude, and the ' venial sin,' be yours; *we* will keep the delight, the exaltation, the loveliness, and the sanctity. It is true this broke down, because life refuses to be arrested mid-way towards its natural issues. But the down-break was the *reductio ad absurdum* of the teaching of the Church. Men soon came to discover that the sprinkling of their food by a holy-water clerk made no difference; and that, in all other respects, the facts of life remained the same, however an institution might excise, tax, manipulate, or throw dirt on them.

IV. It is not easy to miss in the Canterbury Tales a vein of deliberate irony addressed to the notion of ecclesiastically excising certain of the facts of life. Of this irony, the Wife of Bath is the most distinguished mouthpiece. She knows as much of the Bible as the

Parson of the Parson's Tale himself, and she freely uses her knowledge. In her talk we see the natural rebound of the ordinary coarser staple of the English character from the point to which the Parson would strain it. It is exceedingly low and brutal, but it is not vicious. Its vein is very different, for example, from what we get in Boccaccio. However unpleasant we find Boccaccio in certain moods, the extreme levity of that irony (of a certain kind) which runs through the Decameron and prevents its being corrupting,—at least one hopes so,—is very obvious : it has no more weight than a game of shuttlecock ; it is all as unreal as an Arcady of Watteau. But the humour of the Wife of Bath, and the banter addressed by different characters throughout the Canterbury Tales to the same subject as that which so much occupied the mind of this lady, is all solid. Chaucer gives us something like real argument, something like real invective, and stark broad-beamed fun appealing to strong constitutions and defiant tempers ; while Boccaccio is blowing bubbles of scepticism, bright for a moment in the southern sunshine with colours of sense, Chaucer's people really all seem to be trying to believe *something,* however full of nonsense they may be; their humour befits the English habits and the English air, and indicates, however crudely, a real struggle in the heart of the nation.

There is a common-place of discussion when married and single life are compared, which relates to ' having a fixed centre to work from.' There is some-

thing in this common-place, whoever may think proper
to laugh at it.   It points, in particular, to that instinct of force or energy swathing itself round with
tenderness which is the very root of life in a domestic
people.   Women may be chaste, and yet there may be
no such thing as the home ; this we may note in the
gipsies.   Again, women may be chaste, and yet the
home-life may be imperfect in type, and by no means
a source of power ; this we may note in Ireland.   But
when we have extracted all the amusement, to which
dilettante critics of our social life can help us, out of
the Philistine ideal of marrying, settling down, having
a family, and then thinking to one's self, ' Good ! I am
an Englishman,'—when we have got our joke out of all
this,—we know in our hearts that married life is the
root of our power and self-respect, and the school of
the best virtues.   There are many kinds of national
spirit.   There is the national feeling of the Swiss,
which has an intense geographical element in it ; and
the same may be said of the national feeling of America.   But an Englishman, though he is so far a geo-
grapher in his patriotism that he knows he must of
course exist somewhere, and prefers his island, carries
his nationality with him all over the world as a sort of
enlarged domesticity.   He has, somehow, a vague idea,
not only that the English soil is mainly possessed by
married men, but that England is married.   Though
he must know, if he would reflect, that when he goes
abroad, he is the aggressor and the spy, he takes with

him that irritable sense of privacy which only grows up in domestic life, and when he is looking at other people, behaves as if they were looking at him, and is rather apt to break out into rude defiance of their observation. The national spirit of the typical Englishman is, in truth—let whoever pleases call this claptrap—essentially Protestant, and essentially opposed to all mere *toleration* of the domestic life, or the secular-energetic life. To him the Church is in the State, not the State in the Church,—*ecclesia in republicâ, non respublica in ecclesiâ,*—and, since the foundations of the republic are laid in the family, how much that implies !

V. The two most obvious characteristics of Chaucer, it has already been said, are his Englishness and his lightsomeness ; and the part which he played in recording that insurgence of the English spirit proper, which we note in his century, and which was so adverse to the claims of the mediæval Church, is conspicuous. To what extent he was cause, and to what extent effect, it is, of course, utterly impossible to determine. But nobody can help noticing the distinctive place he occupies in the century of Wickliff, or fail to see that unless the heart of England had been then vigorously growing into what it now is, he would not have been possible, such as he is. In vain does he, in his old age, repent of his secular writings, and stick his repentance

on to the end of the Parson's Tale. Nobody reads
his Parson's Tale except out of curiosity; but not all
the repulsiveness of much of his poetry can avail
against its representative character to shut it up from
even the general reader in our own day. The reason
is that, though Literature was then a *European* idea,
and though he gets much of his raw material from
abroad, we find him akin to us in the stress which his
writings lay upon certain qualities and certain ideas.
Prominent among those ideas are the pluck of men,
and the goodness of women, considered as mated or
complementary things. I do not, indeed, think it can
be said, that Chaucer was, even for his age, and making
whatever allowances you please, a chaste or 'domestic'
poet. I only say that the qualities which go to make
most English literature chaste, just as most English
life is chaste, the qualities which flower in the domestic ideal—pluck or bravery, allied with tenderness
—are conspicuous in Chaucer. And the blame of
their not bearing their natural fruit in a man of his
mould, I lay, as the reader knows, upon the disinte-
grating, confusing effect of mediæval faith. If, in fact,
to make an almost ludicrous image, you take Chaucer's
rough Englishness, and steep it in Chaucer's Chivalric
Romanticism, you do get something like the English
ideal. Because, in his case, what a poet would naturally (*i.e.* if unswayed by fantastic dogma), have made
of bravery and tenderness stops short; and then, has

to be supplemented, as well as it can be, by importing something from another province of that which he has left to represent him.

As it is in the mother-chamber, in the striking, however common, incident of that chamber, that the married idea receives its most forcible illustration, so the domestic quality or temper of a nation may be tested by the nurture of children in it. Not necessarily by their education, nor by their culture in any other sense, but their *nurture*. What is the relation of the child to the home and the tendernesses that gather together under the common roof? Nay, there is another question of much force, though it is a very simple one,—How is the birth of a child taken? Is it a great event in the family life, a thing that calls for its own appropriate pomp and circumstance, or is it nothing particular? The natural (not always the necessarily realised) tendency to think much of children is to bind the home-ties tighter. There may be patriotism and strong national feeling without any particular love of children, as is the case, I should suppose, in Switzerland (to take a near example), but the English ideal always gives the children a prominent place.

And it always did. Children are not often mentioned by Chaucer, but wherever he does mention them, his touch is exceedingly tender and sweet. Nothing could well be more affectionate, more motherly, one might almost say, than some of the lines in

the Man of Law's Tale. The passages which relate
to the actual marriage of Constance are so very
English that I wish I could quote them. But I can
only refer to them, and point out (what, indeed, the
reader is pretty sure to note for himself) the very protestant way in which we are told that 'though wyfes
ben ful holy thynges,' they have to bear children
' to folk that hav i-wedded 'hem with rynges :' —

> ' What schuld I telle of the realté
> Of this mariage, or which cours goth biforn,
> Who bloweth in a trompe or in an horn?
> The fruyt of every tale is for to seye ;
> They ete and drynk, and daunce and synge and pleye.'

Here I must stop, not that the verse which follows
is not innocent, but that it is not modern, though it
is, as I have said, quite English. It is to Chaucer's
extreme tenderness in writing of children that I would
solicit attention. Constance, the lady to whose marriage we have been referring, is commanded to quit
the realm, with her child :—

> ' Hir litel child lay wepyng in hir arm,
> And knelyng pitously to him sche sayde :
> " Pees, litel sone, I wol do the noon harm."
> With that hir kerchef of hir hed sche brayde,
> And over his litel eyghen sche it layde,
> And in hir arm sche lullith it wel faste. . . . .'

She then addresses the Mater Dolorosa in words
such as those which have been familiar to ten thou-

and thousand lips in Christendom: she remembers that the LORD was once a child, and that his Mother had seen Him die a death of shame and agony. Once more she turns to the child :—

> ' " O litel child, allas ! what is thi gilt,
> That never wroughtest synne as yet, pardé ?
> Why wil thyn harde fader han the spilt ?
> O mercy, deere constable," seyde sche,
> " And let my litel child here dwelle with the :
> And if thou darst not saven him for blame,
> So kys him oones in his fadres name."
> Therwith sche loketh bak-ward to the lond,
> And seyde, " Farwel, housbond rewtheles !"
> And up sche rist, and walketh doun the stronde
> Toward the schip, hir folweth al the prees ;
> And ever sche prayeth hir child to hold his pees.'

' Yet kiss him once in his father's name,' and ' Ever she prayeth her child to hold his peace,' are touches of the kind which may, indeed, be said to go to every heart, but which, in their contrast, go with peculiar force to the English heart. For a banished mother, like Constance, to ask the instrument of what she believed to be her husband's inscrutably unjust and cruel sentence, to kiss the child once in his father's name, is an idea which belongs to the deepest fantasy (there is scarcely any word for it but fantasy) of a woman's heart : but that the forlorn woman kept on hushing the crying baby, while all the people followed her to the ship, is so simply realistic as to be not less affecting in its way. It does not matter much whether this is all Chaucer's own or not, the tenderness is his, and the simplicity of the language, and the general effect.

Of course, no Englishwoman of the present day, above the lowest class (*in* the lowest class attentive listeners may still hear women talk much in the same vein) would talk as the Wife of Bath talked; but the following passage from her Prologue, in its direct-ness and unflinchingness, may perhaps be taken for English :—

> ' For, lordyngs, syns I twelf yer was of age,
> I thank it God that is eterne on lyve,
> Housbondes atte chirch dore I have had fyve,
> For I so ofte might have weddid be,
> And alle were worthy men in here degré.
> But me was taught, nought longe tyme goon is,
> That synnes Crist went never but onys
> To weddyng, in the Cane of Galile,
> That by the same ensampul taught he me
> That I ne weddid schulde be but ones.
> Lo, herken such a scharp word for the nones !
> Biside a welle Jhesus, God and man,
> Spak in reproef of the Samaritan:
> " Thow hast y-had fyve housbondes," quod he ;
> " And that ilk man, which that now hath the,
> Is nought thin housbond ;" thus he sayd certayn;
> What that he ment therby, I can not sayn.
> But that I axe, why the fyfte man
> Was nought housbond to the Samaritan?
> How many might sche have in mariage ?
> Yit herd I never tellen in myn age
> Uppon this noumbre diffinicioun.'

It is certainly very rough, but it expresses that hearty belief in the fitness of things as they stand, visible and tangible, which goes with what Sir Roger de Coverley called a ' roast-beef stomach.'

The roast-beef stomach is another name for what old writers call stoutness, meaning, of course, not fulness of girth, but pluck, as distinguished from what the French call *élan;* and while, on the one hand, stoutness or pluck in our own mixed but still individual race, tends naturally to family life, on the other hand, family life is a school of practical necessity which is eminently favourable to the cultivation or preservation of pluck as a national quality. Those who, giving woman a share of their lives, yet omit to join themselves to her in the brave sense, and to give her a co-ordinate place in the council of existence, can only learn half their lesson and make half their proper conquests. And the children, too, count for much. A picture of English bravery is not complete without them all. One of the most deeply characteristic of English ballads is that of ' Adam Bell, Clym of the Clough, and William of Cloudesly,' and, for all its wildness, it is one of the most deeply domestic : —

> ' They were outlawed for venison,
>   These yeomen everychone ;
> They swore them brethren upon a day,
>   To English-wood for to gone.

> ' Now lith and listen, gentlemen,
>   That of mirthès loveth to hear ;
> Two of them were single men,
>   The third had a wedded fere.

> ' William was the wedded man,
>   Much more than was his care.'

And the main interest of the story rests with him, and
his wife, and children. In the merry greenwood, he
longs to go and —

> '   .   .   .   speak with fair Alice, his wife,
>   And with his children three;'

and, in spite of the opposition of his brethren, he
goes : —

> ' He took his leave of his brethren two,
>   And to Carlisle he is gone :
> There he knocked at his own windòw
>   Shortly and anon.

> ' " Where be you, fair Alice," he said,
>   " My wife and children three?
> Lightly let in thine own husband,
>   William of Cloudesly."

> ' " Alas !" then saydè fair Alice,
>   And sighèd wondrous sore,
> " This place has been beset for you
>   This half a year and more."

> ' " Now I am here," said Cloudesly,
> " I would that in I were ;
> Now fetch us meat and drink enoug]
> And let us make us good cheer.' '

Can anything be more English, I was going to say
more comically English, than this ? William's wife
tells him he is in danger of his life, and he only
answers that now he is here he may as well spend an
hour with her, and have a good supper : —

> ' She fetched him meat and drink plenty,
> Like a true wedded wife ;
> And pleasèd him with that she had,
> Whom she loved as her life.'

Then, when the house is beset by the Norman officers,
who set fire to it : —

> ' " Yield thee, Cloudesly," said the justice,
> " And thy bow and thy arrows thee fro."
> " *A curse on his heart,*" *said the fair Alice,*
> " *That my husband counselleth so.*"

> ' William opened a back windòw,
> That was in his chamber high,
> And there with sheets he did let down
> His wife and his children three.

> ' " Have here my treasure," sayde William,
> " My wife and children three ;
> For Christe's love do them no harm,
> But wreak you all on me." '

Here, indeed, is a touch in which we recognise a wide

difference between the half-fetichistic faith of the middle ages and our own,—a touch obvious, but worth noticing. In all the bloodshed and tyranny of the time, the name of Christ was assumed to be a name to conjure by; the bitterest foes might ask favours of each other ' for Christe's love.' But there was another name, powerful to conjure by in those days. The king says all three of the men shall be hanged : —

> " Ye speak proudly," said the king ;
> " Ye shall be hanged all three."
> " That were great pity," then said the queen,
> " If any grace might be.

' " My lord, when I came first into this land,
> To be *your wedded wife*,
> The first boon that I would ask,
> Ye would grant it me belyfe :

' " And I asked you never none till now ;
> Therefore, good lord, grant it me."
> " Now ask it, madam," said the king,
> " And granted it shall be." ' '

The queen asks the lives of the three men, which are granted to her. After some incidents which need not be recapitulated,* the king advances and rewards the three yeomen, and the queen concludes her share in the story ' with a characteristic touch : '—

---

* These include the shooting of an apple by William off his son's head. It is no presumption against the truth of the story of William Tell that it has its parallels ; such an incident might naturally have happened in any generation which knew the use of bow and arrow.

' " And, William, bring me your wife," said the queen,
  " Me longeth her sore to see :
 She shall be my chief gentlewoman,
  To govern my nursery." '

In Chaucer we have nothing so quaint and homely
as this. He was a courtly poet; the Romance vein
was strong in him; and it was not until his old age
that he found out where his great strength lay, or at
all events that which has made him remembered as
he would never have been if he had not written the
Prologue to the Canterbury Tales. But in spite of
the bad manners of the court, which may perhaps be
said to have coloured his writing and made him much
of a gallant, and something of a mocker, we can none
of us help warming to him, and feeling that, in face
of his frequent levity and indecorum, he must have a
place in the line of descent in which we afterwards
find Shakspeare, and not in the bad company of the
Wycherleys, Congreves, and the like. In a word, we
feel that the heart of England in his time, if it were
inferred from his writings solely, would have to be
pronounced sound. And in particular, among negative
matters, we may notice that particularly English feature, the absence of treachery. The family, or heart
of the community, is the great nurse of the qualities
which are opposed to treachery; for without truthfulness and the sense of mutual dependence, the institution must go to pieces. There is, I fear, no sign that
Chaucer had caught up the true prophecies of the

insurgent spirit of his time, or that he knew how that
which we now call the English character was beginning, under his eyes, to shake off alien elements and
consolidate itself for the great struggle which, continued through the days of the Reformation and Puritanism, and passing through the middle-class ascend-
ency of the nineteenth century, is even now entering
upon a new phase. Nor was he a moralist. But
his humour alone—the humour, so often, of an exaggerated and reckless virility—is not the humour of
corruption, and would, like that of Fielding, scarcely
be possible in a country of which the heart was un-
sound. It may or may not be true that the flower of the
literature of an age may be taken as representing the
inmost tendencies of an age. Nobody can say authori-
tatively either that it is or is not so ; but if it were,
and Chaucer were the only extant record of his time,
we could reconstruct a good deal of that time out of
his writings. Many of the inferences would be remote
enough ; but we should think we discerned in the
splintered mirror of life, made by the restless humour
of the poet, that very heart of England which likes a
fixed centre to work from, and prefers to make that
centre a home, in which no priest may tithe, or toll, or
have predominance.

CHAPTER VIII.

MOTLEY.

LET us try and imagine, lounging about the Tabard,
some of the patches of the motley of life in the fourteenth century. Imagine, for instance, early in the
morning on the first of May, troops of Mayers pouring
into Southwark in different directions from the fields
around, some of them carrying large boughs of May,
which they humorously call sprouts,—

> ' It is but a sprout, but it's well budded out
>   By the work of our Lord's hand.'

and most of them singing songs, childishly clumsy and irrelevant, to strange music in a minor key,—not so good as the music of the ordinary Christmas carol; more like the tune the cat died of, with very little variety in the tune, or the length of the notes; and much of ' the rhythm of an industrious hammer,' such as that of the old tune which modern Londoners call ' Villikins and his Dinah.' One of these troops of Mayers, largely sprinkled with gawky boys and girls, is sure to find its way into the courtyard of the Tabard, and howl and jump till some of the guests throw them a largess. Or imagine a troop of jugglers or mummers, or a group of morris-dancers, with flags and garlands, attended by very energetic minstrelsy. While the dancing, singing, and mumming are going on, a scene full of movement and colour at all events, a manciple crosses the road from St. Mary Overy, and a nun, perhaps, comes toddling from the Priory at Bermondsey. I think nuns always do toddle, walking as if they had stones in their shoes. Perhaps the beadle comes by, holding by the collar somebody who is going to be put in the stocks; an abbot on a nag; a lady on a palfrey with her wimple down; or a page all in crimson and blue, who being charged with an urgent message, inevitably stops to look at the mummers; and, besides the loss of time, forgets half his business, for which his white-handed mistress, who is just now breakfasting on beef, salt herrings, and beer, will soundly cuff and rate him, later on, swearing at him by Goddes bones or Christes foot. The 'long-haired page in crimson clad,' makes better haste back than he did in going, and on his way hears the bell of St. Mary Overy strike the hour. He is not disposed to linger for so familiar a sound, and perhaps, like Chaucer, he does not care for music ; but in the Ladye Chapel he hears chanting. What he would *like* is a row across the Thames, say to be ferried to the Tower, where he could, perhaps, look at the wild beasts, by favour of some acquaintance of his among the soldiers, whom of course he greatly envies. The river runs bright and clear, between banks which are green enough to keep alive its recollection of the Cotswold Hills; and the gardens of the citizens slope down to the banks. The page is too accustomed to the sight to notice the little boats, laden with piled-up rushes, some of them, perhaps, for the floor of his mistress's boudoir. The Thames eddies and whirls with a great noise around the clumsy piers of the bridge, but he does not notice that either, as we should if we were dropped down upon the London bridge which had a crypt underneath it. From every point the fields are in sight. He can see windmills turning, kine browsing, almost hear the tinkle of sheep-bells ; but all this has no particular charm for him ; he prefers a stroll in Paul's Walk to show off his long hair, his pointed shoes, his new black and red trousers, and the paltock with the gilt edging which he carries jauntily over his shoulder, something like a hussar jacket.

Here comes a black friar, hastening to a death-bed. And here the odd figure that reflects the motley of it all. We all know him in 'Twelfth Night,' and in 'King Lear,' and at the Circus; but how astonished we should be to meet him in the street, himself part of the motley, or in the hall of a friend's house, before dinner, with a cock's-comb, ass's ears, and a bladder full of peas at the end of a stick.

I. This prominent figure in the procession of life in the middle ages, namely the Fool, cannot be overlooked, though it is not in Chaucer's pages that we distinctly hear the ringing of his bells. The apparent confusion of dates in the verses said to be from Chaucer to Scogan has already been referred to; but there seems to be quite as much confusion about Scogan himself. Dr. Doran, in his very entertaining *History of Court Fools*, says Scogan was attached to the court of Edward IV., and then quotes Andrew Borde to the effect that Scogan was a scholar at Oriel, Oxford, 'about a century and a half' after 1326. This brings us to 1476, *i.e.* within seven years of Edward IV.'s death. Of course, however, if Scogan was old enough to have a poem addressed to him by Chaucer, when Chaucer was old, he could not have been a court Fool in 1476; which would make him at least ninety years old. Ben Jonson says Scogan was 'a fine gentleman, and a Master of Arts of Henry IV.'s time,' which make the Chaucer verses possible, so far as Scogan's age is concerned.—

Mere-fool. Skogan ?   What was he?

Sophiel. O, a fine gentleman, and Master of Arts
Of Henry the Fourth's time, that made disguises
For the King's sons, and writ in ballad-royal,
Daintily well.

Mere-fool. But wrote he like a gentleman ?

Sophiel. In rhyme, fine tinkling rhyme, and flowand verse.

The reference to the jester in Shakspeare, 2 Henry
IV. Act III., scene 2, is well known :—

Shall. The same, Sir John, the very same. I saw him
break Skogan's head at the Court-gate when he was a crack,
not thus high.

As Chaucer himself ended his days in the reign of
Henry IV., all this is feasible enough ; but if there was
a Scogan at all at the later dates in which the name is
made to appear, he must have been a descendant of the
Scogan of the fourteenth century. It is possible that
the name, having once acquired a certain significance,
became quasi-generic, and was applied to subsequent
jesters, whatever their baptismal name might be.

II. But these details are of no great interest, nor
are many of the anecdotes about Fools and Jesters of
the middle ages worth quoting ; while too many of them
will not bear it. More important is the question,
What was the real function of this grotesque figure,
with the cap and bells, and ass's ears, and the bladder
at the end of a stick ? It is not improbable that the

best of the good things uttered by Fools have slipped through the coarse sieve of traditionary recollection ; and though it is certainly curious that so important a figure in the scenery of mediæval life has so little that is clever to say for himself, it is inconceivable, perhaps, that the Fool could have been of so much importance unless he served a real use. Wordsworth remarked of the Fool in ' King Lear,' that he ' gave a terrible wildness to the distress ; ' a profoundly true criticism ; but of course kings and barons did not keep Fools for æsthetic reasons. I do not see how we can go farther than the old theory—that the Fool or Jester was a necessary part of the social machinery, a safety-valve and something more, in those days when life needed, as now, to be tempered by epigrams, and there was no printing-press, and no dinner-table, or club *régime* for wit-combats and word-sallies. The only point in which I fancy I differ in my views of the necessity or naturalness of the function of the professional Jester from that of some other critics of mediæval life is this,—that they seem to think of him more as needed and therefore set up, and less as natural and there-fore existing. Given, a sufficient number of men and women to form a community, ever so small, my own imagination immediately finds the Fool there, just as it finds the priest, the soldier, or the physician. He comes like the grass; one ' 'specks he grow'd.' Pau-puk-keewis, Tyl Owlglas, Goroo, Yorick, or Scogan, it does not matter which, he is a natural figure in the procession of life. To push this farther would land us on the shore of that *science des origines,* of which I have elsewhere spoken ; and it is not necessary. We need no more expect to find a society of men without the humourist, a constituted, honoured, active functionary, than we expect to find the individual man totally without sense of humour. Fun, like other metaphysical products, is sown broadcast over life, but here and there, like the others, it lies in a heap.

III. The particular form in which the professed humourist or jester appears before our eyes upon the mediæval platform is incidental, of course. He belongs to a day when functions tended to run into direct contrast, and may be considered as the social antithesis of the preacher. Some people would, no doubt, say,—a necessary make-weight in priest-ridden times. And, indeed, there is a sense in which it may be said that human nature, or at all events human nature in the West, never was and never is—at least in the mass—able to dispense with the application of humour to the most serious of thoughts and interests. It would not be true to affirm that there is no such thing among men as persistent faith in the religious ideas ; but it may assuredly be said they remain for ever in communities —

' Like holy rocks by Druids poised,
The least force shakes, but cannot move,'

and that there is an incessant tendency to shake them with irony more or less explicit. This tendency is more visible just now on the other side of the Atlantic than on this; and it has been said, indeed, that the very essence of American humour is irreverence. But the truth is, that there are moments when the tremendous contrasts of the religious ideas and the story of human life make us all disposed to laugh on one side of the cheek, even if we cry on the other. And there is one perpetual source of humour even among the best men and women, namely, the incongruous, ridiculous difference between what we aim at and what we succeed in doing. Perhaps it may be said that the Fool, as a type, stands for the universal sentiment of fun in those particulars. But, in practice, the Fool of the Middle Ages was himself a long way off from his type. The Fool of genius must have been, of course, a very rare bird: the man, that is, who could with *naïve* and easy mirth, yet without offence or *final* irreverence, banter the incongruities of the human lot, laugh false sentiment out of countenance, and keep all in good humour by slyly hinting, from time to time, that all were rowing in the same boat. Once upon a time a fine lady was discoursing, while the footman waited in the room for some reason, of the superiority of the upper classes, and comparing them to china, the middle classes being delf, and the lower crockery. The lady immediately afterwards requesting John to tell the nursemaid to bring down the daughter

of the house to show to the visitor, John went to the
foot of the stairs and shouted, 'Hollo, Crockery! bring
down little Chaney!'

If this is not true, it is well invented, as the
Italians say; and it is just the kind of thing to say
which lay specially in the function of the mediæval
Fool. But it is obvious, whatever the Fool of genius
might often have said, and in spite of the audacities
we know the Fool often did commit, that his position
kept him very much in check, because he was, in the
very first place, a retainer, a dependant, a hanger-
on, a creature in livery, who formed part of the
pageantry of a big man,—like a chamberlain, or a
castellan, or steward, or mace-bearer. It is quite
possible, that, though often a poor boaster, he was
still more frequently a peace-maker; dropping in
upon the first threat of a quarrel over the flagons,
and giving both sides a chance of escaping from
direct conflict under cover of a joke. But it is clear
that he stood, partly, in place of the drama, not
yet born in England. The Church often denounced
him, just as she did the players wherever they existed;
but he flourished in his poor way,—a sort of vagabond
courtier, who had a location on the 'sport' side of a
great lord's establishment, in fellowship with hawks
and men's-men, and dissolute pages, and sleeping
with the hounds at night. A figure not so very
remote, perhaps, from another,—the pet monkey of
Madame,

     ' In teacup times of hoop and hood,
       Or while the patch was worn.'

It is not at all improbable, indeed, that the Fool
was often a favourite in the ladies' quarter. Who
cannot suppose him to have been an unacknowledged
go-between in many a domestic quarrel—the inter-
cessor that got young master out of a scrape, or that
was sent by my lady with a mock-heroic message to
my lord on the mornings when they had quarrelled
and kept their own sides of the mansion?

    IV. This might happen in a household where there
was only one Fool kept, and that one a man; but
the woman-Fool is an image not unknown in the
history of the middle ages.

    Queens of France kept their *folles,* or female
jesters, who could sing to them and amuse them at
times and in places where the presence of men was not
admissible, or not wanted. In the century of which
we are writing, when King Edward III. was keeping
Pentecost with the usual splendour at Westminster at
Whitsuntide, 1316, a *joculatrix* or *ministrilissa* came
dashing into the banquet-hall on horseback, rode
playfully round the tables, chatting and mimicking
the while, and at last gave the King a letter just before she rode off. The anecdote has been often repeated,—this letter was an expostulation addressed to
the King upon the subject of the undue kindness he

bestowed upon his favourites, while his knights and retainers were left out in the cold. Modern manners would not admit of the existence of a joculatrix in a lady's division of a palace or a mansion, and a joculator or fool in the lord's side; but it was not at all a bad arrangement in the days when the Crusades were barely over, when despotic follies, fighting follies, erotic follies, flagon follies, and priestly follies, were rife. Nor is it always easy, and luckily it is not important, to draw the line between the fool, the minstrel, and the court-poet. Henry Beauclerc, says Miss Strickland, quoting from one of the Tower Rolls, directs the instant payment out of the Exchequer, though it was then shut, of one hundred shillings to 'our beloved Master Henry, the versificator,' for arrears of salary. Edward I. took his minstrel or fool with him to Palestine.

Warton reproduces—from the account-books of the priory of Maxtoke, in the reign of Henry VI.—numerous entries of payments made to joculators and players. ' To a joculator in the Michaelmas week, the sum of fourpence.' ' To the mimes of Coventry, twenty-pence.' ' To Lord Ferrer's mimes, sixpence.' ' To Lord Astley's mimes, twelve-pence.' ' To four of Lord Warwick's mimes, tenpence.' ' To Lord Buckridge's mimes, twenty-pence.' ' To the mimes of Lord Stafford, two shillings.' I have quoted the last six entries, because they suggest how, even after the drama had been created in England by Shakspeare *and his predecessors* (who have, in my opinion, received too little honour for their share in the task), the tradition of the mime's vocation, which allocated him to the household of a 'great lord of the land' (as the phrase was long before Chaucer lived), and yet permitted him to travel about and perform elsewhere, was preserved in the companies of players who afterwards existed in England, from the king's downwards. I need not remind the reader that the Drury Lane Company still style themselves (his or) her Majesty's servants (I am told they may wear a livery, if they choose), and that in the days of Shakspeare great lords had players attached to their persons, who were named after them, ' my lord so and so's company.'

V. Though we should undoubtedly in any case have found this figure of the Fool here, just as we find the vowels in the alphabet, and for reasons of the same order, it is entertaining enough to note that he is, in a fashion, affiliated to the mediæval Devil. The devil, as rehabilitated by Milton in his crystallisation of the Puritan idea, was a grand thunder-scarred figure. The devil of Goethe is (said to be) a gentleman ; but the Devil of the Miracle Plays, like the Vice of the Moralities, which succeeded them, was a butt, a mimic, a coarse joker practical and rhetorical, a mere ' ragamuffin,'* for Christ and the angels to get the

* This word is very old—no doubt as old as Chaucer.

better of. Yet the stage direction, says Strutt, is, to lay about him lustily with a great pole, and tumble the players one over the other with great noise and riot, for disport sake. Vice, or Iniquity, enters upon the scene, ' like Hocus-pocus in a juggler's jerkin, with false skirts, like the knave of clubs.' This is a very different figure from Lear's ' my poor fool'—a pet, as well as a butt, in a king's household; but one can trace the affinity. It is not necessary to insist upon the natural excess of the tendency to pantomime in ages of imperfect culture. Even the love of music and painting, as they exist in coarse minds under our own observation, are little more than a phase of pantomimic passion; forms approaching self-conscious art, but short of it still; forms of that love of loud, staring expression which makes the savage howl and shout, and the gamin chalk the house-wall. In much earlier times I have already remarked that the music or ' minstraulxcie' was often mere noise and display of a pantomimic order; we do not even need to have that suggested by the amusing manner in which the minstrel, the jongleur, and the fool, melt into each other at times as the scene shifts. If there were nothing else, the *loud* life of the middle ages required the practical joker, or Fool, who was also, in due course, very frequently the jokee too—the naughty jack-pudding lad who was whipped, as much for sport as for discipline. In a modern pantomime we see the line of descent unbroken; and the Columbine and the Harle-

quina may be supposed to represent the joculatrix
and the dancer of the generations in which the English
love of 'chaff' made every person of importance, who
could afford it, avail himself of the services of professional jesters and mirth-makers. The religious orders
—practised themselves in the presentation of miracle-
plays—did not turn the cold shoulder to the secular
jack-puddings who were so nearly related to their own
devil, and under-devils.   There are stories of the
welcome the travelling minstrel or Fool received at
the monastery door; bringing with him, as he did,
not only tidings of the world without, but a budget of
fun and frolic.   Nor was the Church unindebted to
the Motley. Rahere, who, however, belongs to the time
of Henry I., not to that of Chaucer, was a Fool or
Minstrel, and, having been urged to the religious life
by a dream which also sent him to the muddy, marshy
land which is now called Smithfield for a site, founded
that Priory and Church of St. Bartholomew, which are
now represented by the Hospital and the Church.   Wal-
den, Bishop of London, and at last primate of England, who belongs to the time of Chaucer, was buried
in the Church, and it is as certain as very high probability can make a thing that Chaucer himself must
have been inside the place.

VI. I do not like to close this chapter without recalling to the minds of those who already know it, and
reproducing for the pleasure of those who do not, a pair,

—distinctly a pair—of counterpart poems in the Rev. Charles Kingsley's drama of the 'Saint's Tragedy,' because they so strikingly exhibit the fool-genius at its proper work. The time is the thirteenth century; the scene is in Thuringia. Guta, a favourite maid in the castle, sings the following beautiful song : —

> ' Far among the lonely hills,
>   As I lay beside my sheep,
>   Rest came down upon my soul,
>   From the everlasting deep.

> ' Changeless march the stars above,
>   Changeless morn succeeds to even ;
>   And the everlasting hills
>   Changeless watch the changeless heaven.

> ' See the rivers, how they run,
>   Changeless to a changeless sea ;
>   All around is forethought sure,
>   Fixed will and stern decree.

> ' Can the sailor move the main ?
>   Will the potter heed the clay ?
>   Mortal ! where the spirit drives,
>   Thither must the wheels obey.

> ' Neither ask, nor fret, nor strive ;
>   Where thy path is, thou shalt go.
>   He who made the stream of time
>   Wafts thee down to weal or woe.'

This song, Guta says, he had ' from a nun, who was a shepherdess in her youth.' The Fool, who is present

with my lady and the rest, interposes in this way:
' Now you shall see the shepherdess's baby dressed in
my cap and bells,' and he proceeds to sing this song : —

> ' When I was a greenhorn and young,
>   And wanted to be and to do,
>   I puzzled my brains about choosing my line
>   Till I found out the way that things go.
>
> ' The same piece of clay makes a tile,
>   A pitcher, a taw, or a brick ;
>   Dan Horace knew life ; you may cut out a saint,
>   Or a bench, from the self-same stick.
>
> ' The urchin who squalls in a gaol,
>   By circumstance turns out a rogue ;
>   While the castle-born brat is a senator born,
>   Or a saint if religion's in vogue.
>
> ' We fall on our legs in this world,
>   Blind kittens, tossed in neck and heels :
>   'Tis Dame Circumstance licks Nature's cubs into
>   shape,
>   She's the mill-head, if we are the wheels.
>
> ' Then why puzzle and fret, plot and dream ?
>   He that's wise will just follow his nose ;
>   Contentedly fish, while he swims with the stream ;
>   'Tis no business of his where it goes.'

A volume of comment could not so well make vivid to
the mind what I have just called the Fool-function.

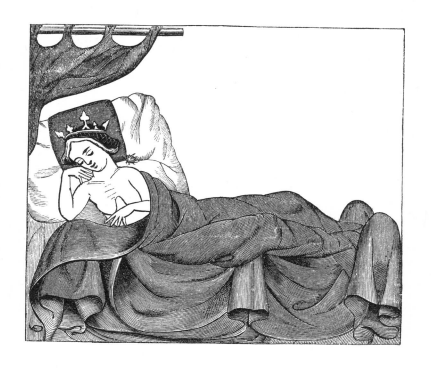

CHAPTER IX.

MEDIÆVAL NUDITARIANISM.

CHAUCER was, to employ a word which is of the coinage, I think, of the Rev. St. John Tyrwhitt, a Nuditarian, and, in my opinion, something worse. Nuditarianism is an open question in art, but grossness is not. There remains, however, a topic of great interest, namely, the extent to which the manners and sentiments of our ancestors are accurately represented by our early Nuditarian, and worse than Nuditarian literature.

I. I cannot help thinking that, on the whole, inferences too strong have been drawn by some antiquarian and historical writers with regard to the rudeness and indelicacy of English manners in early times. Perhaps we are too apt to forget how much depends upon the *suggestiveness* of language, apart from the bare meaning of words. The suggestiveness of the words we employ in common writing and common speech so much depends upon custom, juxtaposition, and a hundred subtle incidents and associations which cannot survive the occasion, or be preserved in any record, however spontaneous and frank that record may seem to be, that it must be very uncertain work drawing conclusions as to manners from any such records or remains. I recollect reading somewhere an anecdote about an aged lady, who said, in answer to some comment upon the changes in recent manners, that in her young days, which were (I fancy) in the early part of George the Third's reign, educated young ladies would sit, and without a blush hear read aloud in company books or narratives which in her older days she found would not be tolerated even in company of a much lower quality. I quote this for the sake of asking the question, would not this lady have keenly resented the charge that in her youth she had been less modest than she afterwards became?

Assuredly she would. Nor, except for short spaces of time, when there is a fashion of indecency, as, for example, when Aphra Behn and Nell Gwyn sat for their portraits in the undress which is so familiar to our memories, do I believe the standard of modesty much varies. It would take strong evidence, indeed, to convince me that a woman stood forth unclad in the streets for the performance of a part in a Mystery, or that any woman in the position of the old carpenter's wife in the Reve's Tale ever performed the trick which is attributed to her in Chaucer's story—in the same age as that in which an insult offered, under cover of a legal errand, to a girl in a similar social position, was fully sufficient to cause the smouldering fire of discontent to break out in the flames of a daring rebellion. Is it easily conceivable that the mother of the maiden of Dartford, whose shrieks, when the girl was affronted, summoned Wat the Tiler to the spot with his hammer, could ever have played Eve before the Fall, in Eve's costume before the Fall, in the presence of a large mob of spectators ?

Again, whether the story of Lady Godiva be true or not, the mere fact that in an age earlier than that of Chaucer it could obtain such currency as could belong only to a legend which justly represented popular feeling on the question of personal display, is enough to remind us that the laws of modesty in women have been substantially the same in England for a great many centuries.

II. A remark which I have made in another page
concerning the large difference in publicity, and in its
effect upon the imaginations and critical faculties of
both its writers and its readers, between a written and
a printed literature, applies not only to the subject of
the marvellous, but to that of decency, modesty,
delicacy, or self-respect in the choice of topics and in
the details of the treatment. Unfortunately, there is
no subject which it is more easy to cant about than
this; no subject which has, in fact, been more cantingly
and superficially handled. First of all, let us have
facts acknowledged for what they are. I, for one,
will not consent to have the occasional grossness of
Chaucer talked out of sight and remembrance by
mere commonplaces about the times in which he lived
and the privileges of the poet's imagination. Frankly, I
hold that the indelicacy and filthiness of Chaucer are in
excess of the license of his time and of the privilege of
the poet. There is every presumption which the nature
of the case admits of that the anticipative apology
which he makes in the Prologue to the ' Canterbury
Tales,' was a deliberate throwing of dust in the eyes of
the reader;* it is conclusive, even if other evidence

---

* ' But ferst I pray you of your curtesie,
    That ye ne rette it nat my vilanye,
    Though that I speke al pleyn in this matere,
    To telle you here wordes and here cheere ;
    Ne though I speke here wordes propurly,
    For this ye knowen al so wel as I,

were wanting, instead of such evidence being abundant, that the poet knew very well the indecency of some of the things he had written. Nor is it possible that the poet, who wrote the sweet, wholesome descriptions and tender suggestions which are to be found in his works could have been unaware of his own grossness when he chose to be gross. That he did at times *choose* to be gross I maintain. His excuse for the gratuitous filth of the ' Miller's Tale ' and the ' Reve's Tale,' may be sought partly in his early training in the *Junkerei* or page's quarter, partly in his camp experience, and partly in other directions. But the mere dirtiness of some of the passages in question is not so unlike an English poet, and not so dishonouring to human nature, as the intrusive, insolent indelicacy

> Who so schal telle a tale aftur a man,
> He moste reherce, as neigh as ever he can,
> Every word, if it be in his charge,
> Al speke he never so rudely ne large ;
> Or elles he moot telle his tale untrewe,
> Or feyne thing, or fynde wordes newe.
> He may not spare, though he were his brothur ;
> He moste as wel sey oo word as anothur.
> Crist spak himself ful broode in holy writ,
> And wel ye woot no vilanye is it.
> Eke Plato seith, who so that can him rede,
> The wordes mot be cosyn to the dede.
> Also I pray you to forgeve it me,
> Al have I folk nat set in here degre
> Here in this tale, as that thei schulde stonde ;
> My witt is schorte, ye may wel undurstonde.'

of certain of the lines which follow the description of the uprising of Emily in the Knight's Tale : —

' Uprose the sun and uprose Emily.'

Up to this point, all is well ; the description is beautiful, and there is nothing indelicate in following the lovely girl to the bath-bower.   The words—

' Her body wessche with water fro a welle,'

only add the idea of purity and lucidity, and the glancing, transparent motion of water to the idea of an exquisite woman's body with the fresh life of the morning in the gentle limbs, though the sacredness of the night hangs like the shadow or the remembrance of a veil from her shoulders to her feet.   But the lines which follow are quite gratuitous, and quite unpardonable in a poet.

III. The law of the case, and of all such cases, I take to be clear.   Human life has no natural incidents which are, in themselves, dishonourable, or things of shame ; but it has incidents which, especially in a state of partial yet considerable civilization, are so frequently connected with accidents of disease, infirmity, vice, or what is quite universally offensive, that when the incidents are openly spoken of, without necessity, the accidents are more or less remotely suggested to the

mind, and a sense of shame or degradation is the consequence. We experience no sense of shame in reading
certain passages in Leviticus or Deuteronomy, just as
we should experience none in reading clauses as plainly
worded in a Public Health Act. Generally, it may
be said that, where the mood or purpose of the speaker
is one of simplicity or unity, whatever his standard
may be, no grave offence is given by plain speech.
But, if we begin by suggesting a contrast between two
aspects of human life and human nature, so as to
create all the watchfulness of a double consciousness,
then all unnecessary reference to the side upon which
the contrast is, by the hypothesis, unfavourably stated,
becomes objectionable. For example, when in the
Miller's Tale the carpenter's wife is described in terms
of express contrast with what is admittedly unpleasant ;
as thus—

> ' Hir mouth was swete as bragat is, or meth,
> Or hoord of apples layd in hay or heth,'

the sequel of the story is beforehand made odious and
dishonouring to human nature. I do not want to incur
the charge of man-millinerism, but I doubt if many
men, even in rude health, could read the description of
the Miller's bedroom in the middle of the night without a sense of nausea. Love and religion, friendship
and modesty, are alike by instinct blind and deaf to
the infirmities of humanity, and will not know them at
all till the knowledge must be crossed by the kind foot

in the path of service : and even then they are silent.
They not only allow, they delight to allow others to
live their lives within wide enclosures, never to be
overstepped except upon needs which gather around
the endings, the beginnings, or the supreme crises of
our lives. Thus treated, the infirmities, or enclosed
circumstantials of existence, become sacred things, which
bring no dishonour and no pain.

It is, I repeat, obvious that, in writing a book
before printing was invented, when a large miscella-
neous audience could not be in contemplation, an
author would be under less restraint than an author
committing to paper what he supposed would be printed
for, possibly, ten thousand eyes. The manners are soft-
ened, and speech on different topics becomes more and
more delicately periphrastic, in proportion as the
scale on which social intercourse takes place grows
wider. So literature has grown more and more reticent in certain particulars, in proportion as the number
of readers has been increased. Many things may properly be both said and written from which the eye
of a tender maid of fourteen or fifteen would naturally
flinch if she saw them ; but Chaucer would not have
written certain passages of his poems if he had had
before his mind any suggestion of a young creature like
his own Virginia as likely to be among his readers.
The truth, indeed, is that literature in the fourteenth
century, and perhaps down to the middle of the
eighteenth, was itself an enclosed thing in the imagi-

nations of readers and writers too. It had its own privileges and licenses, like courts of justice, or places of worship, in which we may constantly see the most modest women hear without a blush what they would not submit to hear anywhere else.

IV. In respect of the subject we are now considering, Chaucer, like some other great writers, has been treated with occasional injustice. It is very wide of the mark, for instance, to blame the poet for sensuality and materialism when he sings thus of Dido in the ' Legend of Good Women :'—

> ' So yonge, so lusty, with hire eighen glade,
>   That yf that God that hevene and erthe made,
>   Wolde han a love, for beaute and goodenesse,
>   And womanhede, and trouthe, and semelynesse,
>   Whom sholde he loven but this lady swete ?
>   There nys no woman to him halfe so mete.'

Chaucer has been called ' gross' and ' material' for this passage; yet, at the worst, it might be defended as a mere hyperbole, natural enough in the days of chivalry, when God, and the Son of God, and Venus, and Love, and the Virgin Mary, were jumbled together in people's imaginations into one supersensible mythology, around which there nevertheless hung an atmosphere or aroma of sense. That Almighty God *chose* the Virgin Mary expressly because she was a lovely, gentle, modest maid, was a fancy quite familiar to the readers and spectators of miracle plays and mysteries. God's mother (Goddes-moder), is as the reader will of course have noticed, a common expression in the literature of the times—Chaucer, among others, employing it with no 'material' or 'sensual' reference; and God's wife (Goddes wyf), is common too. In the miracle play or mystery, 'A Council of the Trinity and the Incarnation,' Cotton MS. pageant XI., the 'three persons of the Godhead' are represented in council upon the fall and the contemplated restoration of man. After the decision is come to, 'God the Son' directs the Angel Gabriel to go to Mary because she is 'full of grace,' and—this phrase is the only appropriate one —-ask her to consent to be the wife of God. The Angel actually gives her time to consider the proposal. And I must observe that this proposal is quite undisguised and real—he 'makyth a lytyl restynge,' and then asks the Virgin what answer he is to take back to heaven—'The Holy Ghost abydyth thyn answer and thyn assent,' and adds that 'all the blyssyd spyrytys, all the gode levers (good livers, or godly people), and the chosyn sowlys that ar in helle,' are also anxiously awaiting her decision. Mary then consents 'with all mekenes.' Gabriel thanks her for her 'gret humylyte,' and then the Holy Ghost descends, 'with three beams, —to our Lady,' the Father and Son attending; after which she declares herself with child, and the Angel Gabriel, calling her 'God's turtle, God's charmer, and his bower,' bids her adieu. In another mystery, Anne, wife of Joachim and mother of Mary, who is said to have a ' gracyous face,' though she is only three years old, asks Mary if she will be ' Goddys wyff,' and Mary answers—' To be Goddys wyff I never was wurthy.'

What precise ideas intelligent people in the fourteenth century attached to language such as this would not, perhaps, be easy to say, and would certainly be difficult to describe in phraseology which would be tolerated in a book for general reading. But one thing is certain, namely, that even in the rudest minds, a halo of mystery would surround the whole subject, and that all attempts to apprehend its secrets would merge themselves in religious awe. The chief difference, indeed, between the old-fashioned way and the modern way of treating the idea of such mysteries, once admitted to the mind, lies in this, that the tendencies of our forefathers were boldly concrete, and insisted on turning whatever they thought of into picture or story, while we are usually content to turn into picture or story only the things of whose representations we can test the reality. But certainly a *poet* —especially a poet of so very concrete an imagination as Chaucer—would not find the subject a difficult one. Both in classical and Christian or quasi-Christian literature he was familiar with the idea of the mingling of the divine and the human in a strictly conjugal sense. However strong a sense of reprobation may have divided such a story as that of Jupiter and Antiope, or Jupiter and Danaë, from the narrative which

is found in one of the three gospels (familiar to the
general imagination of the time in apocryphal shapes,
with plenty of detail), the line of separation would be
a very fluctuating one in the mind of a poet.   For his
purposes, each story would be simply a portion of a
mythology; something which he could employ as picture or imagery.   So that no proof whatever of the sensuality or materialism of Chaucer's mind can be found
in the verses in question.   It was natural for him to
write of a beautiful woman that she was fit for a wife
for ' God ' himself, if one were to be sought for.   All
this may be said to be simply and innocently ' human,' but the same remark will not apply in other
cases where it is frequently sought to make it applicable.

   One of the excuses most commonly made for that
license of expression to which I am myself unable
to give any name but gross indecency is that it is
human—' so human, you know.'   To this it must be
replied that the people who use this or similar language have evidently not taken the trouble to acquire
a clear idea of what they mean by the word human.
It will be seen at a glance, if an honest glance, that
what they really mean by human is precisely what is
common to men and women, and the inferior animals,
and *not* what is truly human, *i.e.* distinctive of humanity.   There is no humanity without ' shame, divine
shame,' nor would I believe upon any evidence, short
of my own vision, carefully checked by long and watch-

ful experience, that the solid earth had a corner, however dark and dirty, where men and women were without its rudiments. At all events, to apply the word human as an adjective of applause to that kind of tone in thought or expression, which is unreservedly free in its references to the points in which the human and the lower animals seem to touch each other, is an abuse of terms. In the well-known dialogue between Adam and the angel in the VIIIth book of 'Paradise Lost,' in the passage beginning—' Neither her outside form'd so fair,' Milton makes an effort to avoid this confusion, and, in fact, does just clear himself; but he does it so barely and so awkwardly that this speech of Adam is a curious study in relation to the subject of which we are now speaking. And yet the line is easily drawn. That only is human in this regard which is not involuntary. Hunger, thirst, nutrition, are not specifically human; and the *accidents* of nutrition are accidents; topics of disease, for science, and not for poetry, or humour either. These topics, the incidents and accidents of nutrition, are excluded by the canon that they are involuntary and compulsory, cannot be modified by our opinions, affections, or sentiments, if we are in health. But the same exclusion does not apply to passion: for the converse reason.

It is, of course, extremely difficult, make what efforts of imagination we may, to place ourselves in the position of our forefathers with respect to what we call the delicacies and decencies of life. Think of halls

strewed with rushes, in which foul things lay long,
visible to the eye and possibly offensive to the nose.
Think of the necessity which must then have existed
for giving directions to servants in much plainer language than we now use ; and that for the simple reason
that offensive things had to be *directly* spoken of, by
the mistress of a household in the ordering of the
day's minor morals. Think of the bedroom, in which both
men and women slept together ; they used frequently,
generally I believe, to go to rest wholly unclad in the
darkness, and it is impossible but that extreme famili-
arity with the aspects and history of the human body
throughout its four-and-twenty hours must have existed
among men and women of all classes.   Again, think of
the absence of drainage, and of the sluttishness of the
average woman, even as we know her now, when employed in menial offices.   And you will have a little
lessened the difficulty of understanding how certain
things would find their way into prose or verse in
the fourteenth century.   But there are words and references in Chaucer which are simply and merely dirty,
and though we can imagine that men and women in his
time spoke much more freely of things with which they
were more familiar, what we have to account for is a
poet's unnecessary references to facts which must,
in any poet's imagination, be enclosed or segregated
facts, whatever they might be in the economy of his
time or of any other time.   Thus, the language in
which the host of the Tabard is made to bid Chaucer

cease his telling of the ' Rhyme of Sir Topas' contains
a vulgarism which serves no purpose whatever. We
know by our own observation that men of inferior organisation and culture are often free enough with such
talk,—it is a thing to be taken for granted of such men
in all ages and countries,—so that the introduction of
similar touches of brutality forms no *necessary* part of
any picture of manners. Can any ingenuity find an
apology for the conclusion of the Sompnour's Tale ?
I confess myself beaten by it. It is in no sense part of
any just picture of manners, for the license of the
time was *inhuman,* if we are actually supposed to
believe that ladies would have sat and heard the story
of ' frere Johan' and the difficulty proposed by

> ' the lordes squier at the bord,
> That carf his mete and herde word by word.'

Perhaps there is one apology to be suggested for this
story, though a rather far-fetched one : namely, that it
was intended to serve a double purpose, to satirise the
greediness of the friars and the subtleties of the schoolmen (or, perhaps, those of the Courts of Love, whether
the courts were ever actually held or not); and, indeed, the question how many angels could dance upon
the point of a needle or whether two or more angels
could occupy together the same point of space is not
more absurd than the problem of the Sompnour. That
some such reference existed in the mind of Chaucer is

made less improbable by the words with which the Sompnour concludes :—

> ' The lord, the lady, and ech man, sauf the frere,
> Sayde that Jankyn spak in this matiere,
> As wel as Euclide, or elles Phtolome.
> Touchand the cherl, they sayd that *subtilte*
> *And high wyt mad him speken as he spak*—
> He was no fool ne no demoniak.'

And also by the terms in which the host immediately addresses the clerk :—

> ' " Sir Clerk of Oxenforde," our hoste sayde,
> " Ye ryde as stille and coy as doth a mayde
> Were newe spoused, sittyng at the bord ;
> This day ne herd I of your mouth a word :
> *I trowe ye study about some sophime.*" '

But whether all this comment of mine be wide of the mark or not, let Chaucer have the benefit, *if any*, not only of the general apology which he has put into the Prologue, but of the more particular, and certainly more humorous excuses which he has alleged in the cases of the Miller's and Reeve's Tales. It will be observed, however, that after all, these excuses go to the morality of the stories, and not to their decency. Whether we ' make earnest of game ' or not, *i.e.*, whether we treat the narrations as fact or fancy, their matter and manner remain as they were.

V. Much must be allowed, difficult as it would be to

say *how* much, for the spirit in which the theology of
the western nations has been apt to speak of the human
body, under sanctions held to be found in the Christian
writings. The uncleanness of the body, the ' corruption'
deemed inseparable from the relation in which all others
are founded, the violent and inflexible separation of life
into two departments,—the department of the spirit and
that of the flesh, the latter being degraded and full of
sin,—these are features which we can trace in nearly all
literature taking the name of Christian, from its very
beginning until now. It is needless again to remark
that the doctrine of the ' Parson's Tale,' namely, that
' marriage changeth deadly into venial sin,' and that sin
there must be whenever there is ' delit' (delight) in which
the body is much concerned, was, in Chaucer's time, supposed to be quite axiomatically true for all Christian men
and women. It is a doctrine which is still abundantly
influential even where it is not received in form, and it
survives in the imaginations and phraseology of the
common people, and in much of our current moral and
religious writing. It is impossible to disentangle the
contradictory threads of dogma and suggestion upon
those matters which are contained even in writers as
great and as diverse as Milton and Jeremy Taylor. Can
any ingenuity reconcile the views of the conjugal emotions implied in Books IV. and VIII. of the ' Paradise,'
and the views of the same emotions which are implied
in the latter portion of Book IX. ? A similar confusion
of ideas inevitably arises when we endeavour to make

sense of the quasi-Protestant doctrine of the Wife of
Bath, and that of the ' Parson's Tale.'   The Wife of
Bath talks very warmly, and lewdly too; but her doctrine is, we may suppose, what Wickliff himself would
have approved, namely, that though ' the dart (*i. e.* the
highest prize) be set upon virginity,' there is no blame
whatever in marriage.   The doctrine of the Parson, on
the contrary, is, that in marriage there is necessarily
sin, because of ' the corrupcioun and delit.'   I need not
enlarge upon this view of life, or trace it through various streams to its source; nor in any case would this be
the place for doing so.   But it is disagreeably obvious
that whenever such a view of life is entertained, there
must be a tendency to treat the body and all its functions with contempt, and to the formation of filthy and
degrading habits and fancies,—the tendency must exist,
I say, and in common minds it will probably run riot.
In the time of Chaucer this way of looking at the facts
of life had the religious sanction behind it, and its influence came into collision with the influence of the
classics, of Italian literature, of the Romance literature,
of the whole spirit of chivalry, of the spirit of revolt
against the Church, which is so abundantly traceable in
the writings and in the events of the times.   The result
was undoubtedly license both of thought and speech.
In Chaucer, as a poet, there could be no tendency to
think meanly of the human body, certainly not of love,—
his descriptions of the beauty of women are conspicu-
ously fine, and he always writes of love with the zest

which belongs only to the finest natures. But he had been familiar with the courtyard and pages' quarter, with the camp, and, in his official capacities, with the common people; and he could not escape the influence of his associations—at all events, he does not show that he escaped it.

VI. There is in the English nature a free rough humour, which makes it not *quite* easy to estimate the value of such evidence as Chaucer's or Shakspeare's writings upon the question of public morality. Both of these poets put into the mouths of some of their personages a loud, brutal banter upon the most serious of facts, which it is impossible to suppose represented their genuine feelings and convictions. Would anybody ever have the patience to count the number of times the word ' cuckold,' or one or other of its congeners, turns up in English dramatic literature, and always in connexion with a jest which implies that scarcely any living man could feel certain the jest did not rightly apply to himself? Look, for example, at ' Much Ado about Nothing,' —not only the bantering of Benedick, but at the whole spirit of the play, including the outrageously absurd suspicions of Claudio, and the disgraceful, unfatherly behaviour of Leontes,—what does it all mean, but that in Shakspeare's time it was held axiomatic that any wife might at any moment be suspected with *probable* cause? It is true this story comes from Italy, but we cannot lay much stress upon that fact without discrediting the

genius of the poet, who chose his material under no compulsion, and deliberately anglicised in his treatment of
it. Chaucer was, even during his lifetime, charged with
outraging womanhood by his pictures of female character (Virginia and Griselda notwithstanding), and he
openly endeavoured to make amends; but the occasional
suggestion of his writing is the same. It is useless at-
tempting to disguise the fact, and no sincere mind will
forgive any such attempt. Yet are we to conclude that
there ever was a time when adultery was more common
than theft, and that a false wife was as frequently to be
found in this island as a drunken husband? Fitzstephen said curtly, that in his time (the reign of
Henry II.) the wives of the citizens of London were
of Sabine virtue—' Urbis matronæ ipsæ Sabinæ sunt,'
and I believe this was always nearer the truth than the
other view,—if we may even use so vaguely positive a
word as ' view.' I attribute the frequent presence of
this kind of jocularity in so much of our elder literature
to causes which are of such a kind as still to leave us
all our faith in domestic purity as an immensely preva-
lent fact in every age and every country that we know
of, including our own. One of those causes is the
exaggerated and exaggerating conceit of men. In the
time of Chaucer—a time when such a tale as that of
Griselda could be accepted as presenting a type of womanhood not unworthy of imitation, however difficult
the imitation might prove,—the conceit of men, ranging
as it did side by side with preposterous ideas of autho-

rity, dignity, and privilege in every direction, must have been, as we can plainly see it was, absolutely enormous. By the conceit of men, I mean their habitual estimate of their attractiveness to women from a low point of view, their superior importance socially, their rights over them, and generally their glory and grandeur in the scale of creation; including such notions as were founded on a false physiology, which, indeed, were, and still are, largely influential among the uncultivated and half-cultivated classes. One of Griselda's reasons for being ready to give up her child to be slain, is that it was *his*, her husband's. A reason founded on a mistaken scientific position—what would the poor lady have said of Parthenogenesis?

VII. But, besides all this, I fear I must add another reason, and that I think it was perhaps the strongest of all. That reason is the factitious prominence which certain topics acquire when the Church of a country and its dominant religious opinion uphold the importance and dignity of celibacy, and large numbers of celibate men and women are present in society, contrasted by their peculiar position with the rest of the social body, and, both by example and precept, casting an irritating and exaggerating light upon the ' secrets known to all.' If the pretence of what was called ' purity ' broke down often, as we know it did,—if, in other words, the ' celibates ' were no celibates at all in a very large number of instances,—

we can imagine how much worse the case became, what perversion of the popular imagination followed. ' If *these* checks, these rigid schemes of discipline, these awful oaths, do not suffice to bind people; and if these impulses are in themselves sinful, so that not even a sacrament of the Church can do more than make them venial sins, and are yet so rife and so deceitful,—why, what can we trust to?' The common people may never have put their thoughts or half-thoughts into this shape; but such thoughts or half-thoughts they must have had —they were natural under the circumstances. To the unnatural and filthy light under which certain topics were commonly presented to the imagination in the days of our forefathers by such religious instruction and example as they were in the habit of hearing and seeing most of, I do greatly attribute the fact to which reference has just been made. The popular imagination, penetrated by inscrutable hints of tradition, and by proverbs and saws of a cosy grandame flavour, though such saws *now* mean little,—has not yet recovered from the imprint of a time when such a preposterous document as the Parson's Tale was acceptable, and accepted as a homily. It is a natural makeweight to the Prologue of the Wife of Bath, and I think nobody can read the two things side by side without feeling that if the domestic imagination of the people was not rotted, it was scarcely the fault of those who had the care of their virtue. The good intentions of a character so beautiful as this ' poore persone,' as he is drawn by Chaucer (and

in England there must have been hundreds like him),
were undoubted; but the effect of such a discourse as
his upon the minds of the majority of men and women
could only be one way.

VIII. To a humourist, much more if the humourist
be also a poet, surveying life in wide sweeps of thought,
with inevitable reference to its contrasts and conflicts,
lights and shades, and striking emotional perspectives,
there is always a seductive topic ready to hand
in the ludicrous incongruity between the external
framework of social order in civilised communities,
and the strong, quick-moving impulses which struggle
for the upper hand beneath the tapestry; between the
accepted hypothesis and the realities of existence. This
topic is a fair one in all its aspects, including those
which concern the very roots and beginnings of society.
Allowing for the difference of manners and habits of
speech and writing in this and the fourteenth century,
it *may* be that Chaucer did not make so bold a use of this
topic on its joyous passional side merely as to degrade
himself or his readers in his own consciousness or in
theirs. And certainly, Chaucer is not, in any part of
his works, to be called a teacher of immoral things.
His breadth of speech does not seem calculated to
stimulate the imagination of an ordinary mind; and
his descriptions of female beauty are rarely what can be
called luscious or sensuous in the usual acceptation of
such phraseology. Take, for example, the description

of the elderly miser's wife, which is put into the mouth of the Reeve, in the Reeve's Tale. It is very pretty; but there is a rude health about it which keeps the air cool. As you read it, you are in a breezy orchard, not in a lady's bower. Accordingly, it is not on this side that, with all his plainness of speech, Chaucer is so condemnable, as on another. He does not so much excite the passions as he degrades life by tampering with its enclosed incidents in a way which could never have been natural to a poet, and by too easily admitting innuendo which, in a more self-conscious age, would be cynical.

IX. After the frequent innuendo of this kind which occurs in writing intended to paint life as it is, it is poor comfort to be referred to such a passage as this in the 'Court of Love,' which is, from the first line to the last, a thoroughly artificial poem:—

> 'It longeth eke this statute for to holde,
> To deme thy lady evermore thy friend,
> And think thyself in no wise a cuckolde.
> In every thing she doth but as she sholde :
> Construe the best, believe no tales newe,
> For many a lie is told, that semeth ful trewe.'

We have ample evidence in other parts of Chaucer's writings that he was by nature intolerant of what some people call 'elevated' or 'idealistic' views of life and duty. He would not have been a poet if he could not have written 'The Court of Love,' and that with the

playful zest, and the peculiar melodious grace which
belongs to the subject; but he seldom seems so
thoroughly happy and so much himself as when he
is laughing in his sleeve at some high-pitched strain
of sentiment or ethics. It was doing no harm (much
the reverse) to ridicule, in his own person, after the
Clerk had finished, the story of Griselda; because
Griselda was a fool, and did very wrong; but, after
all, there is such a thing as the maintenance of a
principle or an ideal, and the first person one meets at
dinner, or in the next thoroughfare, is not necessarily
to be taken as the measure of what human nature is
capable of.

In dealing with this subject, one must not, of
course, omit to allow full weight to passages which
read like disclaimers of serious intent in such loose
talk as we have been noting. For example, in the
broadly humorous squabble between the Reeve and the
Miller, who is drunk, the Reeve rebukes the Miller in
very remarkable language :—

> ' The Reve answered and seyde, " Stynt thi clappe.
>   *   *   *   *   *
> It is a synne, and eek a greet folye
> To apeyren eny man, or him defam,
> *And eek to brynge wyves in ylle name.*
> Thou mayst ynowgh of other thinges seyn."
> This dronken Miller spak ful sone ageyn,
> And seyde, " Leeve brother Osewold,
>   *   *   *   *   *
> Ther been ful goode wyves many oon.

And ever a thousand goode agayns oon badde ;
That knowest thou wel thyself, but if thou madde,
Why art thou angry with my tale now ?
*   *   *   *   *
An housbond schal not be inquisityf
Of Goddes pryveté, ne of his wyf." '

This is the language of chivalry itself, though a
drunken Miller speaks it; and Chaucer's own words,
in his capacity of the story-teller, may be added here
at full length : —

'. . . . . This proud Myllere
He nolde his wordes for no man forbere,
But tolde his cherlisch tale in his manere,
Me athinketh, that I schal reherce it heere.
And therfor every gentil wight I preye,
For Goddes love, as deme nat that I seye,
Of yvel entent, but for I moot reherse
Here wordes alle, al be they better or werse,
Or elles falsen som of my mateere.
And therfor whoso list it nat to heere,
Turne over the leef, and chese another tale ;
For he schal fynde ynowe both gret and smale,
Of storial thing that toucheth gentilesse,
And eek moralité, and holynesse.
Blameth nat me, if that ye chese amys.
The Miller is a cherl, ye know wel this ;
So was the Reeve and othir many mo,
*   *   *   *   *
Avyseth you, and put me out of blame ;
And men schulde nat make ernest of game.'

One would give all this the prominence to which it

is entitled; but, much as I love realism and breadth
of touch, it does not seem to me that the case is much
mended by these disclaimers; because, what *tells* in
the long run is the diffused ethic of a man's work (so
to speak), and it is more to the purpose to inquire to
what keynote he sets his work when he is most at his
ease with himself and his readers, than what particular
sentiments he may deliver at certain times.

Before passing on, in the second volume, to matters
of minuter detail relating to English life in the time of
Chaucer, I will endeavour to select for general comment a few broad features which strikingly illustrate
the difference between the fourteenth century and the
nineteenth. The general use of the language of an
extinct empire is just such a feature.

I. One of the most striking observations made by
Prof. Thorold Rogers relates to the frequent use of the
Latin language for ordinary purposes of business. The
conclusion he came to is, that the knowledge of Latin
was quite general in England up to the fifteenth
century. This is a conclusion which doubtless requires
some defining, and some specific illustration too, beyond that of the bailiff's accounts examined by Mr.
Rogers; but the old practice of teaching Latin to the
young by means of Latin grammars, certainly does

seem to point to some sort of traditional idea that the language was supposed to be much understood, much used, and available for any purpose that any one pleased. Nor must we forget that it was always used in legal proceedings. The observations of Mr. Rogers are as follows :—

'The accounts are, without exception, written in Latin. Of course, the Latin is exceedingly barbarous; the terms used are often no more than English words with Latin terminations; and occasionally they are not inflected at all. But the structure is always grammatical, and the genders are, as a rule, correctly given. Sometimes, indeed, the same document conjugates the verb variously, but this negligence is rare. It is wholly incredible '—and here, of course, is the point— 'that these records were written in a tongue which was not familiarly understood. I have long thought that the fact of the political songs being frequently composed in Latin, is evidence of how widely diffused was the use of that language; but the universality of its use in these bailiffs' accounts seems to be a still more cogent argument for the same conclusion. Is it possible to imagine that a responsible officer should have rendered, even by the hands of a scribe, an annual document, the terms of which he could not himself comprehend? Is it reasonable to think men would have transacted business in an unknown tongue? Besides, most of these accounts contain corrections and interpolations inserted after the fair copy was written.

. . . . After the system of farming by bailiffs ceased, and still more after the Reformation broke up the distribution of the estates possessed by corporations, the single link which connected ancient with later customs,—the general acquaintance with Latin,—may have been severed; but before the fifteenth century, it was, I am persuaded, all but universal, and, till the Reformation, general.'

To what Mr. Rogers has here remarked of the frequent use of the Latin language for the composition of political songs, I may add that some of those songs appear to have been composed in alternate lines of Latin and English, as if in mere playfulness—a fact which would exclude, even if it arose, the supposition that Latin was employed for any purpose of (more or less partial) concealment.

II. Another feature of difference, which has already emerged in the foregoing pages, and which must from time to time emerge again, is more strikingly apparent still upon the surface of all the records aud literature of those early centuries. I mean the preponderance of pageantry and coloured and resonant luxury in the ideal life of the times. It is a subject on which it is scarcely possible to say anything new, and yet upon which it is scarcely possible not to dwell again and again. The contrast between the army of Xerxes and the army of Sparta was not greater than the obvious contrast between the high-pitched and accumulated

splendour of life above stairs in the twelfth, thirteenth,
and fourteenth centuries, and life above stairs in our
own time. It would be trite to observe on the superior
convenience of the modern mode; but it is not quite so
obvious that that mode is much more favourable to
privacy than the other older and more gorgeous
method. The verses I am about to quote are not of
the century of Chaucer, but they are peculiarly illus-
trative for my purpose, and faithfully suggestive of
what may be called the pageantry of life, even in his
days. The passage consists of a speech from the King
of Hungary to his daughter; she has just lost her lover,
the Squire of low degree, and her father endeavours to
console her by promising her all manner of treats.
There are few words which are not intelligible to
modern readers. *Menzie* means *household.* *Yede*
means *go* or *travel.* To *streek* is to *hunt;* and *pight*
means *inlaid.* Anything more juvenile can scarcely
be conceived than the spirit which proposes all these
splendours and luxuries as a cure for the heartache.
First, the princess is to go out hunting in rich attire,
with Spanish ponies, falcons, and bugles:—

> ' To-morrow ye shall in hunting fare;
> And yede, my doughter, in a chair;
> It shall be covered with velvet red,
> And cloths of fine gold all about your head,
> With damask white and azure blue,
> Well diapered with lilies new.
> Your pommels shall be ended with gold,
> Your chains enamelled many a fold,

Your mantle of rich degree,
Purple pall and ermine free.
Jennets of Spain, that ben so wight,
Trapped to the ground with velvet bright. . . .
A leish of harehound with you to streek,
And hart, and hind, and other like.
Ye shall be set at such a tryst,
That hart and hind shall come to you first,
Your disease to drive you fro,
To hear the bugles there y-blow.
Homeward thus shall ye ride,
On-hawking by the river's side,
With gosshawk and with gentle falcon,
With bugle-horn and merlion.'

The young lady is then to have wines enough to
make her very ill, including 'pyment,' which was a
kind of claret-cup, highly spiced, with plenty of honey.
She is also to have venison and wild fowl. Music, of
course :—

' Ye shall have harp, sautry, and song,
And other mirths you among.
Ye shall have Rumney and Malespine,
Both Hippocras and Vernage wine;
Montreśe and wine of Greek,
Both Algrade and despice eke,
Antioch and Bastard,
Pyment also and garnard;
Wint of Greek and Muscadel,
Both claré, pyment, and Rochelle,
The reed your stomach to defy,
And pots of Osy set you by.
You shall have venison y-bake,
The best wild fowl that may be take.'

This puts one in mind of the French nobleman who said that when he had lost a dear relative or friend he invariably ordered pigeons for dinner, and added, ' I always find that after having eaten three pigeons, and drunk a bottle or two of good wine, I rise from the table much less mournful.' However, the splendours are, most of them, to come, and they are *really* splendid. Beginning with the music, we may note that it includes *harmony*—' tenors and trebles, *contre-note* and descant' :—

> ' When you come home your menzie among,
> Ye shall have revel, dances, and song;
> Little children, great and small,
> Shall sing as does the nightingale.
> Then shall ye go to your even-song,
> With tenors and trebles among.
> Threescore of copes of damask bright,
> Full of pearls they shall be pight.
> Your censers shall be of gold.
> Indent with azure many a fold.
> Your quire nor organ song shall want,
> With contre-note and descant.
> The other half on organs playing,
> With young children full fain singing.'

Now note the publicity which attends, of necessity, upon a ' supper ' like the following, which, it will be observed, is in the open air :—

> Then shall ye go to your supper,
> And sit in tents in green arbér,
> With cloth of arras pight to the ground,
> With sapphires set of diamond.

A hundred knights, truly told,
Shall play with bowls in alleys cold,
Your disease to drive away;
To see the fishes in pools play,
To a drawbridge then shall ye,
Th' one half of stone, th' other of tree;
A barge shall meet you full right,
With twenty-four oars full bright,
With trumpets and with clarion,
The fresh water to row up and down.
Forty torches burning bright,
At your bridges to bring you light.'

It must be confessed this is a pretty picture; but
a hundred knights, 'truly told,'—no short counting,
but a full hundred—playing at bowls to comfort a
princess! Nor does she escape when she goes to
bed :—

' Into your chamber they shall you bring,
With much mirth and more liking.
Your blankets shall be of fustian,
Your sheets shall be of cloth of Rennes.
Your head sheet shall be of pery pight,
With diamonds set and rubies bright.
When you are laid in bed so soft,
A cage of gold shall hang aloft,
With long paper fair burning,
And cloves that be sweet smelling.
Frankincense and olibanum,
That when ye sleep the taste may come;
And if ye no rest can take,
All night minstrels for you shall wake.'

There is undoubtedly a charm in all this; the

colour, the light, the odour, and the music.   But
where is the comfort?   Think of a sheet, a 'head-
sheet' too, embroidered with pearls!   And minstrels
'bringing a lady' into her chamber!   The picture is
painted by a poet, and it is, of course, cumulative and.
typical, but that is a reason for selecting it for use in
this place.   We note at a glance the total absence of
the modern spirit, which, in its form of the search after
convenience or comfort, is a reflection of individualism.
To place the ease or well-being of the individual in the
individual's own power, by making life universally convenient ; that is the modern idea, and it is a form of
laisser-faire translated into action.   To *make* the individual happy, or easy, or gay, or jolly, by efforts
addressed *ad hoc* from the outside; that is the mediæval idea, and it is a form of 'protection' translated.
It ran naturally into splendour and gew-gaw, and it
necessarily *hampered* life.   The inventor of such a
simple thing as a fork did more for the emancipation
of the individual (the reader will, with a passing smile,
excuse these fine words) than the makers of a million
tapestries.

On the other hand, when the transition is made, or
about to be made, from splendour to convenience, it is
obvious that the poetic spirit suffers, not indeed an
apparent eclipse, but an apparent occultation.   In its
bearings upon the epoch of Chaucer, and the centuries
that followed, down to the Reformation, and even
onward to that 'glorious revolution' of which Lord

Mayor Beckford has undeservedly the credit of having reminded George III., this last remark is not so barren, perhaps, as it may at first sight appear. It introduces at once to a new topic.

III. Mr. Carlyle, among others, has noted, with peculiar force and explicitness, the transition in Europe generally, from the epoch of poetry proper to the epoch of dogma. In the twelfth and thirteenth centuries, we have all Europe swarming with troubadours, ringing with song, and glittering with splendour. Crusaders, knights, tournaments, pointed architecture, and poetry. But the poetry is mainly the poetry of simple incident, colour, and form. *Ut pictura poesis.* Dante and Petrarch, in opposite directions, slightly confuse the line of distinction, but it is plainly to be drawn ; and, all of a sudden, as it seems, we come upon a time of didacticism. The moralist counts for more, and, apparently, at all events, the poet for less. Here, again, we may note the uprising of the modern or individual spirit. When men in Europe began to assert their rights against power and principle of whatever kind, they naturally resorted to argument as well as invective. The power and privilege of the mediæval Church in particular would necessarily be attacked by weapons of counter-dogma (if such a word may be excused), and morality, as disconnected with sentiment and faith, would begin to assume a new place. This was what did, in fact, happen, and what was prophesied in the insurgent spirit of the time of Chaucer.   Convenience, or facility for independent living for all, rapidly begins to make itself felt as more important than pomp for a few, just as the spirit of commerce and the spirit of private judgment begin to spread.   The vein which runs naturally to mere convenience in the equipage or apparel (*appareil*) of life, and to didacticism in art and the various forms in which the feelings and the intellect express themselves, is naturally strong in the Saxon.   Nay, it is strong in the common people well-nigh everywhere and in all times.   The people are always sententious.   It is not the poetry, or the character painting, or even so much the story and passion of Shakespeare's plays which the multitude enjoys; it is his didacticism. Listen to the hum of approbation which runs through a theatre or a reading-room when the speaker comes to the plain didactic bits.   Such as, ' Use every man after his desert, and who should 'scape whipping ? '   Or, ' Imperious Cæsar, dead and turned to clay, might stop a hole to keep the wind away ; ' or the instructions of Polonius to his son.   The same point emerges in the oldest literature of the common people : in chap-books, in poems like ' London Lackpenny,' and ' Death and the Lady.'   And, again, in company with Protestant-ism, in the prominence given to the sermon as distinguished from the worship.   Who does not remember the Scotchman that, coming late to church, excused himself by saying that he liked the joint, the prayers

and hymns being only the broth?   To this day it may
be said that the spirit of picture-poetry, or natural
delight, has only a small following in England.   The
whole of the spirit which involves that spirit in particular does not show itself much after Chaucer himself,
indeed; and in him we discern the struggle of the new
spirit for mastery.   In his contemporary Gower, *that*
may be said to have been victorious, though the want
of the dramatic element, which in Chaucer is so strong,
has prevented his making any such mark on England as his more illustrious 'disciple;' for so, it will
be remembered, Gower calls Chaucer.   It was, however, by the path of the drama that the stream of
tendency in England manifested itself.   The spirit of
didacticism breathes strong up to the very height of
the Elizabethan period.   Then, even in the drama,
there seems a sort of poise of the two elements.   Suddenly descending the hill on the other side, we come
to Puritanism and Milton.   In Milton, curiously
enough, we find not only the didactic spirit strong,
but also the spirit of picture-poetry, or the mere music
of natural delight (for which see ' L'Allegro ' and ' Il
Penseroso,' in which, too, we recover something of the
artificial air of the troubadour genius).   But the
stream ran on—downwards, as we all know—to
Dryden, Pope, Young, Blair, and the eighteenth-cen-
tury rhymers.   In the great revival at the beginning
of our own century, all the streams of tendency seem
again to be resumed at once in Crabbe, Scott, Byron,

and Moore. Coleridge and Wordsworth inaugurate a new epoch, with which we have nothing here to do, except to note the striking fact that, under the very shadow of the new, the modern spirit turned affectionately back to Chaucer. Perhaps of all modern men, Wordsworth and Leigh Hunt knew him best. But they relished him for different reasons. Wordsworth for, among other things, the antique simplicity of his pathos ; Leigh Hunt (for that too, no doubt, but) because he had himself strong affinities with the Troubadour, or natural-delight, or picture-music vein in Chaucer.

The subject is endless, and my task is done when I have noted the strong rise of the didactic current * in connexion with insurgent currents, political and religious, and the movement (which, indeed, was a lingering one !) for convenience,—which means freedom of every day movement for the individual at his own cost,— a movement which speedily took Discovery into its service, and has, from the first, found Science a faithful servant.

IV. There is one other point, which also lies upon the surface, namely, the extent to which the Bible had already penetrated literature, life, and common speech. Much surprise has been manifested at the extreme

---

* Perhaps undergoing its last transformation for the present in Mr. Tennyson. At all events. we all note in poets like Mr. Swinburne and Mr. William Morris, the growth of the reaction of which Keats and Hunt were the beginners.

frequency with which deposits of Scriptural thought and phrase are found in Shakspeare (Dr. Wordsworth has written a book upon this very subject), and it has been said that he must have been a great reader of the Bible. But we encounter exactly the same phenomenon in Chaucer and his contemporaries, and we are also led to infer that a knowledge of the Bible was general in those days. The tone and language of the ballads and the popular political oratory of the time, so far as we know anything about the latter, point to the fact of a wide, general knowledge of the Bible, which must, of course, have been traditionary; a thing passed on, not learned by book. There is every reason to believe that, whatever Shakspeare read, he had, like other Englishmen, an immense traditionary, reflected, or, so to call it, *gossip* knowledge of the Bible. And it is apparent that this kind of knowledge, carried among the peasantry by the friars, had consequences, political and religious, which were little contemplated by the friars themselves. Thus, we find that not once only, but again and again, the " rebel " and the " heretic " are one and the same person.

THE END OF THE FIRST VOLUME.